NO BULL

THE REAL STORY OF THE REBIRTH OF A TEAM AND A CITY

RON MORRIS

BASEBALL AMERICA BOOKS

Distributed by Simon & Schuster ISBN: 978-1-932391-66-4

DEDICATION

For Kim and Luke,
my biggest supporters through thick and thin,
and the two loves of my life

CONTENTS

PROLOGUE

Somewhere along Interstate 95, perhaps in Georgia, my anxiety about being in the front seat of a Ford station wagon with a former Major League Baseball player was finally beginning to dissipate. We had pulled over for dinner at a truck stop when it struck me that Al Gallagher, the one-time third baseman for the San Francisco Giants and the California Angels and the new manager of the Durham Bulls, was every bit like me, just another person for whom baseball flowed through his veins with the ease of a veteran outfielder settling under a routine fly ball.

Gallagher carried the well-earned nickname "Dirty Al" throughout his major-league career and it stuck beyond his playing days like the tobacco stains that dotted his jerseys and shirts. Gallagher discarded his tobacco chaw before entering the truck stop restaurant, and before he ordered chicken fried steak, mashed potatoes and a medley of vegetables that included sweet peas and sweeter corn. As we awaited our food, a cockroach about the size of my index finger meandered from behind the miniature jukebox against the wall at our booth, sprinted across our table, down my side of the table and into hiding.

Without hesitation, Gallagher summoned the unsuspecting waitress and requested an immediate tableside meeting with the restaurant's manager.

"We just got ourselves a free meal!" Gallagher exclaimed with glee, his crooked smile wildly displaying the deep-seated, black stains on teeth that had endured decades of tobacco chewing.

I was 25 that spring of 1980. To fully understand why I was so awestruck by the mere presence of a former major-leaguer, you must know I was a young — OK, immature — 25. What social skills I possessed had been greatly impaired by the events of my young life, including my family being uprooted and moved from Wyoming to North Carolina prior to my sophomore year of high school. The move represented significant culture shock to me, and the subsequent waves reverberated through my high school days, college and beyond as I slowly attempted — often clumsily — to adjust to the social climate around me.

My wide-eyed view of professional baseball players also had something to do with the misfortune of being reared in a region of the country virtually devoid of the national pastime. The major leagues were something I read about in newspapers, occasionally heard on St. Louis Cardinals' broadcasts on our car radio, and viewed on TV's national game-of-the-week on Saturdays. For the most part, the major leagues and its participants were a part of my imagination. Mickey Mantle and Casey Stengel and even Hector Lopez were gods, their existence known mostly through box scores and statistics lines that appeared in *The Sporting News*, which arrived weekly at my Reed Avenue home in Cheyenne, Wyoming.

My love of baseball, and the softball version of the game as well, was passed along to me by my father, Leo. Dad was a fast-pitch softball legend growing up in Sioux City, Iowa, and he continued to make a name for himself by farming his powerful right arm out to companies such as John Deere Tractor and their touring powerhouses summer after summer. That meant moving with my six sisters and brother from one city to another in Iowa, Missouri, Oklahoma and Colorado before settling in Wyoming for most of my formative years.

Into the twilight of his softball pitching career, Dad turned to radio broadcasting, and his love of sports made him a natural behind the microphone, delivering play-by-play accounts of boxing, football, basketball and even the annual Cheyenne Frontier Days Rodeo. He also created his own University of Wyoming sports network and called every Cowboys football and basketball game from 1959 through 1969. Dad even provided play-by-play of many Wyoming baseball games, back when the Cowboys had a program.

As much as I enjoyed sitting next to him during Wyoming basketball games or in the Knothole Section for Cowboy football games in Laramie, my most treasured memory is that of listening to the wind whistle through the press box at Wyoming baseball games. That is where I learned to keep score. It also is where I learned the finer points of baseball, from knowing why it was important for the first baseman to trail the base runner to second base on a double to one of the outfield gaps, to understanding a balk can be called against the catcher (for stepping outside the catcher's box before an intentional ball is thrown by the pitcher). Dad knew the game. One summer he stepped in at mid-season to coach the Cheyenne American Legion team with my brother, Rick, as the center fielder and guided the Post 6 club to the Wyoming state championship and an appearance in the West Regional tournament.

By the time I was 14, I had a pretty good idea that I wanted to follow in Dad's footsteps — with one exception — by providing accounts of sporting events with a typewriter instead of a microphone. On Sundays during football seasons, I used Mom's typewriter — and carbon copies — to publish my own two-page, double-spaced sports section, distributing it in the evening to each of my brothers and sisters. Then Dad hooked me up with The Associated Press in Cheyenne where I worked on weekends, taking telephone calls from across the state and turning the information into two- and three-paragraph stories. Occasionally, I served as a "stringer" to cover high school track meets or basketball games.

Still, my exposure to baseball was minimal. Because of the difficult winters, baseball is not played as a high school sport in Wyoming. Even our Little League seasons were restricted to 10 games played between Memorial Day and July 4. Denver Bears minor-league games could be heard on the radio, and the re-creation of road games only added to the mythical stature of the game in my mind. Dad and I occasionally drove the Cheyenne streets on summer nights, listening to the voices of Harry Caray and Jack Buck as they described St. Louis Cardinals games on radio station KMOX out of St. Louis.

When I was 8, the magic of the game became reality for one night in Denver. Dad somehow finagled three tickets to an exhibition game at Bears Stadium between Denver's Triple-A club in the Pacific Coast League and the New York Yankees. We sat along the third base line, about halfway up the stands. I was mesmerized by the sight of Ralph Terry and Roger Maris and, yes, Hector Lopez, who won the game with an extra-inning home run.

I had quite an entrepreneurial spirit as a youngster, at one point carrying four newspaper routes, the *Wyoming Eagle* and *Rocky Mountain News* in the mornings, and the *Wyoming Tribune* and *Denver Post* in the afternoons. I also mowed the lawns of neighbors in the summer and shoveled snow from their sidewalks in the winter. One summer, I accumulated enough savings to fly myself to Minneapolis where my aunt and uncle took me to my first major-league games, a Sunday double-header at Metropolitan Stadium between the Minnesota Twins and the Oakland Athletics.

Like most boys, I wanted to play in the big leagues. But we did not have indoor batting cages in Cheyenne, so my baseball skills were not able to develop with such a short season every summer. Not to mention, I was small, slow and could not hit a baseball very well. Knowing my playing days were limited, I aspired to be a reporter for a major metropolitan newspaper with baseball as my beat.

When we moved to North Carolina in the summer of 1969, I immediately became a stringer at *The Salisbury Post*, and began honing my writing skills through high school. Upon graduation from UNC Charlotte in 1977, I went to work for *The Chapel Hill Newspaper*, then hooked on with the *Durham Morning Herald* in what surely was a cosmic convergence because, only a few months onto the job, word broke that minor-league baseball was returning to Durham after a nine-year absence. Everyone on the *Herald* sports staff saw Atlantic Coast Conference basketball as the Holy Grail of writing sports. Everyone, except me. Art Chansky and Keith Drum, our sports editors at the time, did not have to seek out a reporter to cover baseball. I wanted the beat, which I viewed as my ticket to eventually landing a dream job like covering the Orioles for the *Baltimore Sun* or the Braves for the *Atlanta Constitution.*

My first order of business on the beat was to reintroduce our readers to professional baseball, and that meant scouring microfilm to produce a seven-part series on the history of the game in Durham, from the numerous former players who remained in town decades after their diamond days to the exploits of pitcher Eddie Neville, who won 75 games for the Bulls from 1949 to 1954.

Then it was off to West Palm Beach, Florida, to experience a young reporter's dream of covering "his" team in spring training. Before going, I located a copy of Leonard Koppett's brilliant 1967 book *"A Thinking Man's Guide to Baseball,"* believing I could gain immeasurable and invaluable amounts of knowledge about the game before my initial meeting with Gallagher and his pitching coach, the former Pittsburgh Pirates standout, Bob Veale.

My bubble was quickly burst — and my already shaky confidence shattered — when I mistakenly attempted to sound well-versed on the game by mentioning that I had recently read Koppett's book. Gallagher responded, between spits of tobacco juice into the paper cup he was holding, that he had not only never read the book but could assure me that he knew more about baseball than "some dumbass writer." And, he added, "Don't ever call me Coach Gallagher. Ever. Again."

Dirty Al it was, from that day forward.

Also, from that day forward, Dirty Al attempted to make me more comfortable being around him as well as Veale, the other minor-league coaches in the Braves' camp, and Atlanta's front-office personnel. Knowing I had an expense account with the newspaper, Dirty Al invited me to join him for breakfast daily at his favorite West Palm Beach restaurant. The newspaper paid, of course. He also dragged me along to the horse track and dog track, teaching me the rudiments to gambling on sports I knew less about than baseball. He made certain I was invited to occasional evening cookouts among the minor-league coaches, and he must have made it known to Hank Aaron — *Hank Aaron!* — that I was an OK guy who could be trusted.

One afternoon as I was standing behind the backstop of a field at the minor-league complex, Aaron walked up and stood next to me. Aaron was in his fourth year as director of Atlanta's minor-league player development. I could barely contain myself, but was so shaken by his presence that I did not speak a word. Then Aaron began calling out the pitches as they arrived at home plate. "Fastball." "Slider." "Changeup." "Fastball." Finally, I gathered enough gumption to ask a question.

"So, how do you recognize a slider?" I stammered, my voice quivering.

"Watch for the red dot," Aaron told me. Then he ordered the pitcher to throw a few more sliders so I could see precisely what he was talking about. Sure enough, the tight spin of the pitch gathered at some point and the hitter — or me, in this case — could see where the seams formed a red dot on the ball as it approached home plate. The pitch was a slider.

Aaron later invited me into a few meetings, and joined me — OK, I joined him — on occasional morning jogs from the Days Inn to the spring training complex and back. Even after my 10 days in camp, I still could not get to the point of feeling completely comfortable in the company of Aaron, Dirty Al and Veale. They retained their lofty status to me.

So, it caught me off guard when Dirty Al approached me near the end of spring training with a proposal. He had driven his station wagon across the country from his home in Fresno, California, to spring training, and planned to drive the car to his new summer home in Durham. He needed a passenger, and possible driver, for the 15-hour jaunt north. What a grand way, he said, for the two of us to get to know each other better in preparation for my first season on the baseball beat.

I agreed. By the time we arrived at my Durham apartment around 2 in the morning, I not only knew Dirty Al better, but I also knew him to be a lot like me. He enjoyed beer. He had no pretention about farting in the car with a perfect stranger. He made me aware that the accepted language of a recent college graduate was not dissimilar to that of a baseball manager, peppered with profanity and usually centered on the ever-popular topic of women.

But no number of days at spring training, nor any ride halfway up the East Coast could possibly have prepared me for what lay ahead that summer. Just as covering the Brooklyn Dodgers in the 1950s proved to be "*The Boys of Summer*" for author Roger Kahn, the 1980 Durham Bulls provided me with a story that has endured over the next three decades.

The significance of history is so difficult to recognize while it is happening. So it was for me throughout that wonderful summer of 1980. Too much was happening too fast to allow myself to step back and see the bigger picture of the franchise and its impact on minor-league baseball and the Research Triangle area of North Carolina. Nevertheless, I did recognize at times that something very magical was happening in Durham, and more specifically at venerable old Durham Athletic Park.

Thirty-seven years later, it is much easier to see just how enchanting those days were for me, for the Durham Bulls franchise and for the City of Durham. Come along with me as I attempt to recapture that incredible ride.

PART I: 1980

WOW!

Durham Athletic Park was dressed for the occasion. Miles Wolff believed in bunting, perhaps harkening to his days growing up in Greensboro, North Carolina, when the festive decorations in the colors of the national flag signaled a big event was happening at War Memorial Stadium. So Wolff made certain that, if nothing else, his Bulls franchise could afford bunting and it would adorn the old downtown Durham stadium on this special occasion.

This was, after all, the season's home-opener, the much-celebrated return of professional baseball to a city that had been without since 1971. That is when Durham shared a Class A Carolina League team with Raleigh, called itself the Raleigh-Durham Triangles and quietly faded away after 68 home games in which the two locales drew a mere 40,447 fans.

That was ancient history by the time Wolff opened the ticket office and gates to Durham Athletic Park on Tuesday, April 15, 1980. In an effort to promote the occasion and ensure a sizeable crowd, the City of Durham touted the game around the city as "Pack the Park Night," with assistance from the "Durham First" committee of the Chamber of Commerce.

By the time the ceremonial first pitch was tossed by Durham Mayor Harry Rodenhizer, Wolff was looking for any kind of break from the torrent of bad luck that had descended on the club to start the season.

Not long after the club's first workout at Durham Athletic Park, a bandit sneaked into the park through a hole in the fence behind the outfield scoreboard, jumped a chain link fence and pried open the door to the Bulls clubhouse. From there the thief took off with 20 of the team's new spiffy white home uniforms, some gloves and a total of $4,000 in equipment. Shortstop Paul Runge lost his glove, as did pitcher Gil Ryan, who borrowed one from team trainer Gene Lane to use early in the season until a new glove arrived. Catcher Blane McDonald was stripped of two catcher's mitts, five practice shirts, one pair of spikes, a pair of batting gloves, an Atlanta Braves jacket and a pair of socks. "Take a last look at your car," one of the players said as the team bus departed for the season-opener in Winston-Salem.

The most precious of the stolen items were the uniforms because these were not just any uniforms. Thom Mount, a Durham native and one of Wolff's investors in the club, used his clout as president of Universal Studios to commission the design of the uniforms. A friend of Mount's, Marilyn Vance, who later would make a name for herself as a Hollywood costume designer, was working for a clothing company in New York.

"The girls love these guys. Look, these guys have got to look sexy," Mount recalled telling Vance upon asking her to first design baseball uniforms a few years earlier for the Amarillo Gold Sox of the Double-A Texas League. The team's gold lamé socks did not go over well, but both Mount and Vance took to the shiny spandex uniforms the Gold

Sox wore. When Mount came calling again, Vance again went with the spandex look for the Bulls.

They were pure Hollywood. The uniforms had a shiny glow to them, an almost silk-like appearance. Right away, many of the players were OK with the uniforms being stolen, until they learned that Wolff had every intention of getting new ones sewn and shipped to Durham. The uniforms' thickness played well during chilly nights in April, but became more cumbersome than the old wool threads worn by baseball players in the 1940s and '50s under the often-oppressive heat and humidity of June, July and August evenings. The fabric stuck to the skin of players, and with repeated washings the sheen began to fade, and bright whites became dulled to a rusty hue.

Wolff did not want his team to officially display the uniforms for the opening four scheduled games at Winston-Salem, preferring to unveil the unique attire to the home crowd. So, instead of wearing the blue Spandex road uniforms at Winston-Salem, the Bulls sported hand-me-down Braves mix-and-match pants and jerseys. With red pinstripes and blue lettering, the Bulls looked as if they were conducting tryouts for the part of Ronald McDonald of McDonald's hamburger fame.

The opener, played at Winston-Salem's Ernie Shore Field, did not go well. Red Sox outfielder Jim Teller blasted a solo home run with two outs in the bottom of the eighth inning, giving Winston-Salem a 3-2 victory. When asked afterward if the three-ball, one-strike fastball got away from him, Durham relief pitcher Pete Teixeira said, disgustingly, "Yeah, about 400-fucking feet away from me!"

The scheduled games for Saturday and Sunday in Winston-Salem were postponed by rain, but not before the Bulls boarded the team bus each day and traveled the 90 miles west on Interstate 40. Both nights the players played cards in the clubhouse while awaiting word that the games would not be played and they could return to Durham. Following Sunday's cancellation, the bus got stuck in mud outside the ballpark, causing an additional three-hour wait.

While the team was away, city workers gave the Durham Athletic Park grandstand one final power washing — only to see water seep through the cement, which also served as the roof to the clubhouse. Many of the players' belongings were soaked.

The teams made up one of the rained-out weekend games by playing a Monday double-header with both games scheduled for seven innings. Winston-Salem won the opener 3-0. Then Durham notched its first victory of the season when, in the 10th inning, Gerald Perry tripled and scored on a wild pitch before McDonald singled and scored on a double by Runge. Big Ike Pettaway, who for no other reason than to be different, said he would not speak to the media all season, picked up the 4-3 win with three innings of shaky relief pitching.

The bus ride back to Durham was interesting, to say the least. Many of the players on the 24-man roster had played the previous year for the team's manager, Dirty Al Gallagher, in Greenwood, South Carolina, of the Class A Western Carolinas League. Those players knew of Gallagher's desire to win games, somewhat of an unusual practice in the minor leagues. That Greenwood club won regular-season championships in each of the two previous seasons, in part because of the talent the parent Atlanta Braves had sent there, and in part because Gallagher placed as much a premium on winning as on developing players.

To those players who were not aware of Gallagher's managing style, it came as somewhat of a shock to learn he would occasionally storm around the clubhouse after a loss, flinging objects and firing off profanity-laced tirades at any player he suspected was not on board with his desire to win every game. Many had not seen these kinds of antics since their college days. If they had not played college ball, they were either startled by Gallagher's actions or simply amused. Most understood that the minor leagues were about producing players who could one day play for the parent club, and winning or losing these games was largely insignificant.

That, at least, had become the trend in the minor leagues. In the golden age of Minor League Baseball from 1946 to 1951 — after World War II and before the advent of a television set in every home — nearly every community of any size in the United States fielded a professional team. In 1949 alone, there were 448 teams in 62 professional leagues beneath the National and American Leagues. The Brooklyn Dodgers fielded 26 farm teams. Forty-four teams played in the state of North Carolina. Those teams represented the cities they played in, and local fans expected them to win. Chasing a pennant in the minor leagues in the late '40s and early '50s was about city pride. Oftentimes, a local professional player also served as a team's manager and was hell-bent on fielding the best team for the many fans he knew as friends.

That attitude changed dramatically with the advent of TV, and even air conditioning. Baseball fans could now sit in the comfort of their homes to watch Saturday and Sunday afternoon games on TV. A night at the ballpark no longer was the best entertainment in town as the likes of *"I Love Lucy"* and *"The Ed Sullivan Show"* came to every town in the country via nightly and weekly TV shows. Later on, with cable TV, major league games were available at home every night of the week. By the 1960s and '70s, minor-league baseball was dying a slow death. In 1964, the minor leagues were down to a record-low 128 teams as cities such as Durham eventually lost their franchises and went without professional baseball. By 1975, there were still only 130 teams overall, and even in 1979, the season before Durham came back into the pro baseball fold, North Carolina counted only teams in Asheville, Charlotte, Gastonia, Greensboro, Kinston, Shelby and Winston-Salem.

At the time, Major League Baseball teams were all about developing talent through the minor leagues. Winning was secondary. They hired coaches and instructors who were teachers of the game. The Carolina League was a prime example of that and featured old heads like former major-leaguers John Lipon and Jack Aker at Salem (Pirates) and Lynchburg (Mets), respectively. The Winston-Salem Red Sox under Buddy Hunter, the Kinston Eagles (Blue Jays) under Dennis Holmberg and the Peninsula Pilots (Phillies) under Bill Dancy were all led by young managers being groomed for big-league jobs by their parent organizations. They were company men first, and knew their performance would be judged primarily on how well they prepared players for the next level of play.

Gallagher believed the knife cut both ways. Players could be taught the fundamentals of the game while developing an edge about winning. He had the backing of his boss, Hank Aaron, who said he could not recall a single game he did not want to win, even when he played during the winter as a young pro on barnstorming teams. The remainder of Atlanta's front office was not necessarily on the same page with Gallagher's philosophy, and this would lead to head-butting later in the season over personnel moves and lineup decisions.

From the outset of the 1980 season, Gallagher made it known to his troops that winning was important. Teixeira, the pitcher who allowed the game-winning home run to Winston-Salem in the season-opener, was the first to find his way onto Gallagher's "list." Teixeira had been a solid starting pitcher for Gallagher the previous season in Greenwood, compiling a 4-3 record and 3.98 earned run average after the Braves selected him in the 19th round of the 1979 draft out of the University of Florida.

Out of spring training, Gallagher and pitching coach Bob Veale believed Teixeira or Ryan, another right-hander out of Blinn (Texas) Junior College, could be the club's closer. But Teixeira caught the wrath of Gallagher that first night in Winston-Salem, lost the closer job, pitched in only three more games and was released by the Braves by the end of April.

Many on the team were not certain what to expect after losing two of three games to open the season in Winston-Salem. They did know to take their cue from Gallagher as they boarded the bus on road trips. If he pulled a beer out the cooler in the front of the bus, propped up his cowboy boots and was jovial, then it was safe for card games and carrying on to commence behind him. If he was silent and stewing, then it was time for sleep.

It was time for sleep on that Monday night ride back from Winston-Salem. Gallagher knew the Braves had stacked his team with some of the best talent in the organization. Losing two of three in the opening series was unacceptable. He believed this team was capable of winning between 80 and 90 games in the 140-game Carolina League season. It had everything: pitching, hitting, defense, speed. Mostly, it had talent, top to bottom. When he filled out the lineup card for the home-opener, Gallagher had four future major-leaguers — Albert Hall in left field, Milt Thompson in center field, Perry at first base and Runge at shortstop — among his nine starters in the field. By season's end, nine players who wore Durham Bulls uniforms eventually made their way to a major-league roster.

Plus, Gallagher wanted to make it back to the major leagues himself, as a manager. He was 34 years old and believed that his winning ways down on the farm would have a major-league club calling his number once he worked his way through the ranks. Gallagher was hand-picked as a manager in the Braves system by Aaron, who remembered the scrappy third baseman for the San Francisco Giants as a player and thought that Gallagher's dirt-under-the-nails approach to baseball would play well in Atlanta's system.

As far as Gallagher was concerned, the pending six-game homestand afforded the opportunity to get out of the gates fast and establish the Bulls as the team to beat in the Carolina League's North Carolina Division — a four-team alignment that also included Kinston, Rocky Mount and Winston-Salem. Gallagher and those fans who plucked down $2.50 for a general admission ticket — $3 for a reserved seat — had no idea what kind of wild ride they were in for over the next six nights at Durham Athletic Park.

Despite mid-40s temperatures and a frigid wind that made for a chilly evening at the ballpark, 4,418 fans put on their overcoats and snuggled tightly to welcome pro baseball back to Durham. That was a sizeable crowd for a 5,000-seat park. To put some context on its size, consider that the New York Mets drew 3,207 fans at Shea Stadium earlier that same day for their game against the Montreal Expos, and the Oakland A's played before 2,140 fans later that evening at home against the Seattle Mariners.

With their stolen home whites still on order, the Bulls sported their blue-on-blue Hollywood road uniforms for the home folks, many of whom from the outset referred to the togs as "disco suits," a description that would stick throughout the season.

The fans were promised a show by Gallagher, who in spring training said the Bulls would have a chance to set the Carolina League record by stealing 300 bases. Hall, Thompson and Ronnie Rudd, a third outfielder, all were speed-burners, with Hall and Thompson having been clocked under 4.5 seconds in 40-yard dashes. Hall stole 66 bases in 77 attempts the previous season at Greenwood.

The Bulls were successful in all nine stolen-base attempts during the Winston-Salem series, then matched that total in the home-opener. The lone failed attempt occurred in the second inning when Runge was thrown out on the back end of a double-steal. The Bulls scored in seven of their eight at-bats in a wild, 12-8 victory over Salem. They stole at least one base in every one of those scoring innings except the fourth when McDonald's solo home run accounted for the lone run.

Rudd and Thompson swiped three bases apiece as unlucky Salem catcher Scott Kuvinka was the victim of his pitchers' inability to keep Durham runners close to first base and the Bulls' exceptional speed in check.

Durham's first-inning run was representative of how the Bulls would create scoring opportunities all season with their speed. Hall led off with a walk. After three throws to first base by Salem pitcher John Huey, Hall stole second base on the first pitch to home plate. Hall moved to third base when second baseman Andres Forbes hit a grounder behind him, and scored on another grounder to the right side of the infield by Perry. One run, no hits.

"I don't think anybody in any league, including the major leagues, can run with our team," Gallagher said following the game. He credited Durham with scoring 10 of its 12 runs because of speed on the bases.

As smooth as everything seemed to click on the field for the Bulls in their home opener, they went equally haywire for the front office. Early in the evening it was apparent the Bulls had not employed enough concession workers. Lines were long. The water mains in both restrooms on the concourse were not equipped to handle that many visitors, and the women's room backed up. Finally, there was no water in either restroom. Then, when the Bulls were in the midst of scoring three more runs in the sixth inning, three towers of lights went dark. The lights had been upgraded prior to the season to meet minor-league minimum standards, but the electrical current was not strong enough for the ballpark to hold. City engineers were summoned to the main office and went to work to quickly restore power. Once they did, following a 22-minute delay, a city maintenance worker held a screwdriver to a wall fuse box in the men's restroom for the remainder of the game in order for the lights to remain burning.

Not one fan seemed to mind the problems. For the first time in decades, there were no fans in attendance defined by their allegiance to North Carolina, North Carolina State, Duke or North Carolina Central universities. The fans no longer were separated by race or occupation or social status, either. Blacks, whites, men, women, elderly, young, students, truck drivers, doctors and lawyers, all seemed as one. They joined as one in chanting "Al-bert! Al-bert! Al-bert!" when Hall reached first base and set his sights on stealing second. They joined as one in bursts of "Let's Go Bulls!" to ignite rallies. No longer did Durham sports fans have to wait until the fall to pull for their favorite college teams in football or basketball. On one chilly night in April, it became obvious that Durham finally had a team it could call its own.

Of course, that uniting of a fan base does not mean a thing once the home-opener has passed and the same frigid 40-degree weather remains to engulf a baseball park. By the next night, only 642 fans braved the elements. That was more like what Wolff expected for a Wednesday evening, which has long been a traditional church night in the South.

That was too bad for the thousands who did not return for a second night. Rick Behenna, the 20-year-old right-hander with much promise, took the Durham Athletic Park mound and pitched like a veteran. Behenna allowed base runners on an error and a walk in the second inning, another on an error in the fourth, still another on a walk in the seventh and again in the eighth. Then, when he retired Salem's Bill Waag to open the ninth inning, Behenna was two outs from a no-hitter.

Behenna, a fourth-round pick of the Braves in 1978 out of a Miami high school, had something professional coaches could not teach, outstanding natural movement on his fastball. He just needed to learn how to pitch, and how to mature on the mound, which meant not allowing his emotions to overtake his psyche when things went wrong. "He was a little boy on the mound," said Tommy Thompson, who at times caught Behenna in Durham, but more often watched the pitcher from his third base position. "He lost it when shit happened. He just was young. He was just young."

Behenna, who received a $15,000 bonus to sign with the Braves, had taken steps in that maturation process by spending two years in Kingsport, Tennessee, of the Rookie Appalachian League, going 6-4 with a 3.77 ERA after being drafted, then 5-3 with a 4.55 ERA in 1979 in a return engagement before earning a late-season promotion to Greenwood.

Gallagher and Veale saw enough of Behenna in his brief tenure at Greenwood to know they wanted him on their Durham roster in 1980, even though the slender 6-foot-2 pitcher lost all six decisions and posted a troublesome 5.23 ERA. Out of spring training, Gallagher and Veale were in agreement that Behenna could be the ace of the Bulls staff and he earned the opening-night start at Winston-Salem, pitching capably without a decision. He allowed two earned runs while walking three and striking out seven in 6 2/3 innings. Unlike in today's game, where top pitching prospects are not allowed to remotely approach 100 pitches early in the minor-league season, Behenna was under no such restraints. He threw 116 pitches at Winston-Salem, and after keeping his no-hitter alive with one out in the ninth inning against Salem in his second outing, Behenna's pitch count had reached 101.

Only the die-hard fans were on hand to see potential history in the making. The only other Bulls pitchers to throw no-hitters at Durham Athletic Park were Robert "Dizzy" Cruze against Fayetteville on July 14, 1950, and Bruce "Bat Man" Von Hoff against Rocky Mount on Aug. 10, 1966. Cruze and Von Hoff were among five Durham pitchers to ever toss no-hitters.

It was not to be for Behenna on this night. Over Behenna's next 14 pitches, Salem's Mark Riemer singled to end the no-hit bid, Tony Merulla doubled and Kuvinka singled to drive in a run, ending the hopes for a shutout. Gallagher signaled for Pettaway to relieve Behenna, who left to a standing ovation. Leading the cheers was Behenna's No. 1 fan, "Coop," who gathered up his belongings every summer from his home in Miami and moved to whichever city Behenna was pitching. "Coop" would clang his cowbell as he walked the stadium, occasionally stopping to lead a cheer or simply introduce himself as the grandfather of the young Durham pitcher.

Once Behenna retired to the dugout, he watched as Pettaway struck out the final two Salem batters to preserve the 4-1 Durham victory.

To the 884 fans who again braved cold weather for the third game of the homestand, they had to be wondering what could possibly happen next? They had to wait 12 innings to find out, and for the smattering who remained to the end, they were rewarded.

Twice, Durham rallied to extend the game. The Bulls scored three runs in the bottom of the eighth inning to knot the score at 4. Then in the bottom of the ninth inning McDonald's shallow fly ball to right field was enough to score Milt Thompson from third base and tie the game at 5. When Mike Quade led off the Salem 12th inning with a single, stole second and Kuvinka was hit by a pitch, it looked as if Durham would again have to rally from behind.

Salem designated hitter Terry Salazar scorched a line drive off Teixeira, Durham's third pitcher, into the glove of Tommy Thompson at third base. "I was just going to go straight to first with it," Thompson said afterward, "then he (second baseman Jeff Matthews) started yelling at me so I threw it to him." Matthews stepped on second base to catch Quade trying to retreat to the bag, then relayed the ball to Perry at first, retiring Kuvinka, who was more than halfway to second base.

A triple play.

The buzz from that rare play was still cascading around the park when Runge lined the second pitch, a high fastball, from Salem's Crucito Carvajal in the bottom half of the inning 360 feet off the scoreboard behind the left-center field fence for the game-winning home run. There was more than just Hollywood in the Bulls uniforms as the team celebrated a dramatic win.

Already, the Bulls faithful were talking about the "Miracle on Morris Street."

With a weekend of home games scheduled against the Alexandria Dukes, word was quickly spreading throughout Durham and beyond that something special was happening at Durham Athletic Park. In an effort to make certain Duke students were welcome at the park, the Bulls promoted Friday's series-opener as "College Night." Nothing special marked the promotion, other than the allure of one-dollar, 16-ounce beers. With the legal drinking age in North Carolina at 18, there was no cheaper beer in town for college students to go with two-dollar ticket prices and a student ID.

Selling beer at the ballpark was an important obstacle for Wolff and his club to overcome when negotiating a deal to play baseball in Durham. When the Bulls previously played at Durham Athletic Park, alcohol sales were prohibited. Fans routinely purchased cans of beer at Pete's Grill across Morris Street, tucked them in brown paper bags and sneaked them into the ballpark. This time, Wolff was fortunate that the North Carolina General Assembly had recently passed a law that permitted alcohol to be sold at sporting events. The Durham Budweiser distributor landed the first contract with the Bulls to provide beer, and sold all 36 kegs it had earmarked for the opening homestand during the home-opener alone.

So there was plenty of incentive for the Bulls to tap into the Duke student population, other than for the game itself. The weather also had taken a turn for the better, making for a pleasant weekend of evenings, and Duke students responded by accounting for a goodly portion of the 2,316 fans for the Friday series-opener against Alexandria, a team not affiliated with a major-league club but one that had players under contract with multiple big-league teams.

Wolff had little knowledge of Durham's separatist past, one that divided the city between the perceived elite who attended and worked at Duke University and the rest of the city's more-mainstream population. For most of its distinguished history, Duke had an aura like it was on its own separate island, even though it was located inside the city limits. Pete Bock, the Bulls general manager, grew up in West Durham and remembered on occasion riding his bicycle with friends to the nearby Duke campus. The kids would stand in awe while admiring the Gothic-style cathedral and pictorial campus buildings. The school was like nothing they saw in and around Durham, which instead was dotted with tobacco warehouses and not much else.

So Wolff was happy to see Duke students participating in a Durham event, and participate they did. The Friday "College Night" promotion became a staple at Bulls games, and the students adopted

Matthews as their favorite player from the outset, even forming a quasi fan club. Matthews responded in kind, first by delivering a three-run double in the third inning, then by heading for the third-base stands immediately after the game to shake hands with his new band of followers.

"I don't know how they started it, but it's sure nice," Matthews said of the fan club. "I really don't know what I did to deserve it, but it's nice to know somebody enjoys what you do."

That Matthews was a little awestruck was understandable. He was typical of a minor-league player who had never before played baseball in front of sizeable crowds. Kingsport averaged about 650 fans a game during his Rookie ball season of 1977; and Greenwood drew about 600 fans per game in each of his two seasons in the Western Carolinas League.

This was a make-or-break season for Matthews, a Minnesota native and 10th-round selection by Atlanta in the 1977 draft out of Minnesota State University-Mankato. He was two months shy of his 24th birthday, meaning he was one of the older players on the roster and in the Carolina League. He was what baseball folks called a "roster filler," meaning he was not thought of as much of a major-league prospect but was good to have around, both on the field and in the clubhouse. Matthews was not exceptional at any position, but very solid at second base, shortstop and third base. He also was one of the few players who was married and naturally carried with him some respect from the younger players. To the manager, he served as the perfect utility player and model person off the field, thus earning a leadership role on the club that was noticeable even in spring training.

There was not a hint of jealousy from any of his teammates over the new-found "stardom" that Matthews was experiencing early in the season from his legion of Duke followers. Like Matthews, his teammates also seemed to be reveling in the attention they were receiving.

"The crowds are part of the reason these kids are so jacked up," Gallagher said. "These people are behind them."

"These people seem to really miss baseball," said Tommy Thompson, who blasted a two-run homer in the fourth inning of that Friday victory. "They get excited over about anything you do."

"The fans are right on top of you," Runge said. "There's not a better feeling than playing in front of these fans. I've never had so much fun playing baseball."

"It's kind of like a college atmosphere out here," said McDonald, whose two-run homer in the eighth inning was a factor in the Bulls' 11-4 win and also was the first by a Durham player to clear both fences in left field and land on Geer Street. "It makes me want to go out and do my best."

Now that Duke students were solidly on board, Saturday's game served as "Kids Night" with the first promotional give-away of the season. Children 14 years and under received a Durham Bulls rain jacket with a paid admission. The jackets were little more than a piece of plastic with the Bulls logo emblazoned on them. With a per-item cost of less than 50 cents, the club could turn a reasonable profit by drawing an extra 500 to 1,000 fans to the park. Wolff and Bock were expecting a crowd of 3,000, but they grossly underestimated the turnout.

Thirty minutes before the game's scheduled first pitch, the park was already packed, bulging to its 5,000 capacity. Wolff and Bock stood in the parking lot outside the stadium staring in disbelief at what they saw. A line beginning at the ticket window had formed — two-people wide — all the way out to Morris Street, then down the hill, back up the hill and around the corner onto Foster Street, behind the Brame Building far beyond the right field wall. Wolff and Bock began shouting to those in line that the game was sold out, to "go home," and come back on another date when the club would order more give-away jackets.

"You don't do that in the minors," Wolff wrote later in the season for a first-person story that appeared in *Inside Sports* magazine. "Usually, you've got to beat people over the head or kidnap them to bring them in. But tonight, incredibly, we don't have any more room. Every seat is taken. … The best part is that these are paying fans. In the minors, there is a tendency to put out free tickets or do some other mathematical wizardry, where every person is counted two-and-a-half times. But we've got 5,791 people tonight."

The crowd was the largest to see a game at Durham Athletic Park since 1946 and the 10th largest in Carolina League history.

The Bulls extended their winning streak to six games to the delight of the jacket-night throng. This time, the Bulls hero was backup catcher Steve Stieb, mired in a hitless streak to start the season that reached 11 at-bats when he struck out in the third inning. When he came to bat again in the fifth inning, Durham trailed 3-1 when Stieb sent his first hit of the season sailing over the left-field fence to knot the score. Then, in the seventh inning, Stieb doubled to score Matthews with the go-ahead run in the eventual 5-4 decision.

Stieb was best known to baseball fans for being the older brother — by one year — of Dave Stieb, the major-league pitching star. Both Stiebs played at Southern Illinois University, Steve as a catcher who was named to the 1977 all-tournament team at the College World Series, and Dave as an outfielder. Dave was forced into duty as a relief pitcher in a late-season game at SIU, two Toronto scouts liked what they saw and were instrumental in his being selected by the Blue Jays as a pitcher in the fifth round of the 1978 draft. A year earlier, Steve was taken by the Braves in the 13th round. So, while Dave was earning the first of seven All-Star Game appearances with Toronto that summer of 1980, Steve was winning over Durham fans with his late-game heroics.

Stieb was back in the lineup again for Sunday's game, the finale of the six-game homestand, and he contributed a single and a run scored as the Bulls win streak reached seven games. The 7-4 decision over Alexandria was played before 2,722 fans, shooting the Bulls far ahead of the rest of the Carolina League in attendance with an aggregate of 16,769, an average of 2,794 per game.

"Wow!" was all Wolff could come up with to describe the season-opening homestand.

"Fantastic!" chimed in Bock.

It was left up to Gallagher to temper the enthusiasm of Durham's suddenly rabid fan base.

"We're not going to win every game," the manager said. "You don't usually do this in A ball. These kids are doing everything right. And it goes right back to the support we're getting in this town."

No Virgin Territory

A few weeks before the 1980 season I had a chance meeting with Walt Sorgi, whose claim to baseball fame in Durham was that he played in the Bulls' first game in the Class C Carolina League. That was 1945. Durham defeated Burlington 5-0 and the winning pitcher that day was Ray Daedlow, according to Sorgi's vivid memory.

Sorgi knew all about professional baseball in Durham. He grew up in Milton, Massachusetts, and attended Harvard University before pursuing baseball professionally. He began his career by playing in 29 games for a team in Hartford, Connecticut, in the Boston Braves organization in the Class A Eastern League. A year later, he hooked on with the Red Sox organization and was sent to Durham, though the Bulls were not a Boston farm club at the time. Despite playing his final two seasons with Wilson of the Class D Coastal Plain League in 1946-47, Sorgi met and married a Durham girl, Agnes Pleasants, and established his own insurance business in Durham. He played in every old-timer's game possible in Durham thereafter and kept an eye on the game he so dearly loved.

So when Sorgi stood on the grassy knoll outside Durham Athletic Park and offered his take on baseball returning to Durham in 1980 after a nine-year absence, I figured it was worth listening to. This man wanted baseball back in town as much as anyone, yet his skepticism shone through.

"Not going to work," Sorgi said as he shook his head. "Not going to work."

Then he put a couple of exclamation marks on his belief that Durham was not ready to support a professional minor-league baseball team.

"This ain't no virgin territory!" Sorgi said. "It's been fucked before!"

Sorgi was hardly alone in his thinking, at least in Durham and the surrounding Research Triangle area. Professional sports had pretty much died with the advent of the Atlantic Coast Conference in 1953 and interest in men's basketball at Duke University in Durham, the University of North Carolina in Chapel Hill and North Carolina State University in Raleigh was unrivaled nationally. If fans in the area did not attend one of the three schools they at least had some semblance of allegiance to one of them, particularly when it came to men's basketball.

Much like in many areas of the country where college football dominates conversations year-round, talk of college basketball was constantly discussed at coffee shops and around water coolers even during the off-season in the Research Triangle.

Any news of Durham's pending return to minor-league baseball was undoubtedly relegated to the inside pages of sports sections in the area with job searches for college basketball coaches at N.C. State and Duke grabbing the front-page headlines. The opening of the new, 65,000-square foot Durham County Library on Roxboro Street garnered bigger headlines than anything about the Bulls.

News that Al Gallagher would manage the Durham Bulls? Who knew? And who really cared? At least that was the prevailing view of most sports fans in the area. Such ambivalence toward the return of professional baseball represented part of the uphill climb Miles Wolff, the owner of the Bulls, and Jim Mills, the Carolina League president, faced as they located the franchise squarely in the midst of a college basketball hotbed.

Mills was a North Carolina native, raised in the little community of Apex, just outside Raleigh, and educated at North Carolina State. He played for the Raleigh Capitals in the Carolina League during its heyday of 1946 and 1947. Fans would typically fill old Devereux Meadow ballpark in Raleigh one night to see the Capitals play the Durham Bulls, then drive some 25 miles over to Durham the next night to see the same teams play at jam-packed Durham Athletic Park. Devereux Meadow was demolished in 1979 so the city of Raleigh could use the land to park its waste-disposal trucks. Durham, fortunately, never tore down its ballpark thanks to the generosity and foresight of the John Sprunt Hill family. As a condition of donating the land that the ballpark was situated on to the city in 1933, the Hill family stipulated that the property could never be used for anything other than recreation.

Mills loved the ballpark from his playing days, and later during his umpiring career — both at the college and professional levels. He and his twin brother, Joe, also were long-time basketball officials who called many Atlantic Coast Conference games. Jim Mills took over presidency of the Carolina League for the 1977 season at a time that was one the most difficult and challenging periods in the circuit's storied 32-year history. The Carolina League operated with only four teams during the 1975 and 1976 seasons, with Salem and Lynchburg out of Virginia and Winston-Salem in North Carolina playing both seasons. The Rocky Mount, North Carolina, franchise operated in 1975 and then relocated to Hampton, Virginia, for the '76 season. With only four teams, the Carolina League elected to play an inter-locking schedule with the four-team Western Carolinas League both years.

The same four franchises remained intact when Mills took over in 1977, and he knew that without expansion of the league it faced possible extinction. With Mills working hard behind the scenes, the league added franchises in Kinston, North Carolina, and Alexandria, Virginia, for the 1978 and 1979 seasons. But a six-team league was still less than ideal and Mills went in search of additional franchises. He explored possibilities in Macon, Georgia, which had been without pro ball since 1967; Hagerstown, Maryland, without a team since 1955; and tiny Red Springs, North Carolina, which last fielded a team in 1969.

Mills at least had one thing in his favor as the Atlanta Braves were interested in adding a franchise to the Carolina League. The Braves, with only four clubs in their farm system, were looking to expand their minor-league operations and wanted to field a team at the high Class A level, thus diminishing the enormous jump for players from the low Class A Western Carolinas League to the Double-A Southern League.

Durham was particularly attractive as a locale on a couple of counts. It was centrally located geographically, but most important the city had a ballpark, no matter its state of disrepair. Many cities in the southeast, like Raleigh, had torn down their old ballparks believing professional baseball would never be played there again.

As president of the Carolina League, Mills also oversaw its umpires. He handled their scheduling and checked in with them as often as possible to head off any problems they might encounter over the course of a season. One young umpire Mills grew particularly close to was Pete Bock, who was reared and still lived in Durham, and likely was on his way to the big leagues.

To put his plan in motion, Mills requested a lunch date with Bock in early July of 1979 at Bullock's Bar-B-Cue restaurant, a Durham landmark famous locally for its vinegar-based pork and vegetable plates. Mills, as was his direct style, did not mince words and got right to the point of the meeting.

"Do you know a lot of people in Durham?" Mills asked.

"Well," Bock responded. "I've never met the mayor, but I know of him. There's a council person I know. A guy down the street works for the city, and I know the parks and recreation director real well."

Mills commissioned Bock to meet with Wade Cavin, whose term as mayor was coming to an end, for the express purpose of gauging the City of Durham's interest in fielding a professional baseball team. Cavin would soon turn direction of the city over to Harry Rodenhizer, who owned and operated the Pizza Palace, a restaurant located off Ninth Street in Durham near Duke University's east campus. Rodenhizer was a man of great vision and campaigned to be mayor on the promise that Durham would enact changes that would enable it to catch up to its neighbors in Raleigh and Chapel Hill. Both of those cities had prospered with the birth of Research Triangle Park, a high-tech research and development center that was created in 1959 through the cooperative efforts of state and area governments, universities and business interests. Most of those from outside the area who landed jobs in the rapidly expanding park flocked to Raleigh and Chapel Hill, and even Cary, a new suburb of Raleigh located on the fringes of the park, to live. Invariably, they passed on Durham, which had suffered mightily with the steady decline of the tobacco industry in the late '60s and early '70s. By March of 1980, Liggett & Myers Tobacco Company put up for sale two historic warehouses with an asking price of just $450,000, a sure sign that the tobacco industry was dying and Durham would no longer be known as one of the tobacco centers of the southeast.

When Rodenhizer became mayor he inherited a dormant, if not dead, downtown. There were few restaurants, virtually no businesses in operation and block upon block of empty store fronts. Rodenhizer first got approval to expand the Durham Freeway, thus making travel easier from Raleigh and, more importantly, from the Research Triangle Park. He also kick-started discussions about building a sports arena in downtown Durham, hoping to model the complex after one in Lexington, Kentucky, that housed University of Kentucky basketball and became a social gathering spot for Lexington residents. Once deterred on that front, Rodenhizer looked at other options and soon came to the realization that minor-league baseball might be a viable avenue to draw Durham residents and those from surrounding communities into the city's center.

Bock put the wheels in motion when he later met with Rodenhizer and Alex Gilleskie, director of Durham parks and recreation. They continued to meet on a weekly basis and after each meeting, Bock reported back to Mills that there was keen interest in baseball on the city's part. The cautionary tale from the city's end was that there would be financial constraints in refurbishing old, rundown Durham Athletic Park.

"We're not going to put a lot of money in it," Rodenhizer repeated often to Bock.

Next, Mills himself met with Rodenhizer and Gilleskie and offered to bring in a couple of prospective owners of the franchise who could better assess the viability of Durham Athletic Park and perhaps give Mills and the City of Durham a realistic assessment of baseball's prospects.

In early August, Mills arranged for minor-league operators Larry Schmittou and Frances Crockett, who owned and operated successful franchises in Nashville, Tennessee, and Charlotte, North Carolina, of the Double-A Southern League, respectively, to visit Durham and tour the ballpark. A year earlier, Schmittou, a former Vanderbilt University baseball coach, had convinced country music stars Conway Twitty, Jerry Reed, Larry Gatlin and others to invest in the Nashville franchise, and the new Sounds ownership group then spearheaded the building of a new, 10,700-seat ballpark. The team promptly drew 380,159 fans in their first year of operation to not only lead the Southern League in attendance by a wide margin, but all of minor-league baseball. In 1979, they boosted that total to 515,482, while also successfully adding and overseeing a new club in Greensboro, North Carolina, of the Western Carolinas League.

Crockett's father, Jim, was heavily involved in the promotion of professional wrestling for years, and saw a natural tie-in with minor league baseball. He spearheaded the building of Griffith Park in Charlotte for the 1976 season and put his daughter in charge of the club as its general manager. She, too, was interested in helping the Crockett family find another successful franchise.

During their Durham visit, Schmittou and Crockett mentioned to Rodenhizer that they were interested in a partnership to own and operate the proposed new Durham franchise in the Carolina League.

Then Bock, Schmittou and Crockett hopped in Bock's car and drove to Durham Athletic Park, which was located several blocks from City Hall on the fringe of the downtown district. Once inside, Schmittou suggested he take the dirt path behind the grandstand on the first-base side down to the field, with Bock and Crockett doing the same behind the grandstand on the third-base side.

The tour lasted less than a minute, perhaps 45 seconds, as Crockett screamed for Schmittou to meet immediately back on the concourse.

"Let's go!" Crockett said

"What?" Schmittou said.

"I just saw a rat that was as big as a dog."

"Seriously?"

The trio exited the ballpark, got back in Bock's car and rode in silence to Rodenhizer's office.

"That didn't take you long," Rodenhizer said upon greeting Bock.

The four then sat down to discuss the ballpark.

"What do you think of our ballpark?" Rodenhizer asked.

"Well, I think you ought to take about 10 sticks of dynamite and blow that damn thing up," Schmittou said.

The mayor's eyes nearly bugged out of his head.

"Really?" Rodenhizer said.

"Yes," Schmittou responded. "We're not interested."

Everyone shook hands. Schmittou returned to Nashville. Crockett returned to Charlotte. Rodenhizer, Bock and Mills returned to the drawing board, fully realizing that pro baseball's return to Durham might be dead, even before it got off the ground.

While despondent over the news, Mills was not ready to give up.

His next phone call was to Wolff, who was recommended to Mills by the Braves. Wolff had succeeded Mills as general manager of the Savannah, Georgia, franchise, which the Braves owned and operated, nearly a decade earlier when Atlanta took a chance on a 26-year-old with virtually no experience. In Wolff's first season, 1971, he earned minor league "Executive of the Year" honors from *The Sporting News*. Wolff remained in Savannah for three years but since then was in search of a possible team to own and operate himself. Like Mills, he first eyed the Macon, Georgia, market but abandoned that pursuit when Mills called to inquire of his interest in Durham.

A couple of weeks following the Schmittou-Crockett fiasco, Mills set up the same kind of look-see at Durham, only this time with Wolff. Bock first met Wolff at Rodenhizer's office, and then Bock drove Wolff to the ballpark. This time, the prospective owner had a different outlook. Wolff was immediately enamored by the old ballpark, despite its rundown condition. The grandstand area was solid, for the most part. Beyond that, Wolff believed a coat of paint, a few nails to broken boards, a new outfield fence, improved lighting, some sod in the infield … and Durham Athletic Park was ready for baseball.

Wolff particularly liked the asking price for the ballclub. He was virtually broke from six years of working odd jobs across the Southeast, mostly baseball-related, without steady income. His mother had died five years earlier and left him in the neighborhood of $30,000 in various stocks. So he had enough to cover the $2,417 franchise fee to join the Carolina League. The league treasury counted $14,502 at the end of the 1979 season, meaning each of its six existing franchises was worth $2,417. Thus, the entry fee.

"They were almost embarrassed to ask me for it," Wolff said of the league and its entry fee. "Minor-league clubs had no value because it was not a way to make money. You were buying a losing business. If you wanted to do it, fine."

Wolff next needed assurances from Durham officials that the city would contribute to the renovation of the ballpark. By August 16, the city had formulated a proposal to Wolff that included an $8,000 rental fee for use of the park for a 70-game home schedule. Additionally, a $16,000 performance bond was requested from Wolff in the event that the terms of the contract were not met, though the figure was later reduced to $10,000. The city also wanted $6,000 from the club for concessions rights, but that fee later was waived, implemented in the second year and set at seven percent of gross concession revenues for every succeeding year.

For its part, the city proposed $30,479 in improvements to the park, though the club was asked to contribute $4,000 of that total. That might sound like a pittance for repairs, yet calculated for inflation it amounted to about $100,000 in today's dollars. The city's proposed improvements and cost broke down this way:

ITEM	COST
Field lights improvement	$10,000
Bermuda 419 infield sod	$4,000
Outfield fence construction	$3,079
General fence repairs	$3,000
New sound system	$3,000
Painting improvements	$2,500
Electrical system improvements	$1,500
Wooden bleacher repair	$735
Repair/replace restroom fixtures	$735

ITEM	COST
Window security improvements	$630
Protection of building in outfield	$500
Six-foot extension of dugouts	$250
Concrete repair of box seats	$200
Window glass replacements	$200
Scoreboard improvements	$150
Subtotal	**$30,479**
Club payment	**($4,000)**
Total	**$26,479**

On August 23, the Durham City Council Finance Committee unanimously approved the appropriations with the money coming from a reserve for recreation-related capital improvements. The funding approval all but signaled the return of professional baseball to Durham.

One week later, Pat Nugent, assistant to Atlanta Braves General Manager John Mullen, and Paul Snyder, the club's director of scouting and player development, toured Durham Athletic Park and offered Wolff their input — and ultimately their approval. Snyder, who spent his entire 50-year career in the Braves system including seven as a player, loved old ballparks and believed in a baseball philosophy that any park could use a quick, two-step approach to playability: Paint and toilets.

If there was a concern for the Atlanta brass it was the right field area. There was no outfield fence at the time of the tour; instead, a slight incline backed up to the base of the Brame Building, a mere 300 feet from home plate. Major league clubs normally desire to get a true measure of their prospects based on their performance in the minors and generally attempt to avoid playing in ballparks where home run totals can be inflated because of a short porch. By putting an eight-foot fence at the base of the incline, the distance from home plate would be reduced to as little as 285 or 290 feet, at most. The right-center field power alley would be a scant 330 feet. Yet Snyder was undeterred as he saw it from a scout's view. He believed scouts were wise enough to know that unconventional-shaped parks like the one in Durham made hitters look better and pitchers worse than their actual statistics.

Furthermore, he liked the way Wolff and Bock planned to rectify the situation: They would have "305 feet" painted on the new fence at the base of the right-field foul pole, and "340" painted on the fence in the right-field power alley. Problem solved.

With a commitment from the city to move forward on the park, and an affiliation agreement from the Atlanta Braves to send a team of players to Durham, Wolff next hired Bock as his general manager. Unbeknownst to Wolff at the time, he gained an extra measure of free publicity by hiring Bock.

It seems that the past and future of Durham's Carolina League franchise had a common denominator with the past resting beneath the Durham Athletic Park pitching mound and the future now sitting in the front office. Prior to his death in 1967, former Durham pitcher Claude Charles "Buck" Weaver requested that his ashes be scattered on the park's pitching mound. Weaver was Bock's grandfather.

Weaver, the step-father of Bock's mother, produced an 18-8 record with a 3.93 earned run average in 238 innings of work for Durham in 1947 as a 41-year-old right-handed pitcher. Weaver pitched another three years in the minor leagues to conclude a 12-season professional career. When he died 17 years later in Greensboro, his death certificate in the Guilford County Health Department still listed his occupation as "professional baseball player."

Weaver was 61 at his death. On April 28, 1967, Bock was not yet a teenager when he gathered with a handful of relatives at Durham Athletic Park. The Rev. Malbert Smith, longtime pastor of Grey Stone Baptist Church in Durham, spread Weaver's ashes on the pitcher's mound. Later, Fred McNeill, the Bulls trainer and equipment manager, raked the ashes into the red soil.

(In another touch of fate involving Weaver and Bock, Bock's son Jeff signed a professional contract with the Braves organization in 1993, and played for the Bulls in 1994, which turned out to be the final year the club used Durham Athletic Park as its playing venue).

■

On October 7, 1979, the Durham Bulls were officially admitted to the Carolina League as a seventh club. An expansion application from Rocky Mount was approved a short time later, boosting the league to a desirable complement of eight teams. That left Wolff six months to get his new team ready for play and raise enough money to cover start-up costs, which he estimated would be about $30,000.

Wolff's initial phone call was to an old friend, Van Schley, who was willing to contribute $5,000. At the time, Schley was living in California and supplying players on the side to a handful of minor-league teams that were operating without major-league working agreements. Schley had significant Hollywood connections and advised Wolff to contact Thom Mount, who grew up in Durham and was then in his fourth year at age 30 as president of Universal Pictures in California. Mount agreed to toss in an additional $5,000, and recommended that Wolff call his father in Durham to inquire about providing legal assistance in running the club.

Mount's father, Lillard, was a well-respected Durham attorney and a baseball fan who very much wanted pro ball back in Durham. He took over all legal aspects of the club and charged Wolff a mere $600 a year for his services. Mount recommended that Wolff form a corporation with dues-paying stockholders, thereby avoiding the need for bank loans to get the business off the ground. Thus, Durham Bulls Baseball, Inc. was formed.

Wolff contributed $9,000 himself to the corporation, effectively making him the largest stockholder at 30 percent. A friend, Joe Helyar, joined Schley and Mount in contributing $5,000. Helyar was working in ticket operations for the Boston Red Sox at the time and previously had owned several minor-league clubs. Wolff then solicited $1,000 from each of his sisters, Anna Dixon and Lila Wolff, his father, Miles Hoffman Wolff, and three childhood friends in Greensboro, Jim Fulton, Jim McGee, and Johnny Tasker to make up the full complement of $30,000.

Even with the money secured from stockholders, financing operations of the club was difficult in the early months of the team's existence. Wolff went without a paycheck until the season began. Bock was hired at $750 a month, which represented a significant drop in pay as Bock was making a $950-a-month salary as an umpire in the Carolina League and had been promised $1,300 a month the following year in the Double-A Southern League. Although he was employed for only nine months while umpiring, Bock supplemented his income by working at flooring and ceiling companies in Durham during the offseason.

Bock was paid on schedule as the Bulls general manager for the months of October and November, and even promised a raise to $900 a month once the season started. Then Wolff ran out of money, and reluctantly asked Bock to go without a paycheck until the season started — or until he could sell enough advertising on outfield fence signs to cover the club's operating costs. Luckily for Bock, his wife, Cindy, was supporting the family by working a steady job at the Research Triangle Institute outside Durham.

"I would wake up every morning at 4, thinking 'What have I done?' " said Wolff, second-guessing himself. "It was all crashing in. We've got to do this, this and this. We've got no money. I was a wreck. … It wasn't like I could throw in the towel, but it was close. It was a matter of were we going to make it? It was scary."

So scary that six weeks before the season's first pitch Wolff sought a bailout from the Carolina League. Mills reached into the league's coffers without informing the other club owners and loaned Wolff and the Bulls $6,000. Had the other owners known of the illegal undocumented transgression, the league very well could have folded.

The Bulls initially gained financial support from Liggett & Myers because the one-time tobacco giant was desperate to strengthen its foothold in the community with the tobacco industry faltering around it. Liggett & Myers purchased an outfield sign as part of its commitment to the Bulls, and Bock quickly sold out the remaining 25 signs at $800 apiece, netting $20,800.

While Wolff was attending the World Series in Baltimore, he got word from Bock that the Durham Budweiser distributor had purchased eight season tickets. Wolff was thrilled that Bock was selling entire boxes of eight, and the 180 available seats at $125 each quickly were sold out, netting an additional $22,500. At that point, the club decided to add 400 chair-back seats in the grandstand behind home plate and those also sold out at $100 each for 70 home dates, netting $40,000. Wolff was informed that the Durham franchise had historically sold book tickets, or partial season tickets, and the sale of 1,000 of those at $15 for 10 games also significantly aided the cash flow.

"We were generating money, but we still didn't have enough to get to opening day," Wolff said.

Meanwhile, Bock was also securing deals with local merchants to get the ballpark in order. He sold a fence sign to West Durham Lumber Company in exchange for installing carpet in the home team clubhouse. He befriended David Clark, head of maintenance for the city of Durham, and invited Clark and his entire crew to the ballpark one afternoon and presented all with Durham Bulls caps and T-shirts. From that day forward, the crew responded to any needs from Bock without charge to the club.

"You'd change bulbs and they still didn't work," Bock said. "We'd call David, they would find a short in the fuse box and fix it."

The front office, which amounted to two cramped rooms at the top of the grandstand behind home plate, needed furniture. Bock found an office in Durham that was closing, scrounged for a couple of desks and chairs, and the rooms were furnished. Bock convinced a Durham milk company to convert a couple of its retired delivery trucks into beer stands. Again, at no charge to the club.

Wherever possible, the club improvised.

A "colored" restroom from days gone by on the first base side of the main grandstand was converted into a women's restroom. A closet next to the visitor's clubhouse became the umpire's dressing room.

The Braves inquired about building tunnels from the dugouts to an area under the grandstand that served both clubhouses. Wolff refused, believing that it was important for both teams to walk through spectators — and mingle with fans — outside the first base dugout when entering and leaving the field.

Coca-Cola and Miller beer agreed to provide a scoreboard behind the left field fence under a 10-year contract as long as the club installed it. One afternoon, Bock and Bill Miller, the newly hired sales assistant and head groundskeeper, worked a crane and bolted the new scoreboard into place.

Finally, two days prior to the season-opener, a Durham health department inspector showed up at the ballpark and informed the club that it could not use bagged ice. The club needed an ice machine, which cost in the neighborhood of $2,000, money Wolff and the Bulls did not have. Wolff sat in the stands behind home plate with his head buried in his hands believing the Bulls might be out of business before they even got started. Bock again came to the rescue, this time by convincing the health inspector to allow the club to use bagged ice — at least through the opening homestand. The Bulls were back in business.

■

All the while, the Braves began welcoming their minor-league farmhands to spring training in West Palm Beach, Florida, where they shared Municipal Stadium and the surrounding complex with the Montreal Expos. Unlike the major league players who arrived in Florida in mid-February, most of the players slotted for play in the lower minor leagues did not report to camp until the second week of March.

Among those arriving in the Braves camp were Mike Garcia, Tommy Thompson and Lance Gore. Garcia and Thompson became fast friends the summer before, both late-round picks by the Braves stationed in Kingsport, Tennessee, for their introduction to professional baseball at the Rookie League level.

Garcia was selected in the 27th round, a utility infielder who proudly wore the College World Series ring won in 1979 by his Cal

State Fullerton team. Thompson was picked one round later as a catcher-third baseman out of the University of Oklahoma, where twice his teams fell short of playing in the College World Series after winning Big Eight Conference titles.

Their friendship came naturally, mostly because they were college kids. At the time in minor-league baseball, a stigma was often attached to those players who opted for college over professional baseball. Though a new, enlightened era was soon about to pervade college baseball, the game was not nearly as developed in the late '70s as it is today. So the label from front office personnel to coaches about college draft picks went something like this: "Don't know how to play the game properly; think they know everything about the game; believe they are smarter than everyone else."

Some of that assessment applied to Garcia and Thompson, but from the moment of their arrival in Kingsport it was apparent to everyone on the coaching staff that both did, in fact, know how to play the game. They were taught the game's fundamentals well by coaches who ran solid programs: Garcia by Augie Garrido at Fullerton and Thompson by Enos Semore at Oklahoma. Both knew to slide hard into second base, run hard even on routine ground ball outs, and advance a runner with their bats.

Garcia batted .285 and hit six home runs at Kingsport. Thompson batted .307 with nine home runs. They both played well enough in Kingsport to earn promotions in 1980 to either Atlanta's low Class A team, which had moved to Anderson, South Carolina, of the new South Atlantic League, or to the high Class A club in Durham.

They kept in touch over the winter by telephone. When Garcia informed Thompson that he was driving from his home in California to Florida for spring training, the two agreed to meet in Houston, Texas, and travel the remainder of the way together. Gore, a teammate of Garcia's two years earlier at Cal State Fullerton, was part of the traveling party from California. Gore was in his third season with the Braves, a left-handed pitcher who produced an outstanding season in 1979 with a 13-11 record and 2.52 ERA for Greenwood.

All three players were 22 years old and living the dream. They were paid to play a game they loved, and they were sharing the excitement of professional baseball with newfound friends. The meeting in Houston was a moment of euphoria, a trio gathering to celebrate the merry ride they would continue in baseball.

Garcia and Thompson had developed a habit in Kingsport of greeting each other with leaping high fives. So when they met at an underpass along Interstate 10, their excitement in seeing each other could not be contained. They leaped probably higher than ever with Garcia's national championship ring smacking against Thompson's Big Eight Conference title ring.

Unfortunately, Garcia's ring flew off his finger. In the Houston heat of early March, the three searched the cement, the grass and the dirt in a 30-foot radius to no avail. Finally, they decided to return to Thompson's nearby hotel room for the night, drink a few beers and come back in the morning to search again.

A few beers later and Thompson had turned detective. He convinced Garcia and Gore to return to the site and reenact the leaping high-five, this time with Thompson wearing his ring loosely on his finger. The ring flew off Thompson's finger, bounced a couple of times on the cement and landed, believe it or not, right next to Garcia's lost ring in the grass.

"Both rings had a little scar," Thompson said, "but we didn't give a shit. We went crazy. You'd have thought we won the World Series. I was so happy. He was in tears."

The trio returned to Thompson's room and partied into the night. Then the next day they were off to Florida with a story they would tell and retell throughout spring training, into the 1980 season and beyond.

Dawning Of A New Age

The first extended road trip of the young season, a swing through Salem and Alexandria in Virginia, proved fruitful to the Bulls who, thanks to two postponements, returned to Durham without a loss. The Bulls swept four games against Salem, including a complete-game, six-hit shutout from right-hander Mike Smith, then extended the longest winning streak in franchise history to 12 games with a 12-2 win at Alexandria.

The Durham-record 11-game win streak had stood for 26 years. When the Bulls left Alexandria following two rainouts, they had their eyes set on the Carolina League record of 16 consecutive wins, set in 1950 by Winston-Salem. Kinston, a Toronto Blue Jays affiliate, had other ideas, and the streak ended on April 28 at Durham Athletic Park with a 9-5 loss punctuated by Michael Lebo's grand slam in the ninth inning off reliever Pete Teixeira.

Afterward, a dejected Al Gallagher took full blame.

"There's no excuse for stupidity," Gallagher said, "and that was stupid."

Gallagher second-guessed himself about leaving the right-handed Teixeira in the game to fill the bases with an intentional walk to Ron Shepherd, then to pitch to the left-handed hitting Lebo. The Bulls trailed 5-3 with one out, yet Gallagher said he should have called on his bullpen ace, Big Ike Pettaway, to shut the door.

Afterward, the players headed out to the local bars in search of co-eds from one of the nearby colleges, be it Duke University or North Carolina Central University in Durham, the University of North Carolina just 12 miles down Highway 15-501 in Chapel Hill, or North Carolina State University, 25 miles east, in Raleigh. If they were not hitting the local watering holes, a number were holing up in their Duke Manor apartments, listening to music and smoking pot. Recreational drug use had infiltrated the minor leagues by 1980 and most of the players on the Bulls kept a mental scorecard among their teammates, divided by who smoked marijuana and who did not. Cocaine was not much in use, mostly because players at the lower level of the minor leagues could not afford it. The abuse of cocaine was rampant in the major leagues, culminating in the suspension of 11 players prior to the 1986 season for use of the drug.

One morning early in the 1980 season, a few players noticed that a couple in an adjacent apartment had been evicted and much of their belongings were tossed to the curb. The treasure in the trove was a long, tall bong that instantly earned the nickname "Kareem" after the seven-foot-two center for the Los Angeles Lakers at the time, Kareem Abdul-Jabbar. "Kareem" traveled with the Bulls the remainder of the season.

The Durham area offered a plethora of off-field choices for the players, certainly unlike most other Class A-level minor-league outposts. There were plenty of choices in restaurants and recreational facilities.

A few players liked to take advantage of the Durham YMCA,

which offered free membership to any Bulls player. Mostly, players used the steam room to sweat off the previous night's carousing. Players were strictly prohibited from lifting weights then (it was thought to restrict a players flexibility), and few showed much of an interest, anyway. What they really liked to do was exhibit their basketball skills, another activity that was prohibited by the Atlanta Braves organization. The risk of a sprained ankle to a prized prospect while playing basketball was not worth it to Atlanta's brass.

One day, Albert Hall, Gerald Perry, Ronnie Rudd and Tommy Thompson joined a full-court basketball game with a few of the YMCA members. No sooner had the four "stars" on the hardwood arrived at Durham Athletic Park for that night's game and Gallagher came charging into the clubhouse, replete in his trademark cowboy hat, a pair of blue jeans that had not been washed in weeks, and that sleepy eye that seemed to close even further when he was angry.

He was angry.

"Will the four goddamned NBA fucking players come in my office, right fucking now!" Gallagher screamed for all to hear.

The four guilty parties looked at one another. There was a recognition that Gallagher had their names. They dropped their heads and trudged into the tiny manager's office where Gallagher awaited.

"Thompson get out of here," Gallagher said. Thompson later figured that Gallagher did not much care if a non-prospect had broken the no-basketball playing rule. It was the other three prospects Gallagher was concerned about.

"You motherfuckers," Gallagher said. "You've got a chance to play in the big leagues. Don't pull that bullshit on me."

All three waited for the door to Gallagher's office to shut behind them as they departed, and busted out in laughter. All three were in the starting lineup that night, but none ever played pick-up basketball games again at the YMCA.

■

Among the many reasons Atlanta front office officials had warmed to the idea of placing a farm team in Durham was the diversity of the city's population, which had held steady at roughly 100,000 over the previous decade. There existed a nice blend of elderly, working middle class and college students.

Beyond that, Durham long had established a vibrant black community. By the early 1900s, Parrish Street, on the fringes of downtown, became known as "Black Wall Street" with the establishment of North Carolina Mutual Life Insurance Company and Mechanics & Farmers Bank. The former was the first black life insurance company in the country, and the latter was founded by John Merrick and Charles Clinton Spaulding, black men who wanted a bank primarily for African-Americans.

Durham's multiplicity provided a stark contrast to where many of the Bulls players had lived and played the previous season. Greenwood, South Carolina — located midway between Greenville, South Carolina, and Augusta, Georgia — was sparsely populated and offered little in the way of entertainment or restaurant choices for the players. Additionally, the city was still grappling with the early stages of integration and the Jim Crow laws that had been struck down more than a decade earlier were still being practiced in some circles.

Gallagher managed the Greenwood teams of 1978 and 1979 in the Class A Western Carolinas League. Juan Alduey, Andres Forbes and Milt Thompson, along with Hall, Perry and Rudd were the black players on the '79 club. Finding housing for them was difficult. Night-time entertainment for the six was non-existent.

"The six black guys had to live in a rat trap of a house in Greenwood," Gallagher said during spring training. "It was a miserable situation. Not that I want my players out drinking, but our black players couldn't get a drink after the game. They had private clubs in Greenwood to prevent the blacks from getting in."

Bulls owner Miles Wolff and General Manager Pete Bock were made aware of the situation, and while the Braves were in training camp in West Palm Beach, Florida, Bock had no trouble arranging housing for the 24 players who would head north to Durham one month later. Bock reached an agreement with Triangle Communities Realty to rent 13 apartments at its Duke Manor complex. No questions were asked about blacks being housed in the apartments.

"There's a lot of interest about Durham, especially when you're going from Greenwood to Durham. That's a big-time move," Gallagher said. "Hey, Greenwood might have a population of 20,000, counting crows and chickens. Durham has three major colleges in the area and some people the same age as the players. Durham is a very progressive city, especially in its view toward blacks."

Greenwood's population in 1980 was 21,613. Durham's was 100,831. The cultural differences between the two cities far exceeded the disparity in population.

■

Unbeknownst to anyone who worked and lived in Durham in 1980, the city would soon undergo a transformation over the next three decades, taking it from a dying tobacco town of few opportunities to a vibrant community with jobs aplenty and a desirable place to reside.

The implosion of the Washington Duke Hotel on Dec. 14, 1975, signaled the end of an era in Durham, one in which the tobacco industry made the city relevant in the state of North Carolina. The Washington Duke, located downtown, was the city's social identity, its gathering spot. Civic groups met there. Prominent out-of-town guests were housed there, and wedding receptions were hosted there. So, when the grand hotel was leveled, Durham lost a significant link to its past.

"An uneasy feeling crept into the thinking of many of us that somewhere along the way, much that was Durham's heritage had disappeared or was doomed," wrote Jean Bradley Anderson in her 2011 book, *"A History of Durham County, North Carolina."*

"What had happened to our visible roots that had held us so firmly and securely in this hometown of ours?" Anderson wrote. "What did we have left that told the story of Durham — its love affair with tobacco and textiles and Old Trinity and the able men and women who built the foundation of Durham's growth and prosperity today?"

Durham established itself as the center of the tobacco industry in the 19th century primarily through the production and distribution of snuff and pipe tobacco. Then, according to an excellent 2005 PBS documentary *"Bright Leaves,"* a farmer by the name of Washington Duke opened a factory on his homestead and began producing loose tobacco for rolling cigarettes. Soon thereafter Duke moved his factory to downtown Durham where W.T. Blackwell and Company already was marketing a "Spanish" blend of tobacco that later operated under the name Bull Durham, according to the PBS documentary.

Durham soon became the center of tobacco trading for farmers in eastern North Carolina, and Winston-Salem served farmers in the western part of the state. The Duke family established the American Tobacco Company and by 1900 was selling 90 percent of the 4.4 billion cigarettes produced in the world, according to a Main Street Carolina timeline of tobacco in Durham. Two years later, American Tobacco Company controlled 92 percent of the world's tobacco business.

World War I was a boon to tobacco sales. According to Main Street Carolina, the War Department purchased the entire output of Bull Durham tobacco in 1918 for its soldiers. Bull Durham advertised, "When our boys light up, the Huns will light out."

In 1924, the Duke family used a portion of its great wealth to provide an endowment to Trinity College with the provision that the school would forever be known as Duke University.

Soldiers were once again supplied with cigarette rations during World War II and the tobacco industry continued to thrive in Durham into the early 1960s. Then, when the U.S. Surgeon General issued a report in 1964 stating that smoking caused lung cancer and a host of other medical problems, the tobacco industry became embroiled in a major health issue, according to the PBS documentary. Over the next four decades, as the number of American smokers declined steadily and restrictions on public smoking increased, the large manufacturers began cutting costs and laying off large numbers of workers and relocating their factories to less expensive areas, PBS reported.

Fans arriving at Durham Athletic Park for ball games in the summer of 1980 could often catch the waft of tobacco emanating from nearby factories, but that smell was blowing in the wind. American Tobacco Company left Durham in 1987, and by 2000 Liggett & Myers had pulled up its Durham roots.

"In retrospect, two events of 1980 foreshadowed the new character that Durham was quickly assuming: the opening of Duke University Hospital North and the decision of General Electric to build its new micro-electric center in the Research Triangle Park," Anderson wrote in her history of Durham County. "Medicine, with manifold research ramifications, and new computing technology together would be Durham's economic dynamo, basis for pride, and source of new fame."

The landscape was changing in Durham. On March 17, 1980, a new Durham County Library opened on Roxboro Street. The library's 65,000 square feet of carpeted area was more than 12 times the old space on Main Street and included some 100,000 volumes. The old Yille and Watts tobacco warehouses, built by the Duke family, re-opened in 1981 under the name Brightleaf Square and featured specialty shops and offices, and the Burlington warehouses became condominiums a year later.

There was talk in March of 1980 of Durham building a downtown sports arena large enough to entice basketball home dates for both Duke and UNC, much like Lexington, Kentucky, which has a downtown arena that is home to University of Kentucky basketball.

Those discussions never got past the talking stages.

By June of 1982, Durham's City Council passed a $10.5 million bond issue that allowed for renovation of the Carolina Theatre downtown, and ultimately led to the construction of a 15-story office building and nearby hotel.

Sports in the Durham area also were engaged in transition. Ever since Everett Case brought big-time basketball with him from his native state of Indiana to North Carolina State in the 1940s, the sport had captured the hearts of the state's sports-minded population. North Carolina won a national championship under Coach Frank McGuire in 1957 and N.C. State matched it under Coach Norman Sloan in 1974. But the game had been dominated in the area since the late 1960s by Coach Dean Smith and his North Carolina Tar Heels, who reached the NCAA Final Four in successive seasons from 1967 through 1969, returned in 1972, and lost the 1977 national title game to Marquette.

Despite Sloan's success at N.C. State, and Duke's under Coach Bill Foster, who took the Blue Devils to the national championship game in 1978 where they lost to Kentucky, the coaches could not escape the long shadow of Smith and his program. It was Foster who quipped sarcastically that he thought it was "(James) Naismith who invented basketball, not Dean Smith." Tired of playing the undercard to Smith, Sloan and Foster both departed following the 1979-80 season.

While Atlanta Braves' farmhands were training in Florida, Duke and N.C. State athletic officials began their nationwide searches for new men's basketball coaches. Tom Butters, Duke's athletics director, first interviewed Tom Davis of Boston College before appearing to settle on three other candidates: Duke assistant coach Bob Wenzel, Paul Webb of Old Dominion and Bob Weltlich of Mississippi. That prompted this *Durham Morning Herald* headline of March 18: 'Duke's New Coach? He Begins with 'W' '

Instead, unknown 33-year-old Army coach Mike Krzyzewski was

named Duke's head man the following day.

Meanwhile, N.C. State athletics director Willis Casey attempted to woo famed DeMatha High School coach Morgan Wootten out of the Washington, D.C. area. The Washington Post reported that Wootten turned down a five-year, $700,000 contract offer from N.C. State. Other names mentioned for the job included Jack Hartman of Kansas State, Lee Rose of Purdue, Tom Young of Rutgers and Jim Valvano of Iona. Valvano initially was not believed to be interested in the job because his star player, Jeff Ruland, was returning to Iona and Valvano owned a successful discotheque, Fonz's, near the Iona campus in New York City.

Eight days after Krzyzewski was hired, on March 27, the 34-year-old Valvano was introduced as N.C. State's head coach.

So, with coaching searches at Duke and N.C. State crowding the headlines of the *Durham Herald* and *Durham Sun*, it was easy to understand why the return of professional baseball to Durham was an afterthought to not only both newspapers but also to the general sports public. The disinterest was grounded in the fact that Durham, Chapel Hill and Raleigh were college sports towns. The closest professional sports franchise was a minor-league baseball team in Greensboro, 50 miles to the west of Durham.

Yet against that backdrop Wolff believed there was about to be a rebirth of interest in professional baseball, both in Durham as well as nationally. Baseball, motherhood and apple pie had taken a significant hit during the height of the Vietnam War years in the late 1960s and early1970s. Major League Baseball playoff games were not selling out consistently and minor-league baseball was hanging on for dear life.

The rugged world of professional football was more reflective of the violent times of the period and had surpassed baseball as the nation's top spectator sport, if not its sporting conscience. College sports, particularly football and basketball, were booming. But something changed in 1975, specifically with Game Six of a magical World Series between the Cincinnati Reds and Boston Red Sox. Carlton Fisk's game-winning home run in the 12th inning instantly took on legendary status and almost overnight captured the fancy of a national sporting audience, including many who had largely abandoned baseball. Suddenly, baseball mattered again.

Wolff was energized by Fisk's home run and all the drama surrounding Game Six, and almost immediately sensed the renewed interest in baseball at the major-league level might soon trickle down to the minor leagues and provide it a much-needed shot in the arm. But he also saw the moment as a golden opportunity to re-invent the game that he knew growing up, one that catered to and was almost wholly dependent on middle-aged and elderly white men for its survival.

His opportunity to put into practice what he preached coincided with the re-birth of professional baseball in Durham in 1980. From the outset, he sought a different, more diversified audience than the one that previously had "supported" minor-league baseball in Durham and elsewhere.

Wolff sought a younger crowd and, from the outset, wooed Duke students, especially with cheap beer. On specifically designated College Night promotions, the Duke students gathered in the left-field bleachers that had been added for the 1980 season. Soon an additional beer stand was needed beneath the third base grandstand to handle the pressing and unexpected demand.

Before the arrival of the Bulls, social circles for Duke students, a large majority of whom came from out of state, particularly the Northeast quadrant of the country, rarely extended beyond the campus borders. Durham's mainstream population felt similarly isolated and typically only visited the Duke campus for sporting events, and those folks were historically the city's wealthiest citizens who could afford membership in the school's booster club.

Early in that 1980 season it became apparent to anyone attending the Bulls games that a whole new social dynamic was evolving at

Durham Athletic Park, and it was becoming fashionable for people from all different walks of life to attend and be seen at Bulls games.

During that magical first homestand, I telephoned my editor at the *Durham Morning Herald* from the press box to inform him that something really special was happening at the ballpark. Nurses from Duke University Hospital were dancing in the aisles during the seventh-inning stretch with City of Durham maintenance workers. Duke students and professors were joining with retired tobacco plant workers and Durham lawyers in chants of "Let's Go Bulls."

"College students and yuppies mingled easily in the stands with factory workers who no longer had to sit in racially segregated bleachers, although many blacks still favored the old first-base line seats from the pre-civil rights era," reported the *Los Angeles Times* in 1988. The same newspaper story quoted Tom Campbell, then a member of the Durham City Council, as saying the ballpark was "a reflection of the kind of community that Durham is — very divergent groups of people who all have a strong sense of belonging to a community, from Duke professors to assembly line workers."

A new age for the city of Durham had dawned.

Filthy McNasty

Not long after one of Al Gallagher's sessions with the media in his cramped office — OK, it was a converted closet that he shared with pitching coach Bob Veale — the Durham manager stood in front of a mirror for his traditional post-game shave in the dank and dark Bulls' clubhouse beneath the Durham Athletic Park grandstand.

Outside, young girls had learned they could walk the dirt path behind the first-base grandstands, then stand and peer through the glass windows and into the Durham clubhouse below. The sight of Gallagher with only a towel wrapped around his waist was not the attraction. It was the naked players who pranced to and from the showers.

What they might also have seen on this night was a rare address to the team by its manager. Gallagher wanted to make certain all on the 24-man roster were prepared for the next road trip. Seven road games were ahead, the first four in Salem, Virginia, against farm hands from the Pittsburgh Pirates, and the final three in Alexandria, Virginia, against an independent team stocked with players from various teams.

Normally accustomed to residing in downtrodden Holiday Inns and Ramada Inns in the lower levels of the minor leagues while on the road, the Bulls were about to live in luxury for the first time. The club had switched hotels and was scheduled to first stay at the Omega Inn in Roanoke, then the swank Hyatt House in Arlington, just across the Potomac River from Washington, D.C.

"Men, we're stepping up our accommodations on the road, particularly in Washington," Gallagher shouted for all to hear. "So dress accordingly, and bring a sports jacket with you on the bus tomorrow."

Those who partied later that night planned to use the nearly three-hour bus ride en route to Salem for sleep. Painful as it might have been for some, everyone was on board the bus and accountable for the 9 a.m. takeoff. Except Veale and Gallagher.

Veale was five years removed from an outstanding big-league career, mostly with the Pirates. At 6-foot-6 and 230 pounds — just a few over his playing weight — Veale struck the same imposing figure with the Durham players as he did when he stood on a major-league pitching mound. The big, bespectacled left-hander led the major leagues with 250 strikeouts in 1964, the same season in which he registered a career-high 18 wins. He was an all-star selection in 1965 and 1966 when he won 17 and 16 games, respectively.

His hands were huge, capable of cupping five or six baseballs in one of his mitts. His stamina was unmatched, and that is why Gallagher loved having Veale as his dugout sidekick this season as well as the two years before in Greenwood, South Carolina. Veale could stand on the pitching rubber and throw an entire round of batting practice, every single day, from March in spring training through the conclusion of the season at the end of August.

Off the field, Veale spoke little but drew respect and reverence from everyone around him. Most everyone had figured over a period of time that Veale liked to intimidate, but his heart was huge and he delighted in jokingly making some uncomfortable.

Veale had flown all over the country as a major-leaguer and had ridden one too many busses in his minor-league playing days. So he asked for and received permission from the Atlanta front office to take his own car and travel separately from the team on road trips. Veale often drove his 1977 Chevy van directly behind the team bus. Talk about old reliable. Veale owned the van for years, and occasionally would swap in a new engine. Years later, he got its odometer to flip past one million miles.

So with the team bus prepared to depart Durham for Salem, there was Veale sitting in the driver's seat of his van in the gravel parking lot of Durham Athletic Park, all ready to travel along in pursuit. Every team member was nattily attired in dress slacks, an open-collared shirt and a sports jacket tucked into the overhead bin. As card games began in earnest throughout, an occasional glance outside brought a puzzling look from a few team members that begged the question: Where is our manager?

A few minutes passed before a Ford station wagon bounded down Morris Street into the parking lot and came to a skidding halt next to the bus, dust billowing from all tires. Out stepped Gallagher, replete in his traditional cowboy boots and a vintage blue leisure suit complete with some sort of wildly designed shirt with its lapels hanging outside the suit jacket. Naturally, tobacco juice stains dotted his attire.

No doubt, the players believed, Gallagher wore that same suit when he traveled as a player for the San Francisco Giants and California Angels from 1970 to 1973. It was a sight to behold, for sure, although the players were certain folks lodging at the Hyatt House in Arlington had never seen a fashion statement quite like this.

It was so Dirty Al.

■

Gallagher was more than just a minor-league baseball manager when he arrived in Durham. He was a showman and entertainer. He was a public-relations agent for the club. He was a promoter of the game he so dearly loved.

"He knew the fans were there to have fun," Owner Miles Wolff said. "The manager's antics were part of minor-league baseball. They still weren't a bunch of robots. They were colorful guys. In retrospect, I'm surprised the Braves hired him in the first place. He cared about winning and about fans in the stands."

Sometimes the Atlanta brass wondered as well about the decision to bring Gallagher on board as manager of the Greenwood Braves for the 1978 and 1979 seasons in the Western Carolinas League. Hank Aaron, Atlanta's director of player development at the time, sat in the Durham Athletic Park press box in May of 1980, propped his arm on the table and laughed as Gallagher took his position in the third-base coaching box.

"You know," Aaron said, "Gallagher doesn't look like a manager … does he?"

The question was rhetorical. Aaron's implication was that Gallagher's appearance hardly reflected his managerial abilities, which is probably why Aaron telephoned Gallagher in Clovis, California, at 7 in the morning in March of 1978.

Aaron had a job offer for Gallagher, who had been sitting idly since the previous September when the ill-fated Class A Lone Star League — where he had been managing — went belly up. In the interim, Gallagher lined up an elementary school teaching job in Fresno, California, the hometown of his wife, Terry.

"I guess I kidded myself into thinking he was content in a teaching career," Terry said. "When Hank offered Al the Greenwood job, he didn't even look at me. He resigned his teaching job an hour later and was gone."

Aaron had recalled seeing Gallagher play as a third baseman years earlier and loved the fighting spirit in the San Francisco Giants infielder. Beyond that, Aaron saw a competitive drive in Gallagher that he wanted from his managers and coaches in the Atlanta system. When Aaron was named to his post with the Braves in 1977 he believed the organization lacked a will to win, both at the major-league level and in the minor leagues. After winning the West Division of the National League in 1969, Atlanta suffered through difficult times before Aaron was hired in the front office. The 1970s were not kind to Atlanta. The club finished with an 82-80 record in 1971. It also won 88 games in 1974, yet finished 14 games behind the West-Division winning Los Angeles Dodgers. Those were the only two winning seasons of the decade.

Aaron's thinking was that if Atlanta's farm teams began winning, then eventually those players would migrate to the major league club with a belief that winning would be expected. Hiring someone like Gallagher meant it was OK to not only develop players in the minor leagues but also to win games.

Also in Gallagher's corner — at least at the outset — was Paul Snyder, Atlanta's director of player development at the time. Snyder remembered Gallagher well from the 1975 season when the player-coach performed well during an incident that gravely shook the organization.

Gallagher developed his managerial style while playing and coaching under Clint Courtney for two seasons at Richmond of the Triple-A International League. Courtney carried a reputation throughout his 11-year major-league playing career and decade-long run as a minor-league manager as one the game's great characters.

Gallagher and Wolff shared a connection through Courtney, Gallagher as a player and coach under the man most folks called "Scraps" or "Scrap Iron," and Wolff as the general manager in Savannah during the 1972 season when Courtney was its manager. Gallagher and Wolff both carried a deep-seated affection and admiration for Courtney, and were proud to say they came from the unofficial "Scrap Iron School of Baseball."

Wolff liked to recall the time during the 1972 season in Savannah when the next night's starting pitcher for the Braves took the traditional seat in the stands behind home plate wearing civilian clothes to chart pitches. The pitcher, as often happened in those days, sipped on a couple of beers throughout the game. As the game moved into extra innings, though, Courtney realized he was out of pitchers and summoned the next night's starter out of the stands and into the dugout. Much to Courtney's delight, the slightly tipsy pitcher righted himself enough to gain a save for the Braves.

Courtney had an unusual relationship with his players, as Gallagher related of one incident during the 1974 season. You must understand, Gallagher said, that Courtney did not possess a racist bone in his body. Yet Courtney called a team meeting early that season solely to lambast the lack of production from the team's black players. The black members of the team were able to accept Courtney's premise because their low batting averages and high earned run averages backed his claim, with the exception of a promising young infield prospect named Larvell "Sugar Bear" Blanks.

"Sugar Bear is black," Gallagher reminded Courtney in front of the team, "and he's killing the ball, hitting like .400."

"Well, here's the deal," Courtney responded. "Sugar Bear isn't black. He's white."

The club, including the black players, broke up in laughter.

Gallagher was at the end of his playing career that season and the next with Richmond. But his last-gasp chance at returning to the big leagues, this time with the Braves, fell victim to a .248 batting average in 1974 and a .260 mark in 1975. He began to turn his attention to coaching when an incident on Sunday, June 15, 1975, forever altered his life.

Richmond had just arrived in Rochester, New York, for a series. The club was housed at the Colony East Motor Inn, which featured a ping-pong table in the lobby area. Players gathered around the ping-pong table before and after games, many times joined by coaches and their manager. On this evening, Courtney appeared like never before, clean-shaven and freshly showered.

"What the hell's going on here?" Gallagher said. "Scraps is all cleaned up. That isn't like Scraps."

Minutes later, Courtney collapsed to the floor. Gallagher first performed mouth-to-mouth resuscitation on Courtney, then rode by the manager's side in an ambulance to nearby Genesee Hospital. A doctor soon came out of the operating room and asked for anyone who had accompanied Courtney to the hospital. Gallagher raised his hand.

"I've got bad news," the doctor told Gallagher. "He's dead."

Courtney died of a heart attack. He was 48.

The following day, the Braves named Gallagher the team's interim manager until Bob Lemon could arrive to take over the team for the remainder of the season. Gallagher gathered his Richmond team and told the players they would play that night's game in honor of Courtney. Gallagher hung Courtney's jersey in the dugout, where it remained each night for the remainder of that series.

Courtney's death marked Gallagher's strange introduction to his managerial career, one that would take another couple of odd twists over the next two seasons.

Atlanta's front office arranged for Gallagher to manage the 1976 season for the Durango Alacranes in the Triple-A Mexican League. Durango is located about 500 miles due south of Juarez, on the Texas border, and another 300 miles from the Gulf of California in central Mexico. Upon arriving, Gallagher found he was the only one among the team's coaches, players and front office personnel who spoke English only.

"No American was going to succeed there," Gallagher said. "No one spoke English and I didn't care about speaking Spanish. I lasted about 30 days in Durango. I don't know if I couldn't handle it, but I didn't want to."

Red Shuttleworth, Gallagher's childhood friend in San Francisco, claims one early season incident was the tipping point for the manager to either quit, or be fired, depending on who tells the story. Apparently home fans in Durango would urinate in their beer cups and dump the remains on unsuspecting relief pitchers in the bullpen. Gallagher quit.

Back in the United States, he hooked on for the 1977 season as manager of the Texas City Stars, an unaffiliated team in the Class A Lone Star League. There were better things to do in Texas City, which is located just outside Galveston on the Gulf of Mexico, than attend minor-league baseball games and fans stayed away in droves from Robinson Stadium. The Stars drew 12,305 fans for the season, which amounted to fewer than 400 per game.

Strangely enough, when Gallagher was hired, Shuttleworth was living in Texas City. Shuttleworth had just been fired as an English instructor at College of Mainland after he slugged the dean. One of Gallagher's first orders of business when arriving in Texas City was to help Shuttleworth move his belongings out of his college office. It was the first time the two had connected since they left high school a year apart in San Francisco in the early '60s.

Without a job, Shuttleworth joined Gallagher as a bullpen coach that summer, one that entailed Gallagher bringing along a roster of players whose dreams of playing in the major leagues essentially died with their releases from various organizations. So short on talent were the Texas City Stars, Gallagher activated himself for 49 of the team's 76 games and, at age 32, led the club with a .352 batting average in 165 at-bats.

Following the regular-season, the league disbanded. Corpus Christi had won both halves of the league's South Division, but opted out of the playoffs for financial reasons. Then Victoria and Texas City, winners of the two halves of the North Division, cancelled their series with the threat of Hurricane Anita looming off the Gulf Coast.

If nothing else was gained from that season it was the renewal of a friendship between Gallagher and Shuttleworth. The two share the same October 19 birthday, although Shuttleworth is one year older. They were both reared in the hardscrabble Mission District of San Francisco, Gallagher on Church Street in a one-bedroom flat over Jimmy's Bar where his parents long paid $99-a-month rent.

Gallagher's father, Joseph, quit school in third grade to help his father with chores on a farm. Gallagher's mother, Viola, made it through the 10th grade. Joseph Gallagher was a wispy five-foot-six and 160 pounds, but after working most of his adult life in the carpet and linoleum business could dead-lift 300 pounds.

Gallagher's parents wanted "a hundred kids," but after eight years of marriage were still childless.

"The names came out of a bar-room type thing," Gallagher's father said. "All of his uncles wanted Alan named after them." Uncles Alan, Edward, Patrick and Henry were satisfied. And so was Doctor Mitchell, who delivered Alan on October 19, 1945. A confirmation name, George, was added and Alan Mitchell Edward George Patrick Henry Gallagher was the result.

"He wins the duke for the longest name in the major leagues … wrestling the title from Calvin Coolidge Julius Caesar Tuskahoma McLish by one," columnist Furman Bisher of the Atlanta Constitution wrote in the late '70s.

The neighborhoods of San Francisco were divided along ethnic lines. The Gallaghers lived among the Irish Catholics, south of the Italian Fisherman's Wharf District, where the baseball DiMaggios were reared. The black section was nearby on the Avenues.

"It was a rough area," Gallagher said of the Mission District. "We had streets you stayed off at night."

Gallagher learned to do a lot of talking with his fists, even against friends. Shuttleworth fondly recalled the time the two boarded the 10 Monterey bus from Golden Gate Park to the Mission District following a winter league baseball game. Tired of hearing Gallagher's chirping behind him, Shuttleworth stuffed a baseball in his glove, turned and smacked his teammate across the jaw with the weapon. Gallagher jumped Shuttleworth and pummeled him on the floor in the aisle of the bus. The driver pulled the bus to a stop, lifted both kids by the back of their pants and tossed them out the emergency exit in the rear.

"He was always getting in fights down the street," Joseph Gallagher said of his son. "I went to a Japanese friend of mine and told him about these fights and he directed Alan to judo." Gallagher, already a star in Pop Warner football and Little League baseball, was on his way to gaining a brown belt in the martial arts. He was offered a scholarship to further advance his judo techniques in Japan, but refused. Judo, his father said, took a back seat to baseball.

Joseph wanted to be a baseball player growing up, and he made certain that his son would have every opportunity to pursue a career in the game he so loved. It was quite OK for young Alan to be absent from an activity at school, by his father's standards, but no baseball practice could ever be missed. Pickup games were played at Big Rec, a bus ride or cable car trek away, at the corner of Seventh Avenue and Lincoln Avenue on the southern border of Golden Gate Park.

By age 12, Gallagher began playing in the adult baseball leagues. That first season, many of the adults during the summer months were former players for the San Francisco Seals of the Triple-A Pacific Coast League. During the winter months, players on the Seals active roster joined the league. At such a young age, Gallagher occasionally got into winter-league games as a pinch-runner or defensive replacement. During the summer, though, he often worked his way into a lineup as a shortstop.

For at least one year, Gallagher was playing on the same team with some of his idols, since there was no major-league baseball on the West Coast at the time. If he was not playing in a game, Gallagher was taking the 15-minute bus ride to the Potrero Hill neighborhood and Seals Stadium to watch one. He was 11 in the glorious summer of 1957 when the Seals under the guidance of manager Joe Gordon won 101 games and captured the PCL title. Ken Aspromonte led the league in hitting, Leo Kiely won 21 games and Bill Renna cracked 29 home runs in what proved to be the Seals final season.

The New York Giants moved west for the 1958 season and played their games that summer and the following summer at Seals Stadium. By the time the Giants began playing at Candlestick Park during the 1960 season, Gallagher was enthralled by the play of center fielder Willie Mays. Both at St. Paul's Catholic School and later at Mission High, Gallagher often claimed to be one of the few white kids who counted Mays as his favorite player.

Coming out of high school, Gallagher was a spindly six-feet in height and weighed 145 pounds. Although his desire was to play professional baseball right away, a New York Yankees scout at the time steered him elsewhere. There was no draft of amateur players in 1963, so Charlie Silvera sat down with Gallagher and his parents for a frank talk. Silvera said the Yankees were interested in signing Gallagher to a contract, but the youngster simply was not prepared for the rigors of professional baseball. Silvera suggested Gallagher play a couple of years of college baseball and the Yankees likely would be interested in signing a more mature player at that time.

California, San Diego State, Santa Clara and Stanford all offered Gallagher scholarships. Santa Clara fielded a strong program, having advanced to the final game of the 1962 College World Series under Coach Paddy Cottrell. Santa Clara also was the only program to offer Gallagher a full ride. Plus, the school was located only 40 miles south of San Francisco.

As freshmen were not eligible for varsity competition at the time, Gallagher batted .545 during his first year. Beyond that, he developed a reputation as a hard-nosed player on the field and as a hard-driving person off it. It led to the adoption of a nickname that he would carry the remainder of his life.

Early in his sophomore season, Gallagher decided he would not wash his uniform — including undergarments and socks — as long as his hitting streak continued. The streak eventually reached 25 games, and since college teams played only three or four games each week, the grime and stench from his uniform and clothes gathered over a three-month season was unbearable to his teammates.

Prior to that baseball season, Gallagher was seated with his date at a Santa Clara football game. As a promotional stunt, the school's athletics department conducted a greased-pig contest at halftime. When it became apparent no students were going to catch the greased pig, Gallagher left his date in the stands, walked on the field and captured the elusive animal. With little or no thought to cleaning up afterward, Gallagher watched the remainder of the game with his date, then took her to a dance afterward "with the greased pig still on me."

Thus was born the legend of Dirty Al.

Colleges did not practice during the winter months, so Gallagher played in the off-seasons in the Peninsula Winter League on a team sponsored by the San Francisco Giants, and comprised primarily of members of the Giants farm system and other amateur players from the area like Gallagher. During his sophomore season, Major League Baseball instituted a draft of college and high school players to combat the skyrocketing signing bonuses being doled out to untested amateurs, mostly by the wealthiest organizations in the game, notably the New York Yankees and Los Angeles Dodgers. Not much was known about how the draft would work, but the Giants, Dodgers and Cincinnati Reds had all made it known to Gallagher that they intended to draft him.

The Kansas City Athletics selected Rick Monday, a sophomore outfielder from Arizona State, with the first pick of the inaugural draft of 1965. The Dodgers, picking eighth, passed on Gallagher in favor of John Wyatt, a high school shortstop out of Bakersfield, California, who never advanced past Class A ball. Finally, the Giants turn came at No. 14 in the first round and they selected the hometown Gallagher.

Obviously, there was no television, radio or Internet coverage of the draft then, so Gallagher sat in the office of first-year Santa Clara coach Sal Taormina and awaited a phone call from whichever team selected him. Gallagher knew he would sign with the Giants, so there was very little negotiating of a contract other than his and his parents' insistence that his final two years of college be paid by the club as part of Major League Baseball's College Scholarship Plan. In addition to receiving two years of tuition money in cash, Gallagher received a $40,000 signing bonus, which was roughly equivalent to $300,000 in 2016 dollars. It also was equivalent to what Gallagher's father would have made over a four-year period in the carpet and linoleum business.

Gallagher paid $2,500 cash for a 1965 Ford Fairlane for his father, then made the down payment on a $32,000, two-bedroom, 1,000-square foot home for his parents in San Mateo not far from the Bay Meadows Racetrack, some 25 miles south of San Francisco. Gallagher intended to pay the monthly mortgage payments on the first home his parents ever owned, but his father would have none of it and insisted on making all payments himself.

Gallagher waited a year into his pro career before purchasing a 1966 Buick Skylark for himself. Prior to then, he had driven an old pink Rambler through his first year or so of college, converting the back seat into a bed. During his sophomore year, a wealthy student on campus liked Gallagher's Rambler so much he offered a Mercedes in exchange. Rarely has a young man looked so out of place as Dirty Al driving a Mercedes, no doubt most days with pants and shirts that lacked color coordination, and a spittoon near the driver's seat.

Gallagher told his dates in college that he had "star-dust blue eyes," and, yes, he looked a lot like actor Steve McQueen. Most never bought the McQueen comparison, but as his hair began to recede right out of college, Gallagher did gain a striking resemblance to actor Jack Nicholson. Or maybe it was the wild crazy-eye look Gallagher would display in conversation or the smirk that appeared permanently attached to his face like Nicholson's.

Wells Twombly, a columnist for the *San Francisco Examiner* once wrote that Gallagher's looks were "as impishly pseudo-innocent as an altar boy who has just been caught nipping the sacramental wine."

Gallagher also carried a carefree spirit about him, perhaps because he had been so successful at just about anything he attempted all the way through college. But, as is the case with many players making their foray into professional baseball, Gallagher experienced failure on the diamond for the first time in his life.

"I was a slow learner," Gallagher said. "I think they call it pig-headedness."

The Giants undeniably made an error in judgment by starting Gallagher at Springfield, Massachusetts, of the Double-A Eastern League immediately after drafting him, and then by promoting him to Phoenix of the Pacific Coast League late in the season. Gallagher struggled mightily for four seasons in the minor leagues, before finally showing mild signs of progress in 1969 when he batted .293 for Amarillo in the Double-A Texas League. Clearly, the Giants were not getting a return on the investment of their inaugural first-round pick.

Gallagher was in for a surprise when he reported to the Peninsula Winter League following the 1969 season. The Giants informed him that he would not be permitted to play in games. Gallagher marched to Hank Sauer, the Giants' hitting instructor, and voiced his displeasure with the club's decision.

"I agree with them 100 percent," Sauer told Gallagher. "I just spin my wheels with you. You don't listen to a thing anybody says."

Sauer agreed to throw batting practice to Gallagher every morning at 8 sharp, but the player had to be off the field at 9. Gallagher realized, then and there, that he had to shut up and listen. For three weeks, Gallagher absorbed every bit of Sauer's daily instruction. Sauer changed the weight of Gallagher's bat by adding five ounces. That forced Gallagher to swing later at pitches while preventing him from trying to pull every ball. Sauer also knew that Gallagher had a stigmatism in his left eye, the only one in which he wore a contact lens. Sauer figured Gallagher could get a better view of the ball by shifting some weight off his front foot and by opening his stance.

By paying attention to what makes a good hitter, Gallagher was becoming one himself. The Giants liked what they saw and finally allowed Gallagher to be inserted into games. For the remainder of the winter league season, Gallagher batted .325. Beyond that, he showed the Giants he was ready to play in the major leagues. He made the big club the following spring.

On April 7, 1970, at Candlestick Park, with his father watching in the stands, Gallagher took his position at third base in the top of the first inning against the Houston Astros as the first native of San Francisco to play for the San Francisco Giants. He batted second in the order behind Bobby Bonds and one spot ahead of his childhood idol, Mays.

As he left the on-deck circle for his first plate appearance, Mays approached, patted Gallagher on the butt and said, "Go get 'em kid." Gallagher was flying so high he never remembered his first two at-bats, which included a ground out and a single. In the seventh inning, his triple scored Bonds from first base.

From that day forward, Gallagher developed a special bond with Mays. Gallagher later claimed that he was one of the few white members of the Giants who Mays took a liking to. When Gallagher got into managing, he wore No. 24 in honor of his hero. It is the jersey number he donned as manager of the Bulls in 1980.

For 12 seasons, Jim Davenport had manned third base in a steady capacity for the Giants. By 1970, at age 36, Davenport's skills had eroded some and Gallagher was there to win the position. He joined a lineup that featured future Hall of Famers Mays and Willie McCovey in the field and Gaylord Perry and Juan Marichal on the mound.

The '71 Giants won the National League's Western Division thanks in no small part to Gallagher carrying the club in August when he batted a robust .420. But they fell to the eventual World

Series champion Pittsburgh Pirates in the playoffs.

Gallagher was having the time of his life. As the precursor to Ozzie Smith, Gallagher did back flips and handstands when leaving the field after the Giants completed infield practice before games. His showmanship carried into managing. (When he managed the Bulls in 1980 from the third-base coaching box, Gallagher would retrieve a ball in foul territory, wheel and fire a knuckleball back to the dismayed opposing pitcher. Occasionally, he drew the ire of the opposing manager.)

According to a 2011 story in hardballtimes.com, Gallagher soon was called "Pigpen," "Filthy McNasty," and "Sludge" by Giants teammates because of his manner of play on the field and less than sanitary habits off the field. Jeff Matthews was a utility infielder on the '80 Bulls who saw Gallagher play for the California Angels a few years earlier when Matthews was a youngster in Minneapolis.

"He was funny looking," Matthews recalled. "We used to crowd around the third base line and watch him. He pulled his hat down over his eyes and his uniform was always dirty."

Gallagher did not realize it at the time, but the 1971 season was to be the peak of his major-league career, the decline about to commence because of a conflict with the manager and a serious injury.

The Giants were led by Charlie Fox, who was rewarded for 18 years of managerial service in the organization by being named the club's manager after Clyde King was let go early in the 1970 season. Gallagher and Fox routinely feuded, and their differences carried into spring training prior to the 1972 season when Fox named Dave Kingman, a six-foot-six, second-year free swinger as the starting third baseman. Gallagher could not live with the notion he had lost the starting job to a brutal defensive player who also struck out at an alarming rate. Kingman's calling card was towering home runs.

"That may have been something I never recovered from," Gallagher said. "It was the start of my malcontent. I just couldn't get it through my head that Kingman deserved the job."

Gallagher eventually went to Fox with a play-me-or-trade-me ultimatum, and was traded the following season to the Angels, where he batted .273 before a collision with Boston catcher Carlton Fisk wrecked his shoulder and short-circuited his major-league career.

Gallagher later admitted to being the "average major-league player" that once merited an article in "*The New York Times Magazine*" under that heading. His major-league career was finished following the 1973 season at age 27. He posted a career .263 batting average over four seasons and 442 big-league games.

"I was very, very difficult to handle, very moody," Gallagher admitted. "You never knew what I was going to say. I have players who are like I was, always coming in here and complaining. But if I never did that, I might not understand that kid coming through that door.

"I was average, at best, as a major-leaguer. Again, that helps me as a manager. I can understand why certain guys can't do that stuff. I had a lot of shortcomings. So do they."

Years later, Gallagher admitted that his ways as a player came back to haunt him as a manager.

"God paid me back," he said.

Gallagher carried the same love and enthusiasm for the game into the managerial ranks. Unfortunately, Gallagher immediately found that not all players shared the same traits. Even though it might have been impossible for most minor-leaguers to live and breathe the game the way Gallagher did, he nonetheless held them to the same standards he set for himself as a player.

Gallagher in many ways became the minor-league version of Billy Martin, who thrived on confrontation with his players as a way to motivate them. It is a style that works well when a team is winning, but leads to disharmony, dissension and sometimes revolt in clubhouses when a club is losing.

Fortunately for Gallagher, his first three teams as a manager in the Atlanta organization were stocked with talent and his fiery motivational style generally played well to the young prospects. His 1978

Greenwood club, which featured future big-leaguers Steve Hammond, Bob Porter, Rafael Ramirez, Steve Bedrosian, Tony Brizzolara and Joe Cowley, won 82 games and ran away with the league championship. The 1979 Greenwood club again captured the Western Carolinas League title, this time with 78 wins. Among the future major-leaguers on that club were Hammond, again, Brett Butler, Albert Hall, Gerald Perry, Matt Sinatro, Milt Thompson and Rick Behenna.

So the table was set for Gallagher's team to succeed again in Durham in 1980 when Butler, Hall, Perry, Thompson and Behenna all graduated from Greenwood to the Bulls. With a couple of championships in his back pocket, Gallagher had no reason to discontinue his managerial style, one that promoted winning and entertainment as well as player development.

Typical of Gallagher's shenanigans were the events of a Sunday afternoon televised game at Durham Athletic Park. Gallagher, after being ejected, was ready to leave the premises without incident.

"Then it hit me," Gallagher said. "I remembered the game was being televised, so I figured I'd put on a show." He walked to home plate removed tobacco from his mouth and deposited the remains on home plate.

"Family entertainment," he shrugged.

Fantasy Land

As the calendar flipped from April to May it was already quite apparent to sports fans in the Durham area that something special was happening downtown at the corner of Morris and Corporation streets. At the very least, any given visit to Durham Athletic Park was producing an evening of enjoyable entertainment.

The Bulls won 13 of 17 games in April and played eight home dates before an average crowd of 2,500 that included a couple of early games in bitter cold weather that drew fewer than 1,000 fans. The buzz around town was that the Bulls were playing an exciting brand of baseball, the games were family affordable and loads of fun, to boot.

The old ballpark had come alive again.

Yet Durham Athletic Park still had many shortcomings. Parking was virtually non-existent, though there was not much Owner Miles Wolff could do except ask fans to not block driveways of neighborhood residents. Inside, obstructed seats were an inconvenience, though an accepted part of watching baseball in an older park. Restroom stalls were in short supply. Dust became an issue on the dirt "courtyard" area inside the main entrance, as well as along the walkways behind the third- and first-base grandstands. Front office personnel attempted to keep the dust to a minimum by watering the areas prior to every game, much like groundskeeper Bill Miller did with the infield. Also, long lines to purchase beer meant missing some of the game's action.

Once the season moved into June and the oppressive heat and humidity typical of summer in the American South became almost a nightly distraction, the grandstand overhang kept the heat contained and made the best seats in the house among the most uncomfortable. There was little the Bulls could do to remedy the situation as large ceiling fans that once were the staple of many old ballparks had long since been removed from Durham Athletic Park.

By mid-season, beer trucks were added to better accommodate fans in the left and right field bleachers. Additional restrooms were opened down each foul line. Eventually, Wolff contracted with the City of Durham to pave the walkways and courtyard areas, but that was a season away. So, too, was the removal of the light standard in play next to the visitors' third-base dugout. In coming seasons, a building was constructed behind the right field bleachers to double as storage space and an additional concession stand, easing the strain of traffic on the lone stand behind home plate that was operative for that first season.

From the outset, Wolff refused to voice any displeasure about the ballpark — publicly, at least. He insisted on referring to Durham Athletic Park as "historic" and required all Bulls employees to do the same. Outwardly, Wolff loved the "charm" of the park, making certain that the magnolia tree behind the fence in right-center field remained. He even kept the non-operative scoreboard behind the right-field fence intact that first season.

Above all, Wolff had the great fortune to have a manager that first season who believed minor-league baseball could be equal parts player development and sports entertainment. While it was quite OK for an Earl Weaver to argue with umpires, spin his cap and toss it to the ground before being ejected at the major-league level, it generally was unaccepted practice for minor-league managers to do the same. The reason? Well, the games just did not matter as much below the big leagues.

It got to the point where fans never knew quite what to expect from Al Gallagher. He held a closed-door meeting with his team in the clubhouse during the late afternoon prior to a May 2 game against Peninsula. The manager was upset with his team's lack of fight in a 10-2 loss to Kinston the previous night. His message was simple: "Never give up."

That night, Peninsula jumped to a 6-0 lead after two innings and Gallagher's pre-game pep talk was about to be put to a test. When an irate Gallagher and catcher Steve Stieb were ejected by home plate umpire Gerald McCann following a controversial ruling to end the third inning, it looked as if the Bulls were headed to a third straight defeat. Gallagher liked to be ejected from games if it meant firing up his team, and this was clearly one of those occasions. Before departing, Gallagher got nose-to-nose with McCann and made certain his tobacco juice dotted the umpire's face. The crowd of 3,311 loved it.

After his departure, the Bulls rallied for a 7-6 win.

"That's what winning is all about," Gallagher proclaimed afterward as he pointed to a locker room full of celebrating players. "What a super win. Not a good win, but a super win."

Never did Durham fans expect their manager and their Bulls to be upstaged by an opposing manager. Yet that is precisely what happened on May 13 with the Winston-Salem Red Sox in town.

Buddy Hunter, Winston-Salem's manager, was still seething about an umpire's call the previous night that appeared to take a home run away from one of his players. Because the right-field fence, which was eight-feet high that season, rested against the brick wall behind it, umpires had a difficult time discerning whether line drives cleared the fence or not. Determined to get the last word with the same umpiring crew, Hunter questioned another controversial call. This time, Hunter decided to put on a show.

Hunter first grabbed a baseball and raced to the outfield where he rifled it against the fence, then pantomimed a coin flip before giving the finger-twirl signal for a home run call. Hunter then returned to the infield and slid into first base, sat on the base and removed his shoes. He pantomimed pulling a pin on each shoe and tossing each to the outfield as if they were hand grenades. For good measure, Hunter removed first base from its bearing and tossed it into the outfield grass.

He departed to a standing ovation from the home crowd.

In later years, when interest in minor-league baseball had increased and games began to appear on TV, such managerial antics became much more commonplace. Hunter's show was a rarity in the minors and gained recognition nationally with an article later that month in *The Sporting News.*

Hunter had expected to be fined by Carolina League President Jim Mills, but it never came to that.

"I heard that (Mills) got a lot of calls from Durham fans wanting to help pay the fine," Hunter said later. "These fans really get into the game. That's why I put on a show. They deserved it."

■

It clearly was fun again to go to the ballpark, not just because of the team's play and the occasional side shows, but also because Durham Athletic Park — despite its shortcomings — was generally well suited for watching and experiencing the game.

The park's cozy design allowed for easy interaction with players, and fans got an up-close look at the action. When Wolff first looked at the old ballpark as a potential home for his franchise, he recognized the value of interaction between players and fans. He envisioned an atmosphere where the locals could adopt the Bulls as "their team." Often after batting and infield practice, when the field was being prepared for that night's game, home and visiting players would stand outside the non-air conditioned clubhouses and mingle with fans.

Fans also hung around after games to interact with players, and often pat a player on the back for a well-played game. The unusual exit arrangement of players walking among fans to gain entrance to the clubhouse tunnel also allowed for plenty of jeering of opposing players, as well. A visiting pitcher would be removed from a game, retreat to the third-base dugout and then be forced to walk, between innings, behind home plate all the way past the home dugout, through a walkway dotted with fans, and into the clubhouse. Rarely was that a pleasant stroll for a pitcher following a sub-par performance.

Wolff also reconfigured the field prior to the 1980 season, primarily to lengthen the distance from home plate to the right-field fence. In order to gain an additional 10 feet, Wolff simply moved home plate about 10 feet closer to the grandstand. The distance between the plate and backstop was now only about 30 feet — far short of the recommended distance of 60 feet in professional baseball. While baserunners cursed the elimination of any scoring opportunities from third base on a wild pitch or passed ball, fans delighted in the prospect of carrying on conversations from the grandstand with the third baseman or first baseman or with batters in the on-deck circles. The bullpens were located in foul territory down each line and fans in adjacent bleachers also had the opportunity to carry on with pitchers stationed there during games, although in later years security was necessary in the visitors' bullpen as things occasionally got out of control.

The quirks of the park essentially made fans part of the entertainment, part of its charm, part of its fabric.

Seated directly behind home plate for every home game was Frankie Parrott, who placed a transistor radio next to his ear so he could listen intently to the description of every pitch and every play by Bulls broadcaster Dave Slade. Parrott was blind. Pops Baucom never missed a game, either. He sat in a custom-made car seat attached to the right-field bleachers, and nightly distributed "lucky" two-dollar bills to his favorite players.

Three women who returned to Durham Athletic Park that summer were 78-year-old Thelma Inscoe, her 70-year-old sister Roena Crayton, and their 64-year-old cousin, Ethel Lubeck. Their nightly perch was in the last row of the first-base grandstands. They had attended Bulls games off and (mostly) on since 1949, absent for every Wednesday night home game due to a conflict with church services. During pre-1980 games in Durham, the trio carried on a long-standing tradition in the 1950s and 1960s of Ma Gregg, who gained fame over the years for baking a cake for any player who hit a home run. So well thought of was Gregg, the Bulls front office once flew her to the World Series.

As the 1980 season grew on, the fans began to take a greater role in both supporting the home team and becoming an intimidating factor to opposing teams, whose players often were experiencing playing in front of sizeable crowds for the first time.

Three years later, when young Charlie Hudson was called upon as a starting pitcher for the Philadelphia Phillies in the World Series, he was asked by the throng of media if he had ever experienced such pressure. Without batting an eye, Hudson said that he certainly had: in the Carolina League the previous season while pitching for the Peninsula Pilots at Durham Athletic Park.

At first, the Philadelphia writers thought Hudson was kidding. He assured them that he was serious, dead serious. For good reason. Hudson was the losing pitcher at Durham in 1981 in a one-game playoff to determine the Carolina League's South Division championship. Hudson clearly was affected by the environment during his three starts that season in Durham, losing two of three decisions with a 5.21 earned run average. In all other games at all other league parks, the league's pitcher of the year was 14-3 with a 1.46 ERA.

■

Like most downtown ballparks constructed prior to World War II throughout the major and minor leagues, Durham Athletic Park was originally built in 1926 to fit the neighborhood surroundings. Boston's Fenway Park and Chicago's Wrigley Field, the lone two remaining historic ballparks in use in the majors, are the obvious examples of a ballpark fitting the confines of a city block. Thus, the need for a 37-foot high home run wall in left field at Fenway Park. And, what baseball fan does not know that a long home run to left field at Wrigley Field only need clear a few bleacher seats before landing on Waveland Avenue.

Ebbets Field, home to the National League's Brooklyn Dodgers from 1913 to 1957, had the same constraints in its dimensions with the right field fence abutting the passing street. If the blueprints could be found for the field dimensions at Ebbets Field and Durham Athletic Park, it's entirely possible that one could be placed directly on top of the other with little overlap.

In Durham Athletic Park's case, the Brame Building, an old tobacco barn, framed the right-field fence all the way to center field. The fence and berm in left field across to center field backed up to Geer Street, and Morris Street ran along the third-base line all the way to the left-field foul pole. When the stadium was first built, a tobacco warehouse abutted the first base bleachers where West Corporation Street now runs.

■

Much of Durham's professional baseball history can be gleaned from the "*Encyclopedia of Minor League Baseball.*" Durham's first association with professional baseball dates to 1900 and involved participation in the North Carolina Association, an independent league that lasted only five weeks and 21 games. The team was known as the Tobacconists in 1900.

In September 5 and 6, 1901, in Chicago, representatives from seven different minor baseball leagues met and formed a new organization: the National Association of Professional Baseball Leagues. It was the start of the association that would govern minor-league baseball in the 20th century and beyond. The Durham Bulls officially came into existence in 1902, joining the Class C North Carolina League and played 48 games over nine weeks before the league disbanded on July 12. William G. Bramham, a successful Durham attorney and later a judge, was primarily responsible for formation of the short-lived league, and later became instrumental in the growth of the game in the minors by becoming president of the National Association.

The Bulls came back into existence in 1913 when they joined the Class D North Carolina State League, but that league also disbanded on May 30, 1917, even as Bramham took over as president in 1916, because the United States was drawn into World War I. Twenty-one leagues began the season, but only 11 completed it.

In 1920, baseball emerged from World War I and into a boon period. The Class D Piedmont League was formed, with Bramham as its president, and Durham — a charter franchise — remained a member until 1933 and again from 1936 through 1943. The club dropped out of the league during the 1934 and 1935 seasons due to poor attendance, according to J. Chris Holaday in his 1998 book "*Professional Baseball in North Carolina.*"

Meanwhile, Bramham was elected president of the National Association in 1933, and moved the NAPBL offices from their original home in Auburn, New York, to Durham, where he presided over the minor leagues through 1946 and guided them through two particularly turbulent times in baseball's evolution: the Depression of the 1930s and the war years of the early 1940s.

The Bulls played their early games at Hanes Field (now Williams Field) on the Trinity College campus, then at Doherty Park in East Durham until 1926 when those grounds were condemned and declared "unfit for ladies to sit in." That led to the construction of El Toro Park, located on the same site Durham Athletic Park would later occupy. The stadium, built for $160,000 and considered the finest in North Carolina, opened on June 7, 1926. The Bulls defeated the Salisbury, North Carolina, Colonials 4-3 in 10 innings before almost 2,000 fans, including North Carolina Governor Angus W. McLean and Major League Baseball Commissioner Judge Kenesaw Mountain Landis, who rode the Durham mascot — a live bull — onto the field in pregame ceremonies.

El Toro Park was renamed Durham Athletic Park following the 1933 season when a $20,000 donation by Durham philanthropists Annie Watts Hill and her husband, John Sprunt Hill, enabled the city to purchase the park. One stipulation of the donation was that the land on which Durham Athletic Park was situated could never be used for anything but a ballpark, which seemed insignificant at the time but later proved pivotal in keeping Durham Athletic Park from demolition in the 1970s.

A few hours after Durham defeated the Portsmouth, Virginia, Cubs, 7-3, on June 17, 1939, El Toro Park was destroyed by fire. According to a 1993 account in the *Durham Herald-Sun* gleaned from newspaper reports of 1939, "a fire broke out that night in the Big Bull Tobacco Warehouse at the corner of Foster and Corporation streets. The warehouse was leased to a farm equipment company and the conflagration soon reached several gasoline tanks, touching off a series of spectacular explosions that spread the fire to the ballpark's 'tinderbox stands.' Thousands of citizens in pajamas and house robes, many of the men not bothering to put on shirts, gathered to watch the blaze."

Across the street from the park, the Tennessee Lunch Room opened for business at midnight to sell sandwiches and soda pop. No one was hurt in the fire that did between $100,000 and $125,000 in damage, although it nearly claimed groundskeeper Walter Williams as a casualty. He was asleep under the grandstand when the fire began, but managed to escape safely. Despite the possibility of being forced to complete the season in another city — Greensboro badly wanted the franchise — City Manager Henry Yancy found sufficient financing to build temporary wooden bleachers and the Bulls returned home just 15 days later to defeat the Charlotte Hornets 11-4 before a crowd of 1,000.

A new stadium was constructed in time for the 1940 Piedmont League season, complete with 2,000 concrete grandstand seats — the same ones that remain today — and portable wooden bleachers along the first- and third-base lines. Once again, a major source of the funding for the stadium construction came from the Hill family.

The stadium reopened to much fanfare with a major-league exhibition game on April 7 between the Boston Red Sox and the defending National League champion Cincinnati Reds, who the previous fall in the World Series fell victim to the New York Yankees in four games. A crowd of 5,574, the largest in Durham professional baseball history at the time, watched Dom DiMaggio of the Red Sox take the first at-bat in the new park. Future Hall of Famers who played in the game included Bobby Doerr, Jimmie Foxx, Lefty Grove, Ernie Lombardi and Ted Williams.

The official opening came 10 days later against Winston-Salem. Durham won 9-3 before 1,600 fans.

Durham's attendance seemed to ebb and flow with the whims of minor-league baseball from then until the late 1960s when the sport began to fade from the American conscious. To salvage the slipping franchises in Durham and Raleigh, the teams in those communities merged to become the Raleigh-Durham Mets in 1968, the Phillies in 1969 and the Triangles in 1970 and 1971 when they were no longer affiliated with a major-league club. The teams played half of their 70 home games at Durham Athletic Park and half at Raleigh's Devereaux Meadow. The club managed to finish second in the Carolina League in attendance in 1970 with 56,138 fans, but when the numbers fell to 40,447 the following year, pro baseball was dead in the area.

In a desperate attempt to draw fans to the ballpark in 1971, the Triangles announced late in the season that they were prepared to sign a woman to a professional contract, according to Holaday's book "*Professional Baseball in North Carolina*." Jackie Jenson would have been the first woman player in Organized Baseball, according to Holaday, but the club heeded the advice from the Carolina League and did not sign her to a contract.

The Carolina League faced the same hard times as just about every other minor league throughout the '70s. For the 1975, 1976 and 1977 seasons, only four franchises comprised the Carolina League, and in those first two seasons teams played an interlocking schedule with the four-team Western Carolinas League. The Carolina League added two teams for the 1978 and 1979 seasons, and two more with the addition of Durham and Rocky Mount in 1980.

The league was fortunate that old Durham Athletic Park was still standing. Even though professional baseball in Durham had died for nearly a decade, living forever were the memories. When baseball came back, old timers again recalled Luke Easter once hitting a home run over the center field fence, some 500 feet from home plate to Geer Street, during a major-league exhibition game. They remembered that Greg Luzinski matched Easter's feat with a blast of similar distance over the center-field fence.

There were many great players who passed through Durham on the way to the big leagues, not the least of whom was Johnny Vander Meer, who was the Minor League Player of the Year for the Bulls in 1936 when he compiled a 19-6 record with a 2.65 ERA.

Then there was an 18-year-old redhead from New Orleans named Rusty Staub. He essentially saved the Durham franchise in 1962 when the Bulls were on the verge of financial ruin. Struggling at the gate, the Bulls hooked up with the expansion Houston Colt .45s that season.

Tal Smith was the Colt .45s director of the minor leagues at the time, which was good news for Durham stockholders. Smith was a Duke University graduate. Because of his interest in Duke and Durham, Smith helped place a respectable team in Durham, led by Staub. The young first baseman became a favorite of Durham fans that season, not only because of his .293 batting average, 23 home runs and 93 RBIs, but also because of his warm personality.

All of the budding stars who had played field positions in Durham over the years, including the likes of Gates Brown, Luzinski, Dick McAuliffe, Joe Morgan, Charley Lau and Johnny Pesky, were measured against Staub.

Likewise, of all the great pitchers such as Mickey Lolich, Jon Matlack, Vander Meer and Luis Tiant, the standard to which they were compared was lefty Eddie Neville, who never reached the major leagues. Neville won 75 games in four seasons for Durham from 1949 through 1954, including a whopping 25 in 1949.

Durham fans, old enough to remember, never forgot the Aug. 29, 1952 game at Durham Athletic Park in which Neville pitched scoreless baseball through nine innings, but so did the Greensboro pitcher. Neville continued to shut out the Greensboro club through 12 innings, then 13, 14, 15 and, finally, 16 innings. Tired of lack of support, Neville finally doubled and scored the winning run in the bottom of the 16th inning.

Thirty-eight years later, Neville often leaned against the fence down the left-field line in front of the bleachers, sometimes with a glove in hand. He loved reminiscing about his glory days as a Durham Bulls pitcher, and he treasured every chance to attend a game at his old ballpark.

Perhaps author David Lamb said it best in his book "*Stolen Season*," about his tour one summer of minor league parks.

"Durham Athletic Park fulfills our fantasy of what baseball is and should be," Lamb wrote.

Smiley And The Gang

Piecing together a roster for a Class A baseball team out of spring training is mostly an exercise in frustration for a manager, especially one like Al Gallagher who had his eye on capturing the Carolina League pennant even then. In his daily meetings with Atlanta Braves front office personnel, Gallagher attempted to shape his roster around players who could form a winning team. The Braves took a more long-range view and were more concerned about which top-level prospects would perform best at any given level of play.

Typical of the tug-of-war over player personnel involved a decision late in spring training at Atlanta's West Palm Beach, Florida, complex about who would play shortstop in Durham. Albert Hall had manned the position the previous season under Gallagher at Greenwood in the Western Carolinas League but a horrific experience in the field dictated that Hall be moved to the outfield for the

1980 season.

Hall made an astonishing 72 errors in 95 games at Greenwood. Hall's futility in the field may not have been record-setting, although just the thought of him remaining as Greenwood's shortstop for most of the season was an accomplishment in itself. Most shortstops with an abominable .850 fielding percentage would have been shifted to another position sooner than later.

"If nothing else, Albert proved to us that he wasn't a shortstop," said Paul Snyder, Atlanta's director of player development and scouting at the time.

The leading candidate to be Durham's shortstop in spring training was Paul Runge, a soon-to-be 22-year-old out of Jacksonville University and Atlanta's ninth-round pick in the previous year's June draft. The problem with Runge was two-pronged. Although he proved to be an Appalachian League all-star in 1979 while playing for Kingsport, he still had only 66 games of Rookie League professional experience. Playing in Durham would mean having Runge skip playing in low Class A in 1980, which can be a difficult jump even for the most advanced of players. Also, Runge had a terrible time of it in his first spring training with the Braves.

"I was striking out. I was kicking balls in the field," Runge said. "Somehow, some way, I guess Dirty Al liked what he saw. He saw some potential with me."

What Gallagher saw was a player who was a "gamer," in the baseball vernacular of the day.

"He was a tough ass," Gallagher said of Runge. "He played ball, came to play ball every day."

So Runge was placed on the Durham roster, although Gallagher initially batted Runge ninth in Durham's order. Eventually Runge moved up a few spots, sometimes climbing into the No. 3 hole. Runge displayed an aptitude to learn and to adjust. He welcomed the presence of Hall of Famer Luke Appling, a roving hitting instructor for Atlanta at the time. Appling worked with Runge to shorten his swing and drive balls to the opposite field.

Then, upon arriving at the ballpark one day during the season's first half, Runge was summoned to Gallagher's office for a heart-to-heart talk. Gallagher had learned that Savannah of the Double-A Southern League was in need of a middle infielder, and Runge was the likely choice to move up. Gallagher told Runge as much, but said he had reservations about the promotion.

"What do you mean?" Runge responded. "What do you mean?"

"Listen, if you're going to be a major-league player, you don't have the ability to be ready for just 100 pitches out of 110," Gallagher told him. "You have to be ready for 110 out of 110. It's hard to be ready for every pitch when you're an infielder, but you have to be. Sometimes, I think you take seven or eight pitches off during the course of a game, and that's when you're vulnerable to making an error."

Even though he made 24 errors in the 1980 season's first half for the Bulls, Runge proved to be a steadying influence on the infield and his .261 batting average was not indicative of how valuable his bat was to the everyday lineup. He combined 53 walks with 55 strikeouts for an impressive .396 on-base percentage.

Runge also was representative of the kind of player Gallagher liked putting on the field. A big part of Gallagher's ongoing conflict with Atlanta's front office was over playing time. Gallagher wanted to pencil in those players who came to the park ready to compete every night and win games. Most organizations do not work under those principles in the minor leagues, particularly below the Double-A level. Teams at the Rookie and Class A levels generally consist of six to 10 higher draft picks — prospects — and the remainder of the roster late-round picks and free agents, or what generally are known as roster fillers. Gallagher rarely made lineup decisions based on whether a player was considered a prospect or not, and that infuriated his bosses.

His obstinacy led to a particular nasty debate on the final day of spring training about what four outfielders would play in Durham.

Not one to mince words, Gallagher insisted that Ronnie Rudd should be the odd man out and play every day for Anderson, Atlanta's new affiliate, in the low Class A South Atlantic League. Gallagher wanted an outfield in Durham of Brett Butler, Hall, Alvin Moore and Milt Thompson.

All parties agreed that Moore would ideally serve as a reserve, a team player who could accept his role as the backup to the three prospects in the outfield. Moore was 22 years old. He was drafted by the New York Mets in the sixth round in January, 1976 out of a Georgia high school, but instead of signing elected to attend South Georgia Junior College. After one year of school, Moore signed with the Braves as a free agent, and advanced from Rookie ball to high Class A over parts of three seasons. His projected ceiling in minor-league baseball was Double-A, so being sent to Durham as a fourth outfielder likely signaled that he was nearing the end of his professional career. His value to an organization was his ability to stay injury free, be ready to play at all times and mostly carry a happy-to-be-here attitude in the clubhouse. Moore had all of those qualities and proved to be a favorite among his teammates and management.

During the afternoon of June 23, before a Durham Justice of the Peace in a private ceremony, Moore was married to Pat Lawrence of Valdosta, Georgia. Typically, Moore was in uniform for that night's game against Peninsula at Durham Athletic Park. But he did not play.

Gallagher and the Braves brass also came to an understanding that Hall and Rudd would begin the season in Durham.

Hall was extremely raw, but at 5-foot-11 and 155 pounds was a small package of dynamite. When Atlanta selected him in 1977 in the sixth round out of Jones Valley High School in Birmingham, Alabama, Hall's only baseball asset was his legs. He had been timed in the 40-yard dash in 4.3 seconds. The Braves initially sent him to Kingsport and declared that he was a switch-hitter. He had previously only batted from the right side. Braves coaches figured he would need to best take advantage of his exceptional speed by also batting left-handed, and they would teach him how to slap the ball to left field and drag bunt on occasion.

Kingsport was a disaster for Hall. He made 10 errors in 17 games at shortstop, and batted .162 as a switch-hitter. The following year, Hall was dropped down to the Braves' Rookie League club in Florida where he could get more one-on-one instruction in a less-strenuous environment. His fielding did not improve much, but his batting average soared to .293. Then it was on to Greenwood for the 1979 season where Hall had the great fortune of playing for Gallagher.

"Albert can run," Gallagher said. "Oh my God, he can run."

Gallagher worked with Hall on bunting and developing a better eye at the plate, knowing that Hall could only use his speed if he got on base. He batted .288 that season, but his 60 walks against only 43 strikeouts led to a .396 on-base percentage. Once on base, Gallagher believed Hall should learn how and when to steal bases on his own. So Hall had a green light from the manager on the base paths. He led the Western Carolinas League with 66 stolen bases in 76 attempts.

By the time he reached Durham, Hall was tasked by Gallagher to work on reading pitchers' pickoff moves. Again, Gallagher gave Hall the freedom to run anytime, and the speedster learned that it was important not to steal third base with two outs, not to attempt a steal of second base when his team was trailing by a significant margin, and generally how to determine running situations rather than wait for a signal from the manager. More importantly, the move to Durham meant learning to play the outfield for the first time, and that came as a great relief to Hall. "It was a lot of pressure off me," Hall said of the move away from shortstop. "I could relax a little bit. I could use my assets, my arm and my legs, my ability to get on base and steal bases. It took everything off me and gave me everything I needed to go forward."

When Hall swiped nine bases during the season-opening six-game homestand, he served notice to the rest of the Carolina League that this was going to be his breakout season. Only an ankle injury that sidelined Hall for 13 games during the season's first half slowed him. By mid-season, Hall had 50 stolen bases and was fast approaching a couple of Durham records. Pat Haggerty held the Bulls record in the Carolina League with 62 stolen bases in 1949, and Warren Butts swiped 87 for Durham when it played in the Piedmont League in 1916. The Carolina League record of 84 by Salem's Miguel Dilone in 1974 was within reach.

Amazingly enough, Hall's wind was never compromised despite being one of the few cigarette smokers on the team. One afternoon at the ballpark, Gallagher saw smoke billowing from one of the bathroom stalls in the clubhouse. Although smoking was not prohibited by players, it caught Gallagher by surprise when Hall emerged.

"I didn't know you smoked," Gallagher said.

"Well, I couldn't smoke in front of my Dad, and I'm not going to smoke in front of you," Hall responded.

Rudd was somewhat the "golden boy" of the organization. He was a second-round pick in the 1978 January draft out of Sacramento (Calif.) City College. As is still the case in baseball, the players who sign for larger bonuses after being drafted generally get the benefit of the doubt in roster decisions, though Rudd signed for just $4,000.

"They loved Ronnie Rudd," Gallagher said. "It was one of those where they kept telling me, 'You don't know what you're talking about with Ronnie Rudd.' "

It was not as if Rudd was a sub-par player. He had an outstanding 1979 season in Greenwood under Gallagher with a .289 batting average and 41 stolen bases. The left-handed hitter was physically more mature than most of his teammates, his 6-foot-1, 190-pound frame sculpted like no others.

There was something about Rudd that did not sit well with Gallagher, though. Interestingly enough, it had to do with Rudd having been reared mostly in California, same as Gallagher.

"He had what I call a California attitude," Gallagher said. "That

California attitude, white, black, I don't care what color you are, it's a California attitude. It was much nicer having kids from the South (on the team). They're nice kids. Some of the guys from California weren't worth a shit."

Gallagher used as an example a meeting he had early during the 1979 season with the black members of the Greenwood team. He explained to them that the local newspaper was known to run advertisements for Ku Klux Klan rallies. He also told them how their housing rent had to be paid to Gallagher. It seems that the rental agent would only accept the rent money from a white person. There also were certain locales to be avoided by blacks, Gallagher told the players.

"You're not going to tell me where I can go and where I can't go," responded Rudd, who was black.

"If you don't want to listen to me, fine," Gallagher said. "Just tell me where you want the body bag delivered."

Gallagher said the other blacks on the team — Andres Forbes, Hall, Milt Thompson and Gerald Perry — understood fully the ways of the deep South in the late 1970s.

Despite their differences, Rudd performed well for Gallagher and the Bulls in the season's first half while splitting time with Moore in right field and filling in for Hall when the speedy centerfielder was injured.

There was one incident with Rudd early in the season that proved quite humorous. In my desire to add a detailed description about him, I off-handedly wrote that Rudd's legs were shaped like a set of parentheses.

The following day when I arrived at the ballpark, I was greeted by Rudd at the entrance to the field. He had taken great umbrage to my prose and confronted me along the right-field line. Before I realized fully what was happening, Gallagher came charging from the batting cage to forcefully pull Rudd away from me. Gallagher informed Rudd in language not suitable for print that reporters were never,

ever to be touched under any circumstance.

Rudd later apologized. Another word was never spoken about the incident, and from then on I found Rudd to be both pleasant and engaging. We were both working in the minor leagues, and learning as we went.

So the final roster spot for an outfielder really came down to a choice between Butler, a late-round draft pick who few in the organization believed had major-league potential, and Thompson, a multi-talented player who was destined for the big leagues.

Thompson carried the same quiet demeanor in the clubhouse as Hall, and the two possessed a similar skill set on the playing field. Thompson was perhaps a half-step slower than Hall, yet still speedy. Thompson was perhaps a bit more athletic than Hall and he carried more experience as an outfielder.

Thompson came out of the Washington, D.C., suburb of Rockville, Maryland, where as a youngster he wanted to play infield. But he was left-handed, which limited his choices to first base. At age 8, according to a 2008 article in the *Philadelphia Inquirer*, Thompson approached his father about learning to throw right-handed. From that day forward, Wilbert Thompson and his young son played catch in the family's backyard with Milt learning to throw right-handed. By the time the next season rolled around, Milt had earned a spot in the infield as a right-handed second baseman.

It was the kind of determination and desire to learn that proved to be a hallmark of Thompson's after he was selected by the Braves in the second round of the January phase of the 1979 draft after dropping out of Howard University. The Braves initially sent Thompson to Kingsport where they quickly realized — 26 games with a .330 batting average and 13 stolen bases — his talents were far above the Appalachian League. So Thompson finished the '79 season under Gallagher's tutelage in Greenwood.

Thompson was considered a rare five-tool prospect, although his slight, 5-foot-11, 160-pound build would need more bulk before he could hit for power. The manner in which he glided after fly balls was reminiscent of how Hank Aaron did the same in the Milwaukee and Atlanta outfields. It also was occasionally misinterpreted as Thompson not playing at full speed. Yet Gallagher knew better. He loved the way Thompson played the game without flair but with measured intensity.

Unfortunately for Butler, the Braves did not have much money invested in him. He was a 23rd round pick out of Southeastern Oklahoma State University who received a mere $1,000 bonus to sign in 1979. That did not keep Butler from believing he was the best outfielder in the Atlanta farm system, at any level. To describe Butler as confident would do a tremendous disservice to the word.

"He dug himself," is the way Tommy Thompson described Butler.

Then Thompson added a qualifier: "But he backed up his cockiness."

Butler knew he deserved to be in Durham after batting .316 in 36 games under Gallagher the previous summer at Greenwood. He also performed well in spring training while mostly playing with the Double-A Savannah club. While that level of play was out of the question for Butler to begin the 1980 season, there was no doubt in his mind that he was headed to Durham.

Part of Butler's confidence stemmed from being the only person throughout most of his amateur career who believed he was a baseball player. At 5-foot and 100 pounds, Butler was too small initially to play baseball at Libertyville (Illinois) High School, so he turned to wrestling. Butler played JV baseball his freshman and sophomore years, then graduated to the varsity as a junior. Although he had grown some, he was still small for his age and did not gain a single at-bat that season. He kept the scorebook in the dugout while mostly "keeping an eye on the cheerleaders." As a senior, Butler managed only 32 at-bats as a reserve.

"It's been that way my whole life: You're too little. You can't do it. You won't make it," Butler said.

Determined that he could be a baseball player, Butler walked on at Arizona State. He believed the Sun Devils had the best college program in the country, and he wanted to prove himself at the highest level. Of 208 players who tried out, nine were selected for Arizona State's JV club. Butler was one of the nine and he played one season there.

Then he returned home to Illinois where he played semi-pro baseball in Chicago that summer. One of his teammates happened to play at Southeastern Oklahoma State and recommended that Butler do the same. Butler called the school's coach, Don Parham, and signed on to play for the next three years at the NAIA level in the tiny town of Durant in southeastern Oklahoma, about an hour north of Dallas. He batted .437 one year and hit .397 for his career, earning NAIA All-America honors twice. He also led the team to a small-college national runner-up finish in 1977.

There still were not many believers.

After drafting him, the Braves insisted that Butler become a switch-hitter. He was not interested. Then he began to hear chatter within the organization that he did not have enough power to be an outfielder. He was not strong enough. His arm was weak.

There was one coach in the Atlanta system who liked what he saw in Butler from the outset.

"He could play," Gallagher said. "Shit, he could play."

That spring training, Gallagher believed Butler was slightly more advanced than Milt Thompson. He fought hard to have Butler on his Durham roster, and appeared to succeed all the way through the final day of practices before camp broke. That night, Gallagher slipped the Durham roster to me under the condition I sit on it overnight because the players had not been informed of their assignments. I happened to run across Butler later that night in a hallway at the Days Inn where the team was housed in West Palm Beach, Florida. When asked, I informed Butler that he was headed to Durham.

"I had Brett Butler on the final roster. He was voted off," Gallagher said. "They didn't share my value of Brett Butler. So, they sent him down. … They didn't want Brett to be the fourth outfielder and not get to play."

The four outfielders who landed in Durham — Hall, Rudd, Moore and Thompson — constituted the bulk of who the Braves considered major-league prospects on the team. Only Perry in the infield fell into the same category.

From the day Gallagher first set eyes on Perry he was fond of the kid. That was in the spring of 1978, shortly after Perry's senior season ended at McCracken High School in Hilton Head, South Carolina. This was long before travel teams dotted the baseball landscape, and because Perry had not played much high school baseball he faced the prospect of going unnoticed by major-league scouts. Dan Driessen, who also hailed from the Hilton Head area, was a cousin of Perry's. Driessen was playing for the Cincinnati Reds at the time and telephoned Aaron. Driessen asked that Aaron give Perry a look. So the Braves arranged a workout in Greenwood, in front of Gallagher.

Gallagher watched one batting practice session and called Aaron.

"You better sign this boy," Gallagher told Aaron. "This boy can hit."

The Braves drafted Perry in the 11th round that year and sent him to Kingsport for Rookie ball. He was 17 years old. Then in 1979, Perry and Gallagher hooked up again in Greenwood.

"He was special. You could tell that right off the bat," Gallagher said. "He had that the day he was born. That boy could hit. When he got to Greenwood, he started right out smashing the ball. I'm not talking about hitting the ball. I'm talking about smashing the ball. Really, you don't see many kids who could hit like he could hit."

Perry batted .333 for Greenwood that season to lead the Western Carolinas League in hitting before advancing to Durham in 1980. The Braves knew Perry's bat would eventually carry him to the big leagues. But he had some major deficiencies in the field. Ground balls proved difficult for Perry to navigate. Popups were almost impossible for him to catch. So Perry often arrived early to the ballpark in Durham where pitching coach Bob Veale would hit fungo popups one after another after another after another.

Through all the extra work, which proved frustrating at times, Perry maintained a smile that defined his personality.

"Always smiling," Gallagher said. "I called him Smiley."

While the remainder of the infield might have been void of top-level prospects, it certainly was not lacking in characters. None was bigger in that regard than Tommy Thompson, a late-round pick of the Braves in the 1979 draft out of the University of Oklahoma. Thompson was the perfect minor-league player. He offered any club the ability to play just about any position on the field, and was the consummate team leader off the field because of his innate sense of humor and knack for keeping players loose.

At Kingsport the previous season, Thompson played at least one game in the outfield, at shortstop, third base, first base, catcher and pitcher. In Durham, he manned third base, second base, catcher and even pitched in one game. He was not the smoothest of operators at any position, but he generally got the job done. He typically attacked ground balls at third base as if they were venomous snakes in his back yard. Thompson seemingly took as many ground balls off his chest as he fielded with his glove. But he would pick up the loose ball and fire it to first base in time to get the runner. He was exceptional at calling and catching a game because he took charge behind the plate, knowing precisely when and how to pump up or chastise a pitcher during a game.

"The battler. The battler," Gallagher said in describing Thompson. "He didn't give a shit, wherever you wanted to play him. Hell, he'd bring out the water for the guys if that's what you wanted from him. ... Tommy was like another coach. He just wanted to be there, just be on the team."

At one point in the season, rumors in the clubhouse had circulated that Thompson was to be released by the Braves. Gallagher had been on the phone with Snyder about the possibility of Thompson's release.

"Goddamn," Gallagher told Snyder, "whatever you do, don't release this kid. This is a kid who's the heart and soul of this ball club. Don't get rid of Tommy." Snyder finally agreed to keep Thompson for a few days and see how things played out. But when Gallagher approached the team bus soon after for a road trip he found Thompson in tears.

In the end, Thompson stayed, and remained a significant contributor to the team the remainder of the season. There was an early slump in which Thompson could not buy a hit. Finally, as the team prepared for that night's game, Thompson decided to loosen things up.

"OK, I'm oh-for-24," Thompson announced to those in the clubhouse. "I just smoked a big fat doobie and I'm ready to go."

That was Gil Ryan's version of the story. Thompson does not deny it. In fact, Thompson said on occasion he would smoke pot after batting practice to better prepare him for that night's game.

This was an era when the abuse of recreational drugs was rampant in baseball, particularly in the minor leagues. To boot, these Bulls were a fun-loving bunch during that first half of the 1980 season. Accustomed to playing games before a few hundred fans at the lower levels, the Bulls were now performing before thousands of fans nightly. They also were living in a city with four nearby colleges, meaning there were plenty of places to meet coeds after games or simply hang out with students about the same age.

No player on the Bulls had more fun that season than pitcher Mike Smith. He was a ruggedly handsome man of 21 with blond hair and blue eyes who towered over most of his teammates at 6-foot-5. He was the eldest of five children of a Boston police officer. He also possessed a terrific sense of humor and could entertain teammates in the clubhouse, on bus trips and in bars with an ability to tell a story with a classic Boston accent.

Many remembered the good times two years earlier in Kingsport when several teammates shared the use of a worn Oldsmobile Delta 88. Smith, Steve Bedrosian, Lance Gore and Gil Ryan were riding in the car one night when it suddenly went airborne. Upon landing, a hole punctured the gas tank. For the remainder of the season, the tank could hold only a few dollars of gas at a time. When the season ended, the players removed the license tags from the car, placed the keys in the ignition and left it at the apartment complex.

There always was one story in particular that was off limits for Smith. That did not prevent others from talking about the incident in Greenwood. As many as six players lived in a house that season located at an intersection where there was a blinking yellow light. One night, as the players were drinking beer on the house's wrap-around porch, Smith pulled out a BB gun with the intention of taking care of the annoying blinking light.

At about that time, a taxi-cab driver pulled up to the intersection and Smith took aim at the light on top of the car. He missed. Unfortunately, the taxi-cab's driver's side window was open and a BB inadvertently struck the driver in the neck.

A little while later, police arrived at the house and asked if anyone living there owned a BB gun. Smith at first denied owning such a weapon. But when police looked around the house, they found the initials "MS" scripted on one wall with work that looked like it had been done by BB gun pellets. They found their suspect.

"It was an accident. It was an accident," Gallagher told police when he was summoned to the Greenwood Police Department to bail his right-handed pitcher out of jail. "He was just screwing around."

Thankfully for Smith, the cab driver was not seriously injured and willingly dropped charges.

Smith then went back to proving to the Braves that he was a much better pitcher than scouts believed after he was selected in the 23rd round of the 1978 draft out of obscure Massachusetts Bay Community College where he studied — yes, he did — law enforcement.

The Braves drafted Smith on the recommendation of Lenny Merullo of the Major League Scouting Bureau. Merullo, a legendary veteran scout and former major leaguer, was scouting another junior-college pitcher in the second game of a double-header. When Smith tossed a no-hitter in the opening game, the scout departed and recommended Smith to the Braves.

Despite his size, Smith was not a particularly hard thrower, but his fastball had movement and he was advanced in his knowledge of how to pitch.

He and Rick Behenna established themselves as the aces of the Durham staff during the season's first half. Smith was dominant in winning his first eight decisions over 11 starts that included three complete games and a six-hit shutout of Salem in April. He concluded the first half with an 8-1 record and sterling 2.50 earned run average.

Behenna was much the antitheses of Smith as a pitcher. Loaded with talent, movement on his fastball and a nasty slider, Behenna had the tools to eventually pitch in the big leagues. He just had not learned how to pitch.

His teammates referred to Behenna as "Little Boy," in an affectionate way, because of his lack of maturity, both on the pitcher's mound and off. Gallagher often had talks with Behenna's grandfather, Coop, during the season about his grandson's psyche. Behenna was a prime target for pranks by his teammates. One Sunday evening, several players gathered for a party at the home of Len Spungin, the owner of the Grinderswitch sandwich shop in downtown Durham. Early in the evening, Smith placed a couple of hot dog wieners in a microwave oven and cooked them until they were virtually leather. He dropped them into a couple of buns, garnished them with mustard, ketchup and relish and served them to Behenna. All watched in disbelief as Behenna consumed both hot dogs without complaint.

Gallagher and Veale recognized that Behenna had the highest ceiling of any pitcher on their staff, so they were willing to be patient as he matured in the minor leagues. That meant dealing with the enormous swings in his performance. He took a no-hitter into the ninth inning of his second start of the season. He also left without a decision after pitching 10 innings while allowing one run — in the first inning — in another early season game at Lynchburg. Then there were the stinkers. He allowed six runs on 10 hits against Peninsula one night, and near the end of the first half he gave up five runs without getting an out in a start at Alexandria.

Roller-coaster performances generally are the norm for pitchers at the Class A level where they are learning the nuances to the game at the same time they are often dealing with living on their own and away from home for the first time. Pitchers at that level often are scatter-armed and scatter-brained. In one early season game, Rick Coatney charged to the mound at Durham Athletic Park to start another inning only to realize his glove still remained in the dugout.

The mainstays in the Bulls starting rotation were Smith, Behenna, Coatney, Juan Alduey and Al Pratt, the lone left-hander of the bunch. Spot starts were given to left-handers Gary Reiter and Dom Chiti, as well as Ryan.

Who would settle in as the bullpen closer proved to be an issue early in the season. The Bulls broke spring training believing a pair of right-handers, Pete Teixeira and Arcilio Castaigne, could share the duties until one or the other established himself as the most worthy of closing out victories. Veale worked with Teixeira the previous season at Greenwood and saw a mature pitcher who utilized his experience well. Both Teixeira and Castaigne were 23 years old, although there was much suspicion that the latter was probably even older. Castaigne had deep-set eyes and a thick, daily growth of facial hair that made him appear like an older man among his younger teammates. He was born in Cuba and settled with his family in the Dallas area at a young age. He pitched for four different colleges in four years before the Braves selected him in the 30th round of the 1979 draft out of Texas Wesleyan University.

Teixeira got in the bad graces of Gallagher in the season-opener at Winston-Salem when he allowed the game-winning home run in the bottom of the eighth inning of a 3-2 loss. Castaigne had some early season success, but was not the kind of power pitcher that Veale was looking for in a closer. By April 28, Teixeira went down with an arm injury. Not long afterward, he was released. Less than a month into the season, Castaigne was optioned to Anderson.

More importantly, Durham obtained right-handed reliever Ike Pettaway from Savannah one game into the season. Apparently Pettaway was not going to be used often at the higher level, and Veale was more than happy to bring "Big Ike" into the fold. Pettaway was Veale's kind of pitcher. He stood 6-foot-2 and weighed 200 pounds and was an intimidating force on the pitcher's mound.

Veale's pitching philosophy was pretty simple. He wanted all his pitchers to live off their fastballs. He believed pitching to the inside part of home plate was necessary, and it was part of the game to occasionally move a batter further off the plate with a high and hard fastball. Early that season, at a pregame instructional camp for Little Leaguers, Veale preached the value of knocking down a batter with a pitch, "even if it's your mother with a bat in her hand." The wide-eyed youngsters sat stunned as Veale talked and Durham Bulls players giggled.

Pettaway was 25 years old that summer and in his fifth year of professional baseball, mostly as a starting pitcher. There was a bit of a mystery that surrounded Pettaway, who teammates generally steered clear of once they learned that he could sleep on team buses with his eyes open. As part of his mystique, Pettaway also did not speak to the media, thus earning the nickname "Ice Man" from his teammates. Those same teammates also called Pettaway "The Judge," when he began pinning an old jock strap on the locker of any player who made a bonehead play in that night's game.

On the mound, Pettaway was learning, in his new role as a reliever, that he could cut loose with his fastball, which scouts were clocking in the low 90s, on every pitch. Pettaway was signed out of Alcorn State College in Mississippi on the recommendation of Tommie Aaron, Hank's brother, and in four seasons as a starting pitcher he had a 19-26 record and 4.99 ERA. At that point, Pettaway was ready to quit baseball only to heed the advice of his mother and give it one more shot in 1980.

Gallagher and Veale both believed Pettaway was better served as a relief pitcher. Admittedly, at age 25, it was a last-gasp shot at preserving his career, but in the winter before arriving in Durham, Pettaway pitched in Venezuela under Coach Sandy Valdespino.

"(Valdespino) told me Ike was the top pitcher in the league last year," Gallagher said. "I felt, what the hell, if he could do it there, why couldn't he do it here."

Pettaway spent the first half of the 1980 season learning the ropes of pitching out of the bullpen. At the midway point, Pettaway had collected five wins and 11 saves. His earned run average stood at 3.18 and he also had 46 strikeouts in 40 innings. The only real blight on his pitching line were 23 walks.

He was equally difficult for the media to beat. In late May I approached Pettaway in the Bulls clubhouse prior to a game.

"Have you made a smooth transition to the bullpen?" I asked.

"No comment."

"Is relief pitching your ticket to the big leagues?"

"No comment."

"How about the fans in Durham? Do they pump you up?

"No comment."

Dead air.

"I don't know why you keep asking me these questions I'm not going to answer them anyway."

"Is it OK if I just write no comment after every question I've prepared?"

"No comment."

Then he turned to Reiter, his nearest teammate, and whispered that if he reached his goal of 20 saves for the season he would grant an interview. Just one.

Before that, there was the matter of Pettaway being consistent enough as Durham's closer to lead the Bulls to the first-half championship. His showing certainly was among the highlights of the first half.

Also not soon to be forgotten was a tape-measure home run by designated hitter Glen Bockhorn in a May 28 game against Rocky Mount. Bockhorn was known to launch moon shots when he hit the ball, which was not often. This particular one landed atop the Stone Brothers building across Geer Street beyond the left field fence at Durham Athletic Park. Even the old-timers could not recall a player ever hitting a ball that approached that building. The following day a couple of Bulls employees walked off the distance and figured the ball traveled an estimated 450 to 500 feet.

Two days later, Hall stole a Carolina League record five bases in the first game of a May 30 doubleheader at Winston-Salem, accomplishing the feat in seven innings of play.

Durham's early season 12-game winning streak figured to make the team's ride to the first-half championship in the North Carolina Division a smooth one. It was not. A seemingly comfortable 9½-game lead over second-place Kinston quickly disappeared by the end of May.

"We're not hitting, we're not getting good pitching," Gallagher said of a June swoon in which Durham lost 15 of 21 games. "If it wasn't for our good infield play, we wouldn't have a chance. We haven't played good ball in two weeks; pitching, hitting, everything. We're not getting anything in the clutch. Mainly, it's our pitching. That's 80 percent of the game."

Heading into the final four games of the first half against Kinston, the Bulls held gingerly to a two-game lead. That is when a little more magic arrived in Durham.

In desperate need of pitching for a doubleheader on June 17, followed by single games on June 18 and 19, the Braves fortified Durham's bullpen by promoting Gore, a right-hander, and left-hander Larry Edwards from Anderson. The two got the call while Anderson was playing in Gastonia, North Carolina. Just after learning of his promotion, Edwards also found out that his wife was in labor at the hospital in Anderson. So Edwards and Gore sped down I-85 with Edwards arriving at the hospital 45 minutes before his first son, Jason Daniel, was born.

The Braves allowed Edwards and Gore to remain in Anderson through the weekend, and they arrived in Durham on the afternoon of June 17. Edwards came out of the bullpen that night to relieve an ineffective Alduey in the first game of the double-header. Edwards threw 4⅓ innings without allowing an earned run, and picked up the win in an 11-5 decision over Kinston that clinched a tie for the first-half title. When Pratt pitched a complete game in the nightcap, a 2-1 Durham victory, the Bulls secured the championship.

"Next time," Veale said in the locker room celebration that followed, "let's not wait until the final two days to clinch."

Captain Outrageous

For reasons I will never know, Hank Aaron seemed to take a liking to me during my first spring training assignment in Florida in March of 1980. Not long after I arrived for the final week of camp, Al Gallagher invited me to join the minor-league on-field staff following a day of workouts. The Braves' five minor-league managers and their pitching coaches gathered on the grounds of West Palm Beach Municipal Stadium to cook hamburgers and hot dogs on a grill and drink beer.

While it might seem odd today that a reporter would be included in the cookout, the relationship between scribes and athletic personnel was on the back end of a much more cordial and fraternal rapport than we see today. There existed an inherent trust that a reporter understood this kind of get-together was off the record, and the coaches realized they could talk freely on any subject without concern that the conversations would be repeated or appear in print.

That part of attending the get-together caused me little consternation. Much more concerning was the presence of Aaron, the reigning baseball home run king who was just three seasons removed from the conclusion of one of the greatest big-league careers of all-time, one that included 755 home runs and 21 All-Star Game appearances. I admittedly was awestruck, not certain exactly how to address or make conversation with such a celebrity. It helped make me more comfortable when I heard other coaches refer to Aaron as "The Hammer," a name he certainly preferred over "Mr. Aaron," which is how I first addressed him.

Perhaps fueled by a few beers, I somehow stammered to Aaron that I was in attendance at Atlanta-Fulton Stadium for the 1972 Major League Baseball All-Star Game. My father had somehow finagled tickets through his work at a radio station in Salisbury, North Carolina, and we drove down for the game. I asked Aaron about his two-run homer. He told me what he most remembered about that night was that he was removed from the game after the home run, quickly showered and caught a flight to his hometown of Mobile, Ala., and watched on TV from his mother's home as Cincinnati's Joe Morgan drove in San Diego's Nate Colbert with the winning run in the 10th inning.

I quickly learned of Aaron's humble nature, preferring to reference the after-game rather than boast of his sixth-inning home run off future Hall of Famer Gaylord Perry, then with the Cleveland Indians. In future conversations with Aaron he was not interested in talking about his playing career. In his off-setting way, Aaron made it clear that he was the Atlanta Braves' director of player development and that was his current field of expertise.

Aaron played the final two seasons of his illustrious career with the Milwaukee Brewers. Following his retirement, Atlanta Braves owner Ted Turner recognized the popularity of Aaron in Atlanta and promised a position in the club's front office, if Aaron was interested.

Aaron was interested, but only if it was a working position and not one in which he was a mere figurehead for the organization. Aaron liked the idea of being a vice-president in charge of player development.

Unfortunately for Aaron, from the get-go it was nearly impossible for him to do his job, simply because he was Hank Aaron. During spring training workouts at the minor-league complex in West Palm Beach, which were normally open to the public, the Braves were forced to rope off the entrance to allow Aaron to roam from field to field and watch the prospects he was charged with developing. Fans seeking autographs did not understand that Aaron was working when he stood behind a backstop on one of the minor-league fields.

His in-season visits to Braves' minor-league outposts in Anderson, Durham, Savannah and Richmond were virtually impossible for Aaron to navigate. He could not be seen in public for fear of being mobbed by fans. At the ballpark, he was forced to arrive early and hide during games either in the press box or in the front office. After games, he waited until crowds departed before heading from his hideout to the locker room.

There was one night in Durham when Aaron sat in the press box and felt comfortable enough with the writers and front-office personnel to become playful. He began making up names and having Eric Brooks, the public address announcer, ask that the fictitious character please report to the press box.

That is the Aaron I grew to know, both during my trips to spring training and in his visits to Durham. I got wind in that first spring training that Aaron had taken up jogging in an attempt to stay in shape. Before long, the two of us would meet in the lobby at the Day's Inn where both of us lodged, and jog the couple of miles to the spring training complex and back. Once, during a jog around the wall on the west campus at Duke University in Durham, a car with three young men inside stopped us to ask for Aaron's autograph. He politely refused, having to explain that we were in the middle of a jog. Another time, on a rare occasion when Aaron agreed to eat at a Durham restaurant, we found a local ham-and-egger near the Duke campus where Aaron believed no one would recognize him. Sure enough, we sat in a corner booth and he went unnoticed throughout the meal. Then, as we were paying the bill, the waitress summoned up the courage to ask: "Are you Hank Aaron?" Without blinking, Aaron replied, "No. That's not me," and we departed laughing all the way to my car.

Aaron's visits to Durham usually numbered a couple of times each season. His mission was to find out as much as possible about the Braves' prospects on the Bulls' roster. Pregame and postgame conversations with manager Al Gallagher and pitching coach Bob Veale always proved fruitful, and I later figured out that the local sports writer was a good source of insight as well. I did not recognize it at the time, but our conversations usually centered on Aaron wanting to know more about the players' off-the-field conduct. I later learned that Aaron also befriended reporters in Anderson, Savannah and Richmond.

As much as the constraints of his name made Aaron's job difficult, it remained apparent that he was in charge of Atlanta's efforts to replenish its farm system and build a winning team through player development. That was not at all evident three years earlier.

■

If 1980 was the birth of the re-invented Durham Bulls, then the groundwork for the club's inception surely was laid three years earlier on May 11, 1977. The parent Atlanta club was in the midst of a 16-game losing streak, one that had both incensed and frustrated maverick second-year owner Ted Turner.

On an otherwise nondescript Wednesday night at Pittsburgh's Three Rivers Stadium, Turner was so desperate to change his club's sagging fortunes that he dressed in full uniform and took the reins as manager of the Braves. Only 6,816 fans were there to witness this bizarre event that would forever reshape and change the Braves organization.

Earlier that day, Turner had given beleaguered manager Dave Bristol a 10-day leave of absence. Turner, a meddling and hands-on owner, said he wanted to get a first-hand look at his sorry baseball team in his role as an interim manager. He said he also wanted to relieve some of the pressure the players were feeling during a losing streak that at the time was the fourth-longest in major-league history. Bristol was not fired, Turner insisted, though the disposed manager returned to his home in Andrews, North Carolina.

Turner donned jersey No. 27. At age 38, he was a few months older than his starting pitcher that night against the Pirates, Phil Niekro, a future Hall of Famer who took a 0-6 record into the game. At the time, the Braves were 8-21. By contrast, the Pirates were 21-7 and riding a nine-game win streak.

Nothing really much happened regarding Turner, other than his occasional visits to the third-base coaching box where he conferred with Vern Benson about strategies. The Braves lost, of course, 2-1, with a solo home run by Dave Parker in the third inning proving to be the game-winner for the Pirates.

It did not take long for the baseball world to get wind of Turner's latest escapade. Upon hearing the news, former Atlanta player Ken Henderson spoke perhaps for all of baseball. Henderson was then a member of the Texas Rangers.

"I'm not surprised to hear it," Henderson told the *Atlanta Constitution*. "It's *'The Ed Sullivan Show'* over there, a big circus. They treated me right, but I got the feeling it's a mixed-up organization."

Paul Snyder, a member of the Braves organization since signing as an outfielder in 1958, was Atlanta's director of player development at the time, and oversaw the team's minor-league and scouting operations. He was on a scouting assignment, and driving a rental car in Fort Wayne, Indiana. He fiddled with the car radio until he picked up the Pirates broadcast.

"What the hell did I just hear?" an exasperated Snyder recalled saying to himself years later. "So, I called Bill Lucas."

Lucas was Atlanta's general manager, appointed to the position by Turner himself in September of 1976.

"Bill, I just heard the Pirates broadcast," Snyder said. "I think they said Ted's managing the ballclub tonight. Is that right?"

"Duke (that's what Lucas called Snyder), I think that is right."

Turner's dugout gig lasted one game. Commissioner Bowie Kuhn intervened and forbid Turner from continuing in the role, citing baseball rule 20-E, which prohibits a stockholder in a club from managing the same team. Benson filled in as manager the next night in Pittsburgh, Atlanta ended its losing streak and Turner recalled Bristol to his original duties running the club.

The damage had been done, though, if not to the big-league club, desperate for a win under any circumstance, then within the organization and certainly to the reputation of the Atlanta franchise. If those within the game and fans everywhere did not believe before that Turner was a multi-millionaire huckster who treated his baseball team as nothing more than TV programming for his burgeoning WTBS cable network, then they certainly were convinced after this stunt.

Within the organization, the old baseball heads like Lucas and Snyder were fed up. A few days after Turner retired as a baseball manager, Lucas called a meeting with Turner at his WTBS offices near the Georgia Tech campus just north of downtown Atlanta. Turner greatly respected Lucas, the first black GM of a major-league club and the former brother-in-law of Aaron, and treasured the baseball wisdom of Snyder, who joined the meeting.

As the trio sat for the meeting, Lucas and Snyder stared at a "Leave, Follow or Get the Hell out of the Way!" slogan that rested front and center on Turner's desk. Turner always paced during meetings. If he could not walk the room, he could not meet. On this particular day,

Turner paced and paced and paced, and mostly listened to Lucas.

Lucas first wanted to know if the mercurial Turner, a champion yachtsman, was serious about fielding a winning baseball team. If so, Lucas reasoned with Turner, then it was time to turn over complete operation of the club — and all decision-making on baseball matters — to those folks who knew something about running a ball team, namely Snyder and himself.

Turner's frustration with baseball in general, and with the Braves in particular, became evident soon after he purchased the club on Feb. 1, 1976. Around the same time his local TV station, WTCG, was about to go national as the first cable Superstation, which ultimately became WTBS. Turner's belief that throwing money at a product would ultimately turn those dollars into many more dollars worked in the cable TV world. It did not necessarily work in baseball, as he learned immediately with the signing of Andy Messersmith to a three-year, $1 million deal on April 10, 1976 — just three weeks after Messersmith had been declared a free agent in a historic ruling that would have lasting implications on the game.

Upon signing with Atlanta and being given uniform No. 17, Turner discussed with Messersmith the possibility of changing his name to "Channel" and printing that name on the back of his jersey, just above the number "17." Thus, when Messersmith pitched for Atlanta on WTBS, he would prove to be a walking billboard for Turner's TV station. Again, Kuhn intervened, and the first vestige of uniform advertising was halted before it got started.

Turner's way to run the club was to buy the best available talent, or if he took a liking to a particular player to trade for him, no matter the cost. In November of 1976, Turner's primary target was ex-San Francisco Giants outfielder Gary Matthews, who was signed as a free agent. Less than a month later, Turner decided he wanted outfielder Jeff Burroughs on his club, and he obtained Burroughs from the Texas Rangers in exchange for Adrian Devine, Henderson, Dave May, Roger Moret and Carl Morton, plus $250,000 in cash.

Burroughs, the 1974 American League MVP, produced two outstanding seasons with Atlanta and two more sub-par seasons before departing as a free agent. Devine won 11 games for Texas in 1977, then returned to the Braves. The others all washed out. Even though Atlanta might have claimed the upper hand in the trade, it was not the kind of judicious move most baseball executives would have made.

In the case of Matthews, his signing by the Braves came at a significant cost. The impatient Turner was bent on capitalizing on baseball's new free-agent process to provide his struggling club the quick fix he believed it needed, but he was almost immediately accused by Kuhn of tampering in his courtship of Matthews.

As punishment for illegally contacting Matthews before the 1976 season was completed, Turner was suspended for one year, the Braves were fined $10,000 and penalized with the loss of two premium draft picks — the club's first-round choices in the regular phase in 1977, in both January and June.

The Braves forfeited their January pick, but challenged Kuhn's ruling in the courts to retain their June selection (fourth overall), and were successful in overturning it. With the reinstate of the fourth pick, the Braves went for left-hander Tim Cole, who spent 10 years in the minors, including the 1983 season with the Bulls, and never reached the big leagues.

Turner's suspension was initially set to begin on Jan. 18, 1977, but it was temporarily lifted pending the outcome of a suit Turner filed against Kuhn aimed at reversing his ruling. A U.S. district court upheld the suspension on May 18, just after Turner's ill-fated attempt at managing, which led to his summit meeting with Lucas and Snyder.

By meeting's end, Lucas' message had resonated with Turner, who was willing to let Lucas run the baseball side of things. That meant a shift in financial commitment to the organization as well. Free agents would no longer be the path to success. Instead, Atlanta would go about emulating the Los Angeles Dodgers, who for decades had stockpiled talent in their minor-league system, nurturing them along what they called the "Dodger Way."

For the first couple of years under Lucas' direction, Atlanta concentrated on stockpiling talent through the annual amateur draft. To do so, the club expanded its scouting department. At one point in the 1970s, Los Angeles had 33 scouts in the field to Atlanta's five. Within three years, those numbers had evened out. The Braves also needed to sign the players they drafted, and Turner was all in with the financial backing Snyder, as head of the scouting department, needed. Since Atlanta's major-league product was at or near the bottom of the National League annually, the team got to pick at or near the top of the draft rotation each year.

Building through the draft took time, and Atlanta's baseball folks knew their owner had little patience. Getting top-level talent also took time, and the only player of note that came out of the 1977 draft was Albert Hall, a speedy infielder out Birmingham, Alabama, selected in the sixth round.

In 1978, the Braves had the dubious distinction of drafting first overall — a result of their woeful 61-101 record in 1977, the worst since the franchise moved to Atlanta from Milwaukee, effective with the 1966 season. The team narrowed its choice to two college players, Arizona State third baseman Bob Horner, the NCAA single-season and career home run record holder, and Michigan State outfielder Kirk Gibson, a baseball-football standout from Michigan State. In the end, the Braves settled on Horner because they couldn't get a commitment from Gibson that he would sign with the Braves.

Horner signed a rare major-league contract with the Braves, which including a draft-record signing bonus of $162,000, and became just the 12th player in major league history to bypass the minor leagues and begin play with the parent club. He homered in his first game with the Braves, providing the struggling franchise with its most-electric moment since Aaron slugged home run No. 715 four years earlier, and eventually was named National League Rookie of the Year. Horner became the center of controversy a year later, however, when his agent Bucky Woy engaged the Braves in a long, drawn-out and nasty contract dispute, which shook the organization to its core.

Also in that draft, Atlanta signed its first real haul of future major-leaguers: catcher Matt Sinatro (second round), pitcher Steve Bedrosian (third round), pitcher Rick Behenna (fourth round), pitcher Jose Alvarez (eighth round), and first baseman Gerald Perry (11th round).

Following that draft it became apparent to Atlanta's brass that an additional minor-league team was needed within its system to assure a smooth, streamlined development path to Atlanta.

"We could sign players. Money was no object" Snyder said in reflection. "We could get money to sign players. (Ted) never shunted us on the money end of it. But we had to get Durham added through Ted."

The timing was particularly good for Lucas to make his pitch to Turner. By 1979, Turner had conceived the idea of a revolutionary 24-hour cable news network, and much of his time and commitment had shifted by then from baseball to what would become CNN. Turner accepted the idea of adding a high Class A team without giving it much thought, and Snyder is convinced that the advent of CNN eventually led to an unprecedented run of success for the Braves because Turner had finally ceded all authority and decision-making over to the baseball minds.

Unfortunately, Lucas never saw the fruition of much of his legwork or even the addition of Durham to Atlanta's stable of minor-league clubs. Three days after sustaining a brain hemorrhage, Lucas died of cardiac arrest in Atlanta on May 5, 1979. He was 43. The lasting legacy of Lucas was an Atlanta farm system that became one of the most fruitful in all of baseball. Thanks to Lucas' influence with Turner, the Braves expanded their scouting system and began to sink more and more money into their minor-league operation. The addition of Durham was a huge step, but hardly the last one.

The Braves had operated with four teams in their farm system from 1969 through 1975. A second Rookie-level team in Florida's Gulf Coast League gave Atlanta five teams within its system through 1979. Although the Braves dropped a Rookie team for the 1980 season as a tradeoff for adding Durham, they added one back in 1982. By 1986, Atlanta had seven farm teams and even added an eighth for the 1988 season. Only one other organization in the game had as many farm clubs.

By the mid-1980s, the Braves also began adding coaches to their minor-league staffs. Gallagher and Veale were the only coaches in Durham for the 1980 season, but a few years later every club in the system had at least a manager and two coaches, and sometimes a third. The emphasis on development led to enormous success for the Braves in the 1990s at the major-league level, and ultimately proved that Lucas' plan to build from within had significant merit.

None of it likely would have happened had Turner not put on a uniform and managed the Atlanta Braves for one game during the 1977 season.

The Professor

Monday morning came awfully early for Miles Wolff, Pete Bock and the remainder of the Durham Bulls management team following any homestand that concluded with a Sunday night game. The after-game beers around the truck on the concourse at Durham Athletic Park that the staff normally indulged in served as champagne toasts to a successful homestand, which was pretty much every one. The more the front office staff drank, the more they traded stories and often celebrated long into the night and early morning.

Yet Wolff usually conceded only one hour and scheduled a nine a.m. staff meeting on Mondays. Bock was there on time, invariably using a magic marker to shade the baseball-bat-shaped chart behind his desk in the front office. Much like the old United Way fundraising charts, Bock charted the club's attendance with the initial goal of reaching 75,000 fans for the 70 scheduled home dates. That seemed like a reasonable goal, given that Winston-Salem led the Carolina League the year before with an attendance total of 68,702.

By the end of the season's first half, Bock had to construct an entirely new chart with the Bulls having already drawn 81,804 fans, an impressive average of 2,237 per game. The significantly larger-than-anticipated crowds the Bulls were drawing meant Wolff could pay bills on time and also dole out salaries that he was forced to withhold until after the first homestand of the season.

Now, instead of having money issues hang over his head, Wolff had other, more-pressing problems to tackle, although they were a by-product of the unparalleled success the team was enjoying. The club simply could not adequately serve crowds of more than about 2,000 comfortably or efficiently. More staffing had to be added at ticket windows and at concession stands. Water pressure in bathrooms had to be improved. More parking spaces were needed.

As problematic as those tasks seemed, there was a bounce to Wolff's step and a broader smile crossed his face with each passing homestand. Wolff was realizing his lifelong dream of owning and operating a highly successful minor-league baseball franchise.

■

From the get-go, there was little pretense to Miles Wolff. After several telephone conversations with him, my first face-to-face meeting occurred in the dirt parking lot of Durham Athletic Park sometime in the fall of 1979. Wolff arrived in his blue second-hand Chevy Malibu, which was littered with newspapers and discarded fast-food lunch bags. He emerged from the car bespectacled and dressed in his customary khaki pants and cotton, button-down shirt. Members of the 1980 team got to calling him "The Nerd" because of his appearance, but there was a respectful tone even in that derogatory term. Coaches and front-office personnel called him "The Professor." Wolff may not have looked the part of a conventional baseball team owner but in time most everyone developed a reverence for the way he operated a club and conducted his business.

There also was a humbleness about the man, a quality that quickly explained why City of Durham officials and the Atlanta Braves wanted Wolff to own and operate the Bulls. One would never hear him boast of his accomplishments. You came to learn on your own that he had written one book a decade earlier — *"Lunch at the 5 and 10,"* a glimpse into the historically significant 1960 sit-ins at Woolworth's in his hometown of Greensboro, North Carolina — and that his first baseball-themed novel, *"Season of the Owl"* was soon due for release.

You could also find out, though not through him, that in 1971 he was *The Sporting News* Minor League Executive of the Year. When pushed to talk about what was then the highest honor in the minor leagues, Wolff would brush it off. He would tell you it was a fluke, based entirely on a couple of promotions he oversaw that somewhat artificially boosted the team's attendance on the year to 60,712. "There's no way I should have won that," he said.

The previous season, Savannah had a dismal year, suffering through the same general apathy for minor-league baseball that most cities across the country that fielded a team were experiencing. A mere 33,854 fans bothered to show up to watch the Cleveland Indians farm team at decrepit Grayson Stadium. When the Indians opted to move their Southern League affiliate to Jacksonville, Florida, for the '71 season, young first-year Savannah Mayor John Rousakis took it upon himself to find a replacement. He badly wanted an Atlanta Braves farm team to take its place, and the Braves succumbed to Rousakis' pitch when he promised a certain number of season tickets sold. So Atlanta decided to move its Shreveport, Louisiana, franchise out of the Double-A Texas League to the Southern League, and took ownership of the team.

Nevertheless, Atlanta's front office also cottoned to the idea of hiring a young buck — Wolff was 27 at the time — as they believed he could inject some much-needed life into a dying franchise. The Braves paid Wolff $600 a month to run the club, but only during the seven months of the season. Wolff was allowed to hire a 19-year-old secretary at $70 a week to assist in the operations. The front office payroll was scheduled to be $10,800, until Wolff was able to convince Atlanta officials to also hire a concessions manager on a seasonal basis.

While Rousakis was unable to deliver on his promise to sell many season tickets, he at least formed a "Pack the Park" committee for the April 13 season-opener, which guaranteed a sellout. Wolff went about lining up any celebrity he could find to make certain the first game would be one of Savannah's biggest events of the year. Atlanta Braves outfielder Rico Carty led the National League in hitting the previous season with a .366 average, but broke his leg during the offseason and was unable to play by the start of the 1971 season. So the Braves agreed to send him to Savannah and he threw out the ceremonial first pitch. Phyllis George, the reigning Miss Texas, was in Savannah for another engagement, and Wolff coaxed her into attending the game. Five months later, she was named Miss America. Also there was Lou Brissie, a former Savannah pitching hero who spent seven years in the major leagues after nearly losing his leg while serving in the U.S. Army during World War II.

For good measure, Wolff invited every Savannah Little Leaguer and Boy Scout troop member to walk in uniform on the field during pregame ceremonies. Wolff was putting to work what he learned from the baseball bible for executives, *"Veeck As In Wreck,"* the 1962 autobiography of the game's premier promoter, Bill Veeck.

A crowd announced at 10,459 packed the park.

Afterward, Wolff sat on the floor in his office with piles of cash all around him.

"Boy, this is easy," he thought.

He quickly learned the business of minor-league baseball was not that easy. For starters, Wolff dealt with a remarkable 13 rainouts during the season, meaning the club had that many fewer home dates, resulting in fewer revenue dollars.

Wolff resorted to any number of promotions to draw fans, though it took some convincing of Atlanta officials to land Max Patkin for one promotion, knowing the Braves did not want to pay baseball's clown prince his standard $400 appearance fee. When the Savannah club went a month without winning a home game, Wolff publicly asked fans to pray for the team's struggling pitching staff on Sundays and bring their church bulletin to the game that night for half-price admission.

Then there was Union Bag and Paper Company Night at the ballpark. The Savannah-based company, once the largest paper mill in the world, gained national renown earlier in 1971 because of Ralph Nader's book *"The Water Lords."* It annually bought out all tickets to a game at Grayson Stadium and distributed them to its thousands of employees. For this game, Union Bag and Paper paid the club $5,000 for some 15,000 tickets. The ballpark could squeeze in about 8,000 fans, but Wolff knew that not every employee would use the two tickets each received.

Much to Wolff's surprise and delight, though, the company's employees filled the park for the first time since Opening Day. Wolff typically used ticket stubs as a means to gauge attendance and also to give away door prizes. That night, ticket-holders tossed not just their own stub, but often unused additional stubs into the box at the gate. Typically, the ticket counter finalized the count, and he would then report the amount to Wolff and the two would come up with an announced figure. That night, the ticket counter was forced to count tickets in the press box, and came up with a figure of 12,000, even though there were obviously not that many fans in attendance. He happened to mention the number to the sports editor of the *Savannah Morning News*. Before Wolff could adjust the figure downward to more closely approximate the actual of number of fans, the public address announcer informed the crowd that a record 12,000 fans were in attendance.

Add that total to the Opening Day crowd, and Savannah drew 22,459 to just two games. It greatly helped push Savannah's season-ending attendance total to 60,712 — nearly double the previous year, and by Wolff's thinking, earned him Minor League Executive of the Year honors.

■

About the age of 11 or 12, Wolff envisioned running a minor-league baseball franchise. By then, he had become a regular at Greensboro's World War Memorial Stadium, an edifice originally constructed for football in the late 1920s. It also housed minor-league baseball teams sporadically, first in the Piedmont League (1920-42) and then in the Carolina League (1945-68).

Wolff's father, Miles Sr., once served as managing editor of the *Baltimore Sun*. While living in Baltimore, he met and married Nan Webster, and soon after the couple began raising three children. In 1950, the Wolff family relocated to North Carolina when Miles Sr. became executive editor of *The Greensboro Daily News*. The job paid a modest, middle-class annual salary of $12,500, which was enough for the family to live comfortably in Greensboro but certainly did not allow for many frills.

Baseball really did not play much into Wolff's life until 1954 when the family moved into its North Elm Street home in the Fisher Park neighborhood of Greensboro. A Sunday school teacher, who recognized Wolff's developing passion for baseball, presented him with a gift book of 10 tickets to the Greensboro pro games and he used them enthusiastically. His parents soon began dropping off young Miles at the ballpark late on summer afternoons. Furthermore, they trusted him that he could walk or ride his bicycle the two miles home following the nightly games.

Young Wolff was new to the neighborhood, so he sought solace at the ballpark and in the game itself. Like many young American boys in the early 1950s, he dreamed of one day wearing the uniform of a professional team, even if it was only the Greensboro Patriots.

This was when Little League Baseball conducted tryouts before placing players on teams. For three consecutive years, beginning at age 10, the gangly Wolff was cut.

"I wasn't going to be a big-league player," Wolff said. "So what else was there? Well, I could run a minor-league team."

He truly loved going to the games, soaking in the action as well as the activities away from the field. Yet he often thought of himself as a stranger in a strange land. "I'm the only one who is liking this?" Wolff often asked himself. "Why don't more people like this?"

Wolff attended many Greensboro games with his neighborhood buddy, Bob Godfrey. Each was about 14 years old when Wolff turned to Godfrey during one game and said, "Bobby, I can tell you now, I am going to stay in this game the rest of my life," according to bobspoint.blogspot.com.

The Patriots led the Carolina League in attendance in 1954 when the turnstile count reached 81,607, which averaged to about 1,200 fans a night. Home attendance dipped to 58,282 in 1955 and dropped a year later to 39,738 — a mere 500 or so ticket-buyers per game.

If nothing else, Wolff figured, it was worth going to the ballpark to see stars on other teams, such players as league MVP Curt Flood of High Point-Thomasville in 1956 and Leon Wagner, who hit 51 homers for Danville the same season. By 1960, Greensboro had become a New York Yankees farm club and Wolff found renewed interest in the local team, especially when it won the league pennant behind infielder Phil Linz, who led the league in hitting with a .321 batting average, and ace pitcher Jim Bouton, who went 14-8 with a league-leading 2.73 earned run average.

Wolff was fascinated by the action on the field, and had become more keenly interested in keeping an eye on the team's general manager and how he operated the team and promoted the product. He watched in disbelief as the GM often chased kids, including Wolff, in his efforts to retrieve foul balls for further use in games. Even to a 10-year-old, that smacked of bad public relations. Wolff also grew to despise the night or two each season when the club papered the city with free tickets and opened the gates.

"I hated free tickets, and still do," Wolff said. "Three thousand or 4,000 would show up. Then, the next night none of them would come back. It was just a very negative crowd. They would get a free ticket, and then would complain that the hot dog wasn't any good, or it was too cold. I hated those nights. Why were they taking my seats, complaining and taking my foul balls?"

By age 15, Wolff figured it was time to make some money at the ballpark by peddling soft drinks in the stands. But he chickened out, purchased a ticket and continued to watch the game as a fan while chasing foul balls.

Two years later, Wolff made a much more pivotal decision about his future as it involved baseball. He had applied to and was accepted at both Princeton University and the University of North Carolina. His third choice to submit his SAT scores was Johns Hopkins University in Baltimore, mostly because the school's campus was a few long Brooks Robinson home runs from Memorial Stadium, home of the Orioles. Wolff's parents had gone to Baltimore one summer, and returned home with souvenirs that made their son an Orioles fan forever. His decision to attend Johns Hopkins was sealed.

Wolff saw plenty of Orioles games while attending Johns Hopkins. Every spring, he walked the one mile from campus down East 33rd Street to the ballpark and volunteered his services to the club's farm director, first Harry Dalton and then Lou Gorman, both future major-league general managers. Nearing graduation, Wolff prodded the Orioles brass for a job in their minor-league system. No offer came. Wolff also mailed letters of inquiry, with a resume attached, to more than 40 minor-league clubs. Not a single club offered a job.

While at Johns Hopkins, Wolff also played basketball and worked at the student-run radio station. He called the school's football games for the station and might have been the only play-by-play announcer of lacrosse. None of that work played into a job when Wolff graduated in the spring of 1965.

Believing the Vietnam War was nearing an end, when in fact it was only escalating, Wolff took advantage of a student exemption to avoid being drafted and enrolled in the graduate history program at the University of Virginia. Upon completion of his master's thesis, Wolff avoided joining the infantry by enlisting in the Navy.

Wolff first attended Officer Candidate School at Naval Station Newport in Rhode Island, then Supply Corps School in Athens, Georgia, and finally was sent to Bremerton, Washington, where he shipped out on the USS Puget Sound as a supply officer. In his role, Wolff was enlisted to handle all business functions of the ship, including providing food and supplies for the 1,500 men aboard. Wolff was a 23-year-old ensign, dealing with 20-year veteran petty officers.

"I learned how to deal with being in charge," Wolff said. "I learned really good business principles in the Navy, organizational skills and how to deal with people."

He served his duty by 1970 and immediately used money saved from the Navy to travel the country and eventually to France. At the same time Stein and Day Publishers of New York were releasing *"Lunch at the 5 and 10,"* his master's thesis, as a book.

Wolff attended the Carolina League meetings in the fall of 1970 in Lynchburg, Virginia. He connected during the meetings with Marshall Fox, the general manager of the Peninsula Phillies. About a month later, Eddie Robinson, the farm director of the Atlanta Braves, telephoned Fox and asked him about a couple of potential candidates to be the general manager for their new Double-A franchise in Savannah, for the 1971 season. Both had listed Fox as a reference.

Instead, Fox suggested to Robinson that he should talk to Wolff. The Braves decided to take a chance on Wolff, believing it was time to inject some young blood into a minor-league front office at a time when the average age of the typical general manager probably was closer to 60 than 50.

Wolff flew to Atlanta and Robinson interviewed him for two hours at Hartsfield Atlanta International Airport. The next day, on New Year's Eve, Robinson called to offer Wolff the Savannah job. On Jan. 4, Wolff packed all his belongings in his car and reported the following day to work.

The move by Atlanta paid dividends when attendance at Savannah games nearly doubled from the previous year. For his efforts, Wolff was rewarded with a $100-a-month raise to $700, and was put on the payroll year-round.

Attendance jumped another 18,000 during Wolff's second season in Savannah, to 78,147, but slipped slightly in 1973. More noteworthy was the managerial change that season when the parent Atlanta club replaced Clint "Scrap Iron" Courtney with Tommie Aaron, the first black manager of a minor-league team in the deep South. Aaron's presence barely drew notice, other than his being Hank Aaron's younger brother.

On April 14 that season, Savannah and Columbus played a 23-inning marathon in the first game of a scheduled double-header. A big fireworks display was set for between-games entertainment. Undaunted, even with the game concluding around 1 a.m., Wolff ordered the fireworks to go off amid complaints from neighbors and city officials. The second game was postponed.

Three years of running the Savannah club was enough, so Wolff left his baseball job and lived at the nearby beach on and off for most of the next five years. His thinking was that he had satisfied his thirst for working in baseball, and at age 29, he believed it was time to find a real job like many of his fellow Johns Hopkins graduates who were now lawyers and doctors.

He spent some of his time writing what eventually would be his first novel, *"Season of the Owl,"* which again was published by Stein and Day, in 1980. Wolff also kept his hand in baseball by picking up odd jobs with minor-league clubs in the southeast. In Savannah, he occasionally filled in as the public address announcer and official scorer. When the Anderson (South Carolina) Mets of the Western Carolinas League needed a general manager to finish the 1974 season, Wolff was there to step in. In 1975, the general manager of the Jacksonville Suns of the Southern League left to work with the fledgling World Football League, and Wolff again had a job. He ran a soccer club in Toronto one summer, and another summer used his announcing skills from college to call radio play-by-play for the Richmond Braves of the International League.

Through his friendship with league president Bob Freitas, he also sought to gain the rights to one of the two new expansion teams in the short-season Class A Northwest League in 1974, with the intent of putting a team in Victoria, British Columbia. But he was the odd-man out as two other suitors, with considerably deeper pockets, trumped his modest offer and landed the two available franchises. Wolff had been attracted to Victoria, located on the southern tip of Vancouver Island, from his days in the Navy, when he was stationed a short distance away in Bremerton, Washington.

He also spent a week in Vancouver, British Columbia, in 1978, as the short-lived general manager of an expansion team in the Pacific Coast League. His tenure there was unusually short as he simply quit rather than work under the team's irascible owner, Harry Ornest, who later owned the National Hockey League's St. Louis Blues and Canadian Football League's Toronto Argonauts.

Wolff's career was at a crossroads in 1979, and his limited options included continuing to write for a living or pursuing a front office position in baseball.

The minor-league front office landscape had not changed much over the previous four decades. The St. Louis Cardinals, who once oversaw the most expansive minor-league system in the game, no longer owned their farm clubs, and the minor leagues of the 1970s were dotted with community owned franchises. Very few of those clubs were operated as business ventures, instead taking on a mom-and-pop flavor more geared toward simply keeping professional baseball alive in the town or city. Most owners and general managers were mere carnival operators who would suck a town dry for two or three years, then move on to the next city. Minor-league baseball teams had little or no value, either to the operators or to the cities that fielded the teams.

Wolff represented a new breed of owner who would soon take over minor-league baseball. He was a businessman first, and saw an opportunity to make money. Wolff's first choice to get his renewed career off the ground was owning a club based in Macon, Georgia. The Southern League was considering expansion, and Macon as well as Birmingham, Alabama, were considered the prime prospects for moving the league from 10 to 12 teams. Instead, Macon, which had been without professional baseball since 1967, joined the newly named South Atlantic League — successor to the Western Carolinas League — for the 1980 season. Birmingham, without baseball since 1975, would join the Southern League a year later.

Meanwhile, the Braves were on the cusp of expanding their farm system, from four to five clubs, to better streamline talent as part of a renewed emphasis on player development that hopefully would lead to great success later on. Key to that transformation was adding a club to bridge the gap for players moving from low Class A to Double-A. That meant adding a high Class A team in the Carolina League, and Durham was seen as the ideal location with Wolff as the perfect young executive to own and operate the club.

What made Wolff such a good fit was his belief that he could make it work for Atlanta in Durham. While other prospective owners looked around at Durham Athletic Park in 1979 and saw a dilapidated stadium with little promise, Wolff saw a charming old ballpark that could be embraced and brought back to life.

"I don't know if I believed baseball was coming back in the minor leagues," Wolff said, "but I believed I could run a ball club."

Fertile Ground

Miles Wolff is not certain why, when or where he conceived the idea. It could very well have just been happenstance. Yet following every home game during the 1980 season, the beer truck located in front of the concession stand on the main concourse at Durham Athletic Park was the gathering spot for assorted front-office personnel, coaches and the media. The taps flowed, sometimes into the wee hours of the night, as that night's game and any other happenings in baseball were digested and discussed.

You never knew from one night to the next who might show up to drink a couple of free beers and talk baseball. On one of those nights Rube Walker, an instructor in the Atlanta farm system, was in town. The conversation with Walker was compelling, particularly when he reminisced about his days as pitching coach of the New York Mets. Walker freely gave a pitcher-by-pitcher scouting report on every member of the 1969 World Series Champion Mets to the delight of a young reporter and unabashed Mets fan.

Then I struck a nerve in my line of questions for Walker. I had recalled that Walker was the catcher for the Brooklyn Dodgers on that fateful day of October 3, 1951, at the Polo Grounds in New York. Walker was called into duty in the finale of the best-of-three series against the New York Giants to decide the National League pennant when starting catcher Roy Campanella was sidelined by injury. So it was Walker who watched helplessly when Bobby Thomson's famous "Shot Heard 'Round the World" in the bottom of the ninth inning left the park and gave the Giants a pulsating 5-4 victory and the National League flag.

"I don't talk about that," Walker said sternly, thus concluding what previously had been a joy-filled, fun and informative conversation.

Three decades had passed yet Walker still carried a deep-seated hurt, a scar on his baseball career that he never could remove. When I later recounted the conversation with Walker to Wolff, the Bulls owner merely smiled, for it was the kind of story that further deepened Wolff's love and appreciation for baseball and respect for its history. It was a reverence for the game that shone through in all of Wolff's decision-making as the owner and operator of a minor-league team. In short, he was a traditionalist — almost to a fault.

In the early years of his ownership of the Bulls, in particular, Wolff detested the idea of promotions or on-field activities that might in any way take away from the purity of the game. He believed the public-address system was for informational purposes only. Instead of catering to the wonts of players and fans when it came to music, Wolff insisted on playing old baseball classics — The Harry Simeone Chorale's 1960 rendition of *"It's A Beautiful Day For A Ballgame"* and Homer and Jethro's 1970 country hit *"Daddy Played First Base"* — as fans found their seats prior to games.

He relished the opportunity of having the game's "old heads" around the ballpark even if it was only for his own enjoyment at the beer truck following games. Wolff would not commercialize the name of a visiting Hall of Famer for the sake of boosting his gate. He fully understood that when Hank Aaron and Luke Appling were in town, they were working for the Atlanta Braves, Aaron as the director of the club's farm system and Appling as a roving hitting instructor. They were not there to sell tickets.

Protecting the retired stars from the public played to my benefit. Appling loved to talk baseball, and invited reporters to stand next to him at the batting cage while he told stories between spits of tobacco juice and words of wisdom to Durham hitters. His memory of games played during a 20-year career with the Chicago White Sox was impeccable. He was able to recall in uncanny detail how an official scorer in Chicago once cost him a six-hit game, or that he collected two doubles and a single on the day in 1947 when Larry Doby broke the American League color barrier.

There were, I thought, no restrictions on interviews with the celebrities Wolff brought to town with the express purpose of selling tickets to the games. The likes of baseball Clown Prince Max Patkin and Hall of Fame pitcher Bob Feller fell into that category. I believed Wolff brought in these acts because he preferred the old guard of celebrities over the newer wave of mascots such as the San Diego Chicken or Phillie Phanatic. Truth be known, Wolff could not afford or was unwilling to pay the multi-thousand dollar price tag attached to the new breed of entertainers. The $500 fee for Patkin and Feller were much more in line with Wolff's financial constraints.

Patkin, who later gained more fame for his brief appearance in the movie *"Bull Durham"* than he did over 35 years of performing at minor-league parks, was more than happy to abide the wishes of a young reporter for a lengthy interview. Patkin once was a big draw around baseball, his act of coaching first base for a couple innings drawing laughter no matter how many times a city had witnessed his water-spewing antics. By 1980, though, Patkin's appearances had dwindled to the point of being booked by owners such as Wolff who were doing the performer a favor to keep his career alive. "There have been nights where it was cold, drizzling and 30 degrees and I was performing in front of 300 people who had seen my act 15 straight years," Patkin said, "but I still go out there and try to get people to laugh."

The same could not be said of Feller, who carried a hard edge to him as he made appearances around the minor leagues throughout the 1960s, 1970s and 1980s. Feller's show included signing autographs for a fee and then pitching batting practice to the local media before that night's game. I interviewed Feller the afternoon before his first appearance in Durham and he reminisced about his remarkable career in baseball. He, no doubt, repeated the same rehearsed lines in answers to my questions that he had fielded thousands of times previously. Then I made the mistake of asking Feller about an ugly incident between him and Jackie Robinson during their playing days. Feller turned angry and stormed from the interview.

Later, Feller allowed every member of the media to make contact with the meatball pitches he lobbed to home plate, until I came to bat. Then the 60-year-old Feller put everything he could behind three consecutive fastballs, making certain that I swung and missed at all three.

The fans loved it.

I did not recognize it at the time, but by bringing the likes of Patkin and Feller to town, it was a final salute by Wolff to the past in minor-league baseball, to a time when the game and its heroes were the attraction. Wolff also was beginning to recognize a new era emerging in the minor leagues where the game on the field was often secondary to the promotions, the loud music between batters on the public address system, the concessions fare and anything else that once was considered sacrilege to the selling of minor-league baseball.

The minor leagues were undergoing a dramatic change.

■

Attendance figures in minor-league baseball notoriously have been suspect. Unlike in the major leagues, where an actual count is made of tickets sold or used for each game, minor-league executives customarily have strolled around a ballpark and come up with an estimate of the number of fans in the stands. That number often is greatly exaggerated because most general managers want to create a sense in their community that fans are flocking to games, that the ballpark is the "place to be" on summer evenings.

The minor leagues also use season-ticket sales as a base for calculating attendance. So if a club sells 500 season tickets, there never will be fewer than that number in a nightly attendance figure, even if only a fraction of the tickets are actually being used. By taking into account that base number, executives then add the number of folks actually in the stands, and often tack on a few hundred — or even a thousand or so — to come up with the "official" announced attendance for a given night. So where there are actually 480 folks in the stands, an attendance figure might end up being as much as 1,200 or even 1,500.

Every minor-league club has exercised the same deceitful practice for decades, prompting reporters in press boxes around the country to immediately follow the announced attendance with the proclamation: "Where they at?"

Durham padded its attendance figures during the 1980 season, although Wolff and General Manager Pete Bock were generally less exaggerated in their estimates than most clubs. Wolff did not believe he could fool the public. So when he announced a crowd of 3,000 at Durham Athletic Park, there likely were at least 2,500 tickets sold. At the same time, Wolff had a couple of chances that season to announce record crowds for Durham Athletic Park on those nights when every seat in the house was occupied and fans stood in every available space and also sat on the grassy banks beyond the outfield fences. Wolff believed that the 6,237 who attended a Sept. 2, 1946 Carolina League game against Raleigh at Durham Athletic Park was a sacred number and should forever stand as the record. The closest Wolff came to challenging that record in 1980 was the announced crowd of 5,791 that showed for a Jacket Night give-away on the season-opening home stand and the 6,101 who attended a Merchants Night game in mid-July.

Even with padded figures, there was no doubting that fans were attending Durham Bulls games in record numbers in 1980. The Bulls surpassed their preseason goal of 70,000 fans by their 28th home date on June 7. On July 3, John R. Corne of Raleigh won an all-expense paid trip to attend a Braves game in Atlanta when he was announced as the season's 100,000th fan. Midway through the season's second half, the Bulls surpassed the franchise record of 152,095, set in 1947. By season's end, the Bulls had drawn 175,963 fans, an average of 2,588 for 68 home dates.

Minor-league baseball was back in Durham in a big, big way.

Durham's season total ranked second nationally in attendance among Class A franchises. Not surprisingly, Greensboro of the South Atlantic League, located an hour to the west of Durham, drew more fans with an announced attendance of 255,130, though the actual total was probably more in line with the figure the Bulls reported. The Greensboro franchise was owned by a group headed by Larry Schmittou, a young entrepreneur who, like Wolff, was instrumental in sparking the rebirth of minor-league baseball.

Schmittou and Wolff were among a new breed of minor-league baseball owners that also included Jim Paul in El Paso, Texas, and George Sisler Jr. in Columbus, Ohio, who were in on the ground floor, just as a renewed wave of popularity was about to take over the minor leagues.

"All of us believed baseball should be fun," Wolff said. "We all believed the sport could draw. We weren't just caretakers anymore, like the mom and pop operations who just tried to break even every year."

Club owners throughout the 1950s and 1960s, and late into the 1970s, operated under the philosophy that little or no money should be spent on the product. The less overhead — employees, uniforms, stadium upkeep — the greater chance of turning a profit. It was not uncommon at minor-league parks across the country at the time to see general managers in the parking lot during games, beating the neighborhood kids to foul balls that could be returned to play. An old trick was to pour milk on a scuffed baseball to give it the appearance of being as good as new.

There also was a reason teams carried the nickname of their parent club — the Winston-Salem Red Sox, for instance — and it had nothing to do with identifying with a more-established major-league team. Rather, it had everything to do with saving money by having the parent club pass uniforms down following each major-league season. Beyond that, major-league clubs were almost wholly responsible for the players' salaries.

That is the management environment and image of minor-league baseball that permeated when visionaries like Paul, Schmittou, Sisler and Wolff entered the game in the late 1970s. Above all, they seemed to be cognizant of a swing in momentum taking place nationally that gave a more favorable status to baseball, which fell behind football, both college and pro, in fan following in the political and social turbulent time of the 1960s. Perhaps it was the counterculture movement during the Vietnam War and through President Richard Nixon's impeachment that all but killed the old axiom of "Mom, Apple Pie and Baseball" being at the heart of America.

Whatever the reason, baseball had lost its prominence in the American sports psyche. Attendance at every level of professional baseball had been in slow decline for a quarter century. By 1975, seven of the 24 major-league clubs failed to draw one million fans, including the San Francisco Giants and Braves who barely drew half-a-million. Only the Los Angeles Dodgers and Cincinnati Reds topped two million in attendance. At the minor-league level, only Rochester in the Triple-A International League, and Hawaii and Sacramento in the Triple-A Pacific Coast League topped 200,000 in attendance. Below the Triple-A level, a mere five clubs announced attendance figures above 100,000.

But something happened in the 1975 World Series that seemed to spark a renewed interest in baseball at all levels. Cincinnati's "Big Red Machine" featured future Hall of Famers Johnny Bench, Joe Morgan and Tony Perez as well as soon-to-be all-time hits leader Pete Rose. The Boston Red Sox, which had not won a World Series since 1918 after falling previously in 1946 and 1967 were led by future Hall of Famers Carlton Fisk and Carl Yastrzemski, a precocious rookie in Fred Lynn and a wily old pitcher in Luis Tiant. It was a terrific series, a back-and-forth affair that included dramatic one-run decisions in Games Two, Three and Four. Cincinnati, leading three games to two, appeared on its way to the title when it forged a 6-3 lead in a drama-packed Game Six, but Bernie Carbo's timely three-run, pinch-hit homer in the bottom of the eighth inning tied the score at 6 and forced extra innings.

Fisk's game-winning home run in the 12th inning off the left-field foul pole at Boston's Fenway Park not only forced a decisive seventh game but was so sudden and dramatic that it captured the fancy of a national TV audience. Fisk's hand-waving to will the ball fair, as seen from a camera inside the "Green Monster" left-field wall proved to be both compelling TV but an image for the ages. It signaled to a nation that the sport could again be electrifying and fun to watch.

While that change in momentum in the nation's conscience and attitude toward baseball did not occur overnight, it certainly provided a different look and appreciation for America's national pastime and signaled a shift in the game's status from being considered a "tired, boring" sport that appealed mainly to middle-aged white men to one that could be enjoyed by all walks of American life.

The new breed of owners in the minor leagues was quick to recognize the impending shift. The pioneer among these young owners was Paul, who landed in El Paso, Texas, in 1975 as owner of the Diablos in the Double-A Texas League. Paul purchased the team for the token sum of $1,000 and assumed the team's $52,000 in outstanding debt, according to *Texas Monthly* magazine. So strapped was the club financially, Paul lent his personal credit card on road trips to Manager Jimy Williams, who later managed in the big leagues, to cover transportation, food and lodging, according to David A. Berchelmann III in his 2012 book, "Legendary Locals of El Paso."

Paul created a carnival-like atmosphere for every home game in El Paso, from loud, taped music over the public-address system that replaced the standard organ tones of years past, to young women in hot pants dancing atop dugouts between innings, to giveaways of all ilk, including jackets, hats, bats, balls and T-shirts. The idea was to get as many fans as possible into the ballpark and keep them entertained as much by what was happening off the field as on.

"El Paso seemed an unlikely place to stage the revival of minor-league baseball and Jim Paul, a Vietnam veteran who thought the infield fly rule had something to do with zipping up your pants, appeared an improbable candidate to be its guardian saint," wrote David Lamb in his 1991 book, "*Stolen Season*."

"If I had to pick one franchise that placed a premium on fun, that made every game a rollicking adventure, the El Paso Diablos were the winner, hands down. No one else even came close," Lamb wrote.

Under Paul's leadership, El Paso's attendance jumped from 112,477 the previous season to 162,399 in 1975. Then, in successive years, it went to 181,746 in 1976 to 217,346 in 1977 to 251,086 1978, and to 266,475 in 1979. Paul became so successful at peddling his product to the El Paso public, that he soon began conducting offseason seminars in El Paso for other minor-league executives on how to promote baseball. The seminars were attended for years by front-office personnel from major-league and minor-league teams, as well as athletics department officials from colleges across the country.

As El Paso's success at the gate was gaining national attention,

Sisler was serving from 1966 to 1976 as president of the International League. But in 1977, Sisler left the presidency to oversee the return of professional baseball to Columbus, Ohio, after a seven-year absence. He became general manager of the newly formed Columbus Clippers franchise in the same league he once ran. A crowd of 15,000 jammed Franklin County Stadium for the return in April of 1977, and through Sisler's promotions — "Dime A Dog Night" was a huge hit for years — the Clippers almost overnight became the biggest draw in the minor leagues. At a time when 100,000 was a good gate for a Triple-A season, Columbus drew an astonishing 457,251 that first season. The next highest attendance figure in the International League was 245,693 in Rochester, a city that had a team since 1902, the longest continuous run in the minor leagues.

■

By observing the success of the El Paso and Columbus franchises from afar, Schmittou and Wolff began plotting ways to jump on the bandwagon. Schmittou was the head baseball coach at Vanderbilt University in Nashville, Tennessee, at the time, and Wolff was renting a house for $100 a month on the beach in Savannah, Georgia, while writing a novel.

To fully understand what Paul, Sisler, Schmittou and Wolff faced in attempting to resuscitate minor-league baseball in the late 1970s and early 1980s, one must know the depths the game had reached by the mid-1970s. The outstanding book "*The Encyclopedia of Minor League Baseball*," termed the years 1946-51 as The Golden Age of minor-league baseball, followed by The Second Decline (1952-62), The Subsistence Years (1963-77) and The Revival (1978-1991).

The path the Carolina League took through those eras was representative of the ups and downs all of minor-league baseball was experiencing. The league, which began operating in 1945, enjoyed unprecedented success before the advent of television sets and air conditioning in almost every home in the early 1950s. Minor-league baseball had been one of the best forms of affordable summer family entertainment nationwide and franchises were located in just about every city and town of any size.

In 1946, the Carolina League fielded teams in the North Carolina cities of Burlington, Durham, Greensboro, Leaksville-Draper-Spray, Raleigh and Winston-Salem, and the Virginia cities of Danville-Schoolfield and Martinsville. All but two of the franchises drew more than 100,000 fans each for the season. There were 43 minor-league baseball teams in the state of North Carolina alone that season, a number that would shrink to a mere five three decades later.

The Carolina League continued to operate with eight teams through 1956. From 1957 through 1974, that number fluctuated anywhere from six to 12 teams each season. Then from 1975 through 1977, only four franchises existed, and the highest attendance figure in any of those seasons was the 55,123 drawn by Lynchburg, Virginia, in 1977.

Minor-league baseball was all but dying, if not already dead. Developing players in the minor leagues was a significant financial drain for major-league clubs, and minor-league operators mostly hung on to their franchises because they were enamored with the idea of owning a team. Few, if any, minor-league franchises were profitable. Staying home in the mid-'70s to watch *"The Love Boat," "Three's Company"* or *"Lou Grant"* on TV was a much more viable and attractive option than paying to watch a baseball game with little if anything at stake in a dank, run-down ballpark. Going out to watch *"Star Wars," "Close Encounters of the Third Kind"* or *"Annie Hall"* in the comfort of an air-conditioned movie theater was also much more appealing than battling the sweltering heat and humidity at an old ballpark in the Southeast.

It was then that Tal Smith believed the time had come for baseball to consider shutting down the minor leagues altogether. Smith was a longtime, respected baseball executive, who had worked in the front office of the Houston Astros since their inception in 1962, when they were known as the Houston Colt .45s. Smith had interned at *The Sporting News* while a student at Duke University, and went so far as to write a story for the publication in the mid-1970s that proposed abolishing all of the minor leagues, with the exception of the Triple-A level, and forming a major-league wide complex of baseball fields at spring-training sites in Florida and Arizona where the vast majority of minor leaguers would train and play games at the same site. Smith wrote that it no longer made sense financially for major-league clubs to continue to field and underwrite teams in the outreaches of the country where games were being played in front of maybe 300 or 400 fans a night. Minor-league baseball, he wrote, no longer had relevance.

Indeed, the minor leagues were floundering.

Then along came Paul and Sisler and Schmittou and Wolff.

Schmittou was reared in Nashville, on the city's west side. He was the youngest of five children and named Larry in honor of Larry Gilbert, the owner and manager of the Nashville Vols club in the Double-A Southern Association from 1939 through 1948. Gilbert, a player on the 1914 "Miracle" Boston Braves, eventually managed in the Southern Association at New Orleans and Nashville for 25 seasons, and continued to own the Nashville franchise through 1955. Once or twice a summer, Schmittou's mother would take her young son to Sulphur Dell, the ballpark located just outside Nashville's downtown district. The two would ride the city bus to the park and Larry would gain admission in the 25-cent knothole section.

Sulphur Dell had a few unique characteristics, most notably a home run porch in right field that was 235 feet from home plate and an incline that ran all along the outfield fence from the left-field line to the right-field line. The top of the terrace in right field was 22 feet above the playing surface. Right-fielders were commonly referred to as "mountain goats" because they routinely chased fly balls and even ground balls up and down the terrace.

Most all ballparks of the day had some sort of quirky design, whether it be a terrace or a tree in deep center field or light poles in play, but they were all part of the appeal of attending minor-league games in a bygone era, where on any given night a fan might see some unusual play or occurrence.

That appeal had gradually worn off, though, and as attendance dwindled throughout the minor leagues so, too, did the number of franchises. The Vols' and minor-league baseball's 62-year run at Sulphur Dell concluded following the 1963 season. Schmittou was 23 years old and a recent graduate of Peabody College, near the Vanderbilt campus. He became a teacher in the Nashville public schools system and coached baseball, football and track at a junior high school. He previously had established a name for himself as a youth baseball coach in Nashville, accumulating more than 500 wins, 20 city titles and eight state championships. Righthander Wayne Garland, who pitched nine seasons in the major leagues for Baltimore and Cleveland, played 10 seasons of youth baseball in Nashville under Schmittou's direction.

Coaching was in Schmittou's blood and Vanderbilt hired him as its head baseball coach in 1968. In 11 seasons at the helm, Schmittou twice won Southeastern Conference coach of the year honors and led the Commodores to league titles in 1973 and '74. Among those who played for Schmittou at Vanderbilt was righthander Scott Sanderson, who later pitched for seven major-league teams over 19 seasons.

Even while coaching at the college level, Schmittou never lost his affinity for minor-league baseball. He was told by the Southern League in 1977 that if he could build a baseball stadium in Nashville, it would arrange a working agreement with a major-league club and award him a franchise. The City of Nashville balked at the idea of building a ballpark, so Schmittou went to work on his own and immediately hooked up with an old friend, Conway Twitty, the country music legend who also was a fan of Schmittou's Vanderbilt baseball teams. Schmittou mortgaged his home for $150,000 in capital and sold 20 shares of stock in the soon-to-be-ballpark at $15,000 apiece. In all, Schmittou and Twitty lined up 14 investors in the ballpark, including the likes of country singer Jerry Reed, Richard Sterban of the Oak Ridge Boys and country entertainer Cal Smith. Schmittou and Twitty were the team's majority owners, and eventually bought out all the other stockholders.

The City of Nashville agreed to lease a tract of land two miles south of town on the grounds of Fort Negley to Schmittou's group if it built a stadium within 10 years that had a minimum seating capacity of 6,500 and construction costs of at least $400,000. The club also agreed to pay the city seven percent of the team's total revenue over the first 10 years of its operation. With those conditions met, the Southern League expanded to Nashville and Memphis for the 1978 season, with the Cincinnati Reds relocating their Double-A affiliate from Trois Rivieres, Quebec, of the Eastern League to Nashville.

"I'd say 99 percent of the people told me it wouldn't succeed," Schmittou said. "That didn't bother me. I believed, and the people who invested with me believed. If you didn't do anything because somebody said you couldn't do it, nothing would ever get done."

Schmittou had done his homework, and by 1981 his plan had become the blueprint for successfully run franchises throughout the minor leagues. By then, his Sounds were affiliated with the New York Yankees. In an article written by Pat Embry of the *Nashville Banner* for *Baseball America* in its May 1981 issue, Schmittou outlined both his steps for locating a team in a particular city and for operating the club. Here is what Embry wrote:

POPULATION BASE. "Hopefully, there is a base where you can always count on drawing one third of the population," Schmittou explained. "For example, if you're a Class A city with 60,000 people, and it takes 60,000 attendance to break even, then I wouldn't go in there. That's why the New York Yankees can draw 14,000 people by just turning on the lights and people stopping to see what's going on.

It's because of their huge population base."

MEDIA COVERAGE. "Media is very important, especially the morning newspaper. Every survey we have taken has shown that many people decide if they're coming to the game that morning, particularly the casual fan." Schmittou has enjoyed a glut of press coverage from both the morning and afternoon papers, and the television and radio stations in Nashville.

NUMBER OF BUSINESSES. "It's very important that you have 100 businesses that employ 100 people. The more ads you sell controls the ticket prices."

STADIUM. "I wouldn't recommend building a stadium like we did to anybody (the cost was three times higher — $1.5 million — than first estimated). A man would be crazy to do that. You should have a good relationship with the parks and recreation department. It's very important that you get a lease that's fair to you as a private business, fair to them, and fair to your players and spectators. There must be clean facilities, adequate parking."

After selecting a city, Embry wrote, the next steps were:

HIRING A GENERAL MANAGER. "The GM is the key man of the operation. He's in the spotlight. You make yourself visible and available to the press, but not too available. You must allow time to walk through the stands and meet the people. You must be able to handle complaints personally," Schmittou said.

SIGNING A GOOD WORKING AGREEMENT THAT WILL GUARANTEE A CHANCE AT A WINNING TEAM. "It's almost essential. You should associate yourself with a competitive (major-league) team, one that has acceptance locally and puts emphasis on the minor leagues. They also must supply players who are solid citizens.

PROMOTING AND MARKETING THE TEAM WITH ITS OWN LOCAL IDENTITY. "If you're going into a business, you have to market it as a business. We do that with the Sounds colors and logo (a distinctive design featuring a cartoon player swinging a guitar as a bat) marketed through our souvenirs and promotions. The reason we don't like to have the same name as the parent club is you go uptown and you hear people ask how the Yankees did last night. I believe people will immediately think of the New York Yankees. But if you go uptown and ask how the Sounds did last night, then everyone knows who you're talking about."

CONCESSIONS. "Lots of owners don't like to mess with it, but if you can I would strongly suggest it. You can't really control how good the team is or if it wins and loses, but you can control how good the food is. Others may not want to admit it, but they're more in the restaurant business than the baseball business. It will make up at least 30 percent of your total revenue ... but 30 percent of your heartaches, too."

PERSONNEL. "You must control the ticket-takers, the concessions workers, the security. A grumpy-old ticket-taker can turn more fans away than a .180-hitting shortstop. A bad hot dog will turn a mother away quicker than a pitcher with an 8.20 ERA. Pretty girls sell more programs than some 82-year-old man. We have rules in dress and personal appearance and they're followed by everyone or they don't work here."

Schmittou's Nashville franchise quickly was the model for those keys to success. The Sounds drew 380,159 fans for their inaugural 1978 season and 515,482 the next. That overwhelming success prompted led Schmittou to locate a team in Greensboro, North Carolina, of the Class A Western Carolinas League for the 1979 season and the Hornets drew 165,596 fans — nearly three times as many as Gastonia, the next closest club in the league.

That led Schmittou and Wolff to Durham, another city that had been without professional baseball in recent years, in the fall of 1979. Schmittou informed the Durham mayor that at least $200,000 was needed from the city to get the ballpark in suitable condition for professional baseball. The mayor instead found Wolff, who was more than willing to accept the $54,000 in expenditures that the city was agreeable to putting into park renovations.

"I couldn't be picky," Wolff said. "I just needed a club."

While Wolff did not have the kind of detailed plan for Durham that Schmittou used in Nashville, the new Durham owner did share the same vision of minor-league baseball being on the brink of making a comeback. But like Schmittou in Nashville, Wolff had no idea that the minor leagues were on the verge of such a widespread renaissance.

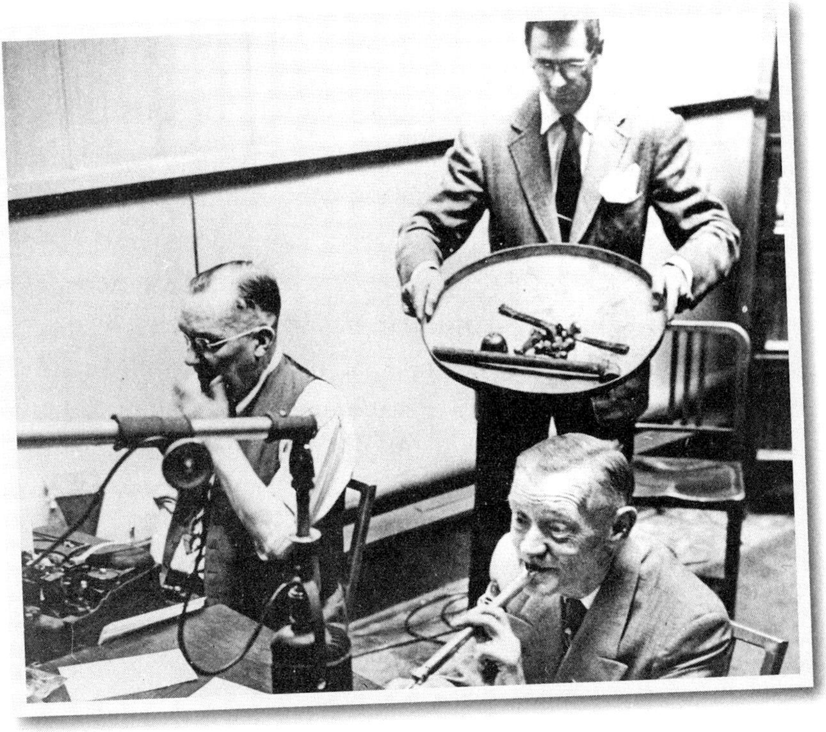

Not-So-Live From Durham

I arrived at Durham Athletic Park every afternoon at 4 o'clock and immediately made my rounds in search of any news about the Bulls — on or off the field. I first checked in with the front office staff to see if anyone special might be attending that night's game, then headed to the clubhouse area where Bill Miller, the club's groundskeeper, usually was a fountain of information regarding player moves or clubhouse activity.

A big part of my job was to know more about the team and its players than everyone except perhaps the coaching staff and maybe Dave Slade, the radio play-by-play announcer whose wife, Lois, worked in the front office. Standing around the batting cage and hanging out in the clubhouse prior to each game, while considered mindless activity to some, was often the most challenging part of working the beat. The closer the game got to first pitch, my office for the evening became the press box located at field level directly behind home plate at Durham Athletic Park.

That locale and its unique location actually made for difficult viewing of the game, and I occasionally moved to a bleacher seat. Because I was seated below ground level in the press box, some plays in the outfield simply could not be seen, particularly those fly balls to the deepest reaches of the power alleys. Those of us in the press box often had to take the word of the base umpire on diving catches in the outfield. Johnny Moore, the official scorer for home games during the 1980 season, occasionally had to check with players after the game before making final scoring decisions.

Beyond the difficulty of simply viewing the game from a quirky press-box location was the matter of keeping up with cumulative playing statistics, both for the Bulls players and for those in the Carolina League.

Before that season began I recognized that gathering statistics on the Durham team was going to be difficult. So I devised a data sheet in which I could chart each player's game-by-game results, using pencil to record any number that could be taken from a scoresheet. The problem was securing the scoresheet from each game. Home games were easy to obtain, obviously, but road games meant relying on Slade, who kept a meticulous book for every game that he broadcast, whether in person or through re-creation. At the conclusion of each broadcast I copied Slade's scoresheet into my scorebook and transferred those numbers over to my own data sheets.

It was Moore's duty to deliver the official scoresheet following each home game via telecopier — a primitive machine that transmitted copy — to Boston-based Howe News Bureau, the official statistician for the league. Howe, in turn, compiled all of the league's statistics, as it did for most of the minor leagues that operated east of the Mississippi River, and it then provided a printed summary of league statistics at the conclusion of each Friday's games. Unfortunately, those statistics were sent via the U.S. Postal Service to each club, meaning batting averages and earned run averages were normally at least a week old by the time they arrived in Durham, and essentially outdated. Thus, my efforts to cover the Bulls on a daily basis in 1980 was not only difficult, not having daily access to current statistics, but unacceptable as well.

To make matters worse, *The Sporting News* had begun to cut back considerably on its baseball coverage by 1980, and the minor-leagues in particular. Its weekly listing of league leaders and statistics package generally were out of date and virtually useless by the time the publication arrived in the mail. As strange as it seems now, the Internet and the instant access to statistics and information were not even a pipe dream.

Miles Wolff recognized the value of information being disseminated, not only to the media but to fans as well. The more informed they were, the more likely they were to embrace the product. It pained Wolff to see *The Sporting News*, long considered the bible of baseball news, shift its focus in the 1970s to encompass all sports. Expanded coverage of other sports such as basketball, football and hockey, and even fringe sports like bowling and auto racing, meant less baseball news.

In its heyday as an all-baseball publication, *The Sporting News* covered the game in considerable and unparalleled detail. It devoted extensive coverage to not just the major leagues, but the minor leagues, as well. The St. Louis-based publication was a labor of love for the Spink family, which owned the weekly publication from its inception in 1886 to 1977, when it was sold to The Times Mirror Corporation, a publishing conglomerate.

By 1977, *The Sporting News* had begun to scale back its coverage of the minors. Where once it would publish box scores of most minor-league games, it had discontinued the practice altogether in the 1970s, and the amount of space it allocated to the minors generally slipped even further when the publication was sold and new ownership decided to broaden the paper's appeal by covering all sports in much greater detail. Then in the early 1980s, *The Sporting News* discontinued its longstanding tradition of printing major-league box scores. That signaled the final straw for long-time baseball readers who looked to the publication for news it could not previously get anywhere else.

The idea of creating a new, baseball-only publication festered with Wolff throughout the 1980 season and led him to a like-minded entrepreneur in Allan Simpson, himself a former minor-league general manager living in Kelowna, British Columbia. It eventually led the two to hook up with each other and resulted in the creation of a publication that would not only rival the staid, old *The Sporting News* as the baseball paper of record, but one day even surpass it in its impact on the game.

Until the two could unite on that front, Wolff had a more pressing problem with getting the word of the Durham Bulls out to baseball fans in the Chapel Hill-Durham-Raleigh area. Wolff was pleasantly surprised, though, that in a hotbed for college athletics, the two local newspapers, the *Durham Morning Herald* and the *Durham Sun*, covered his team as a viable sports entity. The two papers covered the team as if they were reporting on a major-league franchise in a big city. In fact, Wolff found that the local newspaper coverage was beyond fair to the point of being almost boosterish, as journalism seemed to be giving way to the prospect of covering a team that drew the allegiance of all area sports fans. Television coverage was much the same as that of the newspapers. Raleigh's two major stations routinely joined the two Durham stations in providing nightly reports before and after home games from the ballpark.

Radio was a trickier proposition. Play-by-play broadcast of games can be a costly venture in the minor leagues. Advertising is difficult for both radio stations and the club to sell because the listening audience is generally slim, restricted mostly to homebound fans of the team. Additionally, a club must pay an announcer a salary and cover the cost of travel expenses for 70 road games. The return — advertising dollars and a sizable listening audience — rarely matches the outlay.

Prior to the 1980 season, Wolff hammered out a deal with WDBS President William Dix for radio broadcast rights on the Duke University, on-campus FM station. WDBS welcomed the summer programming while students were away. While Wolff would have preferred a station with a stronger signal, he believed at the outset that the team's fan base would not likely extend beyond Durham's city limits. So, the initial arrangement was OK, as were the financial terms. The Bulls paid nothing for the broadcast, and kept all advertising revenue, which was virtually non-existent. Had the Bulls been able to sell out the broadcasts, they would have provided a live play-by-play account of all 140 games, home and away.

To trim costs, Wolff opted to re-create road games, at least the 40 scheduled to be played in Virginia. The play-by-play account of road games in Kinston, Rocky Mount and Winston-Salem would be provided just like home games since those bus trips were up-and-backs. The play-by-play announcer would receive the same per-diem as the players, mainly to cover meals, and could ride the team bus. He did not need a hotel room for those games. For games played at Alexandria, Lynchburg, Peninsula and Salem, Wolff would save money for travel and telephone broadcast lines by providing play-by-play from the WDBS studios.

Wolff had previously witnessed re-creation of games in Savannah, Georgia, and hired Slade as his play-by-play announcer partly because Slade was familiar with re-created games while working in Rochester, New York.

"From the first time they talked to me, they said there was going to be re-creations," Slade said of his early discussions with Wolff. "I was fascinated by it. That's something I had never done and I looked at it as a challenge."

■

Headset secured, Slade adjusted his scorebook, neatly penciled in the lineups for the Durham Bulls and the Salem Redbirds and awaited a cue.

"Hi, everybody, tonight the Durham Bulls play the first game of a four-game series at Salem," Slade said, his voice transmitting onto the airwaves. "The Durham Bulls seek their eighth win in a row in tonight's game being played at Salem Municipal Stadium in Salem, Virginia."

When Slade glanced up from his scorecard he obviously did not see Bulls' outfielder and leadoff hitter Albert Hall adjusting his cap before stepping into the batter's box in Salem. Instead, Slade peered through a dirty glass window in the WDBS studio off Markham Avenue, about a mile from Durham Athletic Park. The green infield grass and freshly painted stadium described by Slade were borrowed descriptions of other baseball parks he had visited, lent to an audience in an effort to make the game seem real.

As Slade described the first pitch from Salem's Jeff Zaske, the clock above his head inched past eight o'clock. In Durham, WDBS listeners heard Slade describe Hall's fly out to left field in the first inning. One hundred and sixty-two miles away, Hall was actually batting in the fifth inning.

This was re-creation, a lost art likely forgotten even to baseball fans whose memories scanned to the post-World War II period when it was commonplace. That is when Gordon McLendon, aware that travel and broadcast costs were too high to permit live broadcasts, instituted the Liberty Broadcast System.

The foundation of the Liberty network was built on a system of broadcasting Major League Baseball games in a studio where an announcer received information and relayed reports to his audience over the air. The reports, direct from the ballpark where the game was being played, consisted of scant information transmitted by a Western Union ticker machine in a code that any baseball fan could interpret.

Former President Ronald Reagan once re-created Chicago Cubs games in the mid-1930s from a radio station studio in Des Moines, Iowa. Les Keiter, who re-created New York Giants broadcasts for years in the 1950s, continued the same practice into the 1980s for the Hawaii Islanders Triple-A team in the Pacific Coast League because the club could not afford to send him to the mainland for road games.

The concept for re-creating Bulls' games was essentially the same. In Durham's case, the official scorekeeper in Salem, Virginia, telephoned the WDBS studio every 20 minutes. In his report, which was received in the studio by Wolff, the scorekeeper included the count to each batter and a brief description of each play. Wolff, in turn, prepared a score sheet account for Slade. A first-inning account of the April 21 game at Salem read:

Albert Hall	LF	3-2	F-7	
Milt Thompson	CF	0-2	K-S	
Alvin Moore	RF	3-2	BB	steals 2nd
Gerald Perry	1B	3-1	6-3	

Thus, Slade could describe for his listeners that leftfielder Hall had flied to left field on a 3-2 pitch, Thompson struck out swinging on three pitches, Moore walked on a 3-2 pitch and stole second, and Perry grounded out shortstop-to-first base on a 3-1 pitch. Slade was at liberty to describe each pitch prior to the actual play. Whether a ball was a "fastball high and outside" or a "slider low and away" was pure speculation on his part.

"That's the beauty of this," Wolff said. "You can make a dull game exciting. A routine fly ball to right field can easily be a long fly ball caught against the fence in a crucial situation."

Slade concurred.

"It's theatrics," he said. "I don't think it's lying, it's colorful. It's poetic licensing."

Slade's voice alone could not carry the broadcast.

In the studio across the hall, a WDBS disc jockey had two tapes of crowd noise playing in the background. One tape ran 40 seconds, the other 70. By interchanging the two, the listener got the impression he was hearing the shouts and cheers of the 396 fans attending the game in Salem. "I poured over an hour of crowd noise and picked out something that didn't stand out in the average listener's mind," Slade said. "Ideally, the audience is listening to what you're saying and the crowd is just the background."

Slade also provided a re-created crack of the bat. When the situation called for it, Slade tapped a Nicholson file against the borrowed Stanley Hercules hammer belonging to his wife, Lois. The sound projected over the airways as something similar to that of a bat hitting a ball. There were minor problems to iron out early in the season, such as a crack of the bat on the soundtrack that had to be deleted.

There long have been glitches in re-creations. Many a play-by-play announcer provided details of dogs being on the field or sudden thunderstorms that delayed action, when in fact information from the source at the ballpark was delayed or slow in arriving to the studio. During Slade's re-creation of Durham's April 22 game at Salem he found himself in a radio announcer's version of a baseball pickle.

With two outs in the second inning of that game, the Bulls' Jeff Matthews was on third base and Steve Stieb on second when Milt Thompson came to bat. Slade misread the information provided by Wolff and told his listeners that Thompson walked to load the bases. Thompson had actually grounded out to shortstop, ending the inning.

"I didn't know what to do," Slade said. "I had to get somebody out so Alvin Moore could still lead off the next inning. I didn't want to pick Milt off first base because he hadn't been picked off all year and had stolen 12 bases in 12 attempts. So I picked on Stieb, the poor old catcher."

According to Slade's account, the Salem pitcher wheeled and threw to second base where Stieb was caught flat-footed and tagged for the third out of the inning. Apparently all listeners that night were fooled. Slade never received a call about his boot, one that could not be found in the box score that appeared in the newspaper the next day.

Three nights later, any alert listener could have picked up one of Slade's errors in the box score. The fault was not Slade's on this occasion. He simply was not provided proper information. Slade was never told of a pitching change in Durham's April 25 win at Alexandria when, in fact, Gil Ryan pitched the final four innings in relief of Juan Alduey.

"It was a surprise to me when I picked up the paper the next morning," Slade said.

On another occasion, the information was late being relayed to Slade. To fill time, Slade had a Salem pitcher change undershirts in the middle of an inning. Luckily, it was a humid day in Virginia and Slade could use the 80-degree temperature as an alibi.

Amazingly enough, perhaps because there were so few listeners on the radio, Wolff heard virtually nothing from fans the entire season about Slade's re-creation of the games. Most apparently never knew it was happening.

■

By mid-June, media outlets in the Research Triangle area had recognized the Durham Bulls as a legitimate news story. In addition to the *Durham Morning Herald* and *Durham Sun* covering all home games with a reporter, the *News and Observer* of Raleigh and the *Raleigh Times* occasionally sent a reporter to a home game in search of a feature-story angle. Area weekly newspapers had jumped on board with coverage, and TV stations filled their nightly sports segments with highlights from home games and scores when the Bulls played on the road.

All the attention was almost too much for Wolff to ask for. While he had not budgeted any spending in the preseason for advertising

— mostly because he simply did not have the money — it turned out that the Bulls did not need to advertise their product. The media coverage of the team sold the Bulls better than any newspaper, radio or television advertisement. Word of mouth proved to be quite a powerful advertising vehicle for the club.

Then WTVD-Channel 11 in Durham decided to take coverage of the Bulls to another level, one not before seen in the Carolina League. The station approached the Bulls and the league about televising a league game. At the time, it was believed no Class A minor-league game had ever appeared live on TV. Because Wolff and the Bulls were thrilled to be gaining another source of exposure to their fan base, there were no rights fees assessed to the TV station. So WTVD officials began plotting when and how they could pull off the major undertaking for a local station. This was in the pre-ESPN days when live telecasts of sporting events were not an everyday occurrence, particularly in baseball, which has always been considered the most difficult sport to televise because the action can shift instantly to anywhere in the park.

"We could have picked a Durham game against Rocky Mount, which is in our viewing area," said WTVD sports anchor Don Shea, who would provide the game's play-by-play, "but they are not a good club. We decided on Peninsula."

Because the lights at Durham Athletic Park were sub-par for a telecast, the Bulls agreed to move the Sunday, June 22 game against Peninsula to the afternoon. The broadcast was an expensive project for WTVD, which employed 23 people for the game and stationed five cameras around the ballpark, one each behind first and third base, one atop the grandstand, one atop the press box behind home plate, and one on the bank beyond the center field fence. The cameras were valued at $250,000 and were hooked up by 2,500 feet of cable. Two production vans, each valued at $110,000, were stationed in the parking lot behind the first-base grandstands where Paul Guffey as director and Bob Johnson as production manager called the shots.

The station sold 53 commercial spots to help recoup their outlay for the broadcast, but advertising fees were low enough "to give the guy who never advertises on television the chance to do it," according to Shea.

Shea was teamed with fellow WTVD sports staffer Stan Saunders in the booth, and surprisingly the station provided viewers with a top-level broadcast. All were treated to a thrilling, 8-7 Peninsula victory after the Pilots rallied from a 4-1 deficit. As they had all season, the weather gods smiled on the Bulls with a picture-perfect afternoon of clear skies and temperature in the 80s.

Typical and expected for a local production, WTVD cameras missed several plays during the game. In the bottom of the seventh inning, the TV camera was on batter Paul Runge when Hall was picked off first base, so viewers at home could not tell if Peninsula pitcher Daryl Adams balked on the play. When Al Gallagher charged out of the dugout to argue, he was immediately ejected by home plate umpire Tom Hallion. Gallagher had placed black licorice in his mouth prior to the inning and splattered juice across the front of Hallion's shirt. As we learned later, Gallagher had actually planned to be ejected from the game but had forgotten it was being televised until the seventh inning.

No matter, it made for solid TV entertainment for those Bulls fans who were watching out of curiosity and for those who were seeing Durham Bulls baseball for the first time. Whatever the audience, no one smiled bigger following Durham's foray into TV than Wolff, who had found yet another avenue for advertising and promoting his baseball team.

Tears To My Eyes

As often happens in minor-league baseball, the team that wins the first half of a split-season schedule does not resemble the one that completes the season. Roster shuffles are commonplace, given to the whims of injuries, promotions, demotions and the influx of talent from the annual June major-league draft.

Thus was the case with Durham's roster. From April 11 through June 15 — the bulk of the first half — Durham made a mere five player transactions. Then from June 16 to July 15, the Bulls made 18 transactions. Only a few key components remained with the Bulls the entire season, most notably outfielders Albert Hall and Ronnie Rudd, first baseman Gerald Perry and pitchers Rick Behenna, Mike Smith and Ike Pettaway. Even with the roster shakeup there were no fewer characters on the team and no less excitement during the season's second half.

Less than a week after Durham clinched the North Carolina Division title in the first half, Atlanta's front office began making moves. The moves coincided with the draft held the first week of June. The Braves were a good three years into their concentrated efforts to develop players through the minor leagues with a heavy emphasis on accumulating pitching talent. It showed that June when Atlanta took left-handed pitcher Ken Dayley out of the University of Portland, followed by right-hander Jim Acker from the University of Texas, and right-hander Brian Fisher out of Hinkley High School in Aurora, Colorado, with its first three picks.

As is customary in baseball, draft picks were first sent to Atlanta for physical exams, then to a Rookie club to determine what level they should compete at for the remainder of the season. In this case, most of Atlanta's 28 selections were sent to Bradenton, Florida, for a minicamp in front of coaches. Daley and Acker, because they were coming out of college, were advanced enough to be assigned to Savannah in the Double-A Southern League. Fisher went to Anderson, the Braves' low Class A affiliate.

Right-handed pitcher Craig Jones, a fourth-round selection out of the United States Military Academy, came to Durham along with 12th-round pick Johnny Lee, a third baseman out of Florida Southern College, and 15th-round selection Paul Zuvella, a second baseman out of Stanford University.

In acquiring those players, Durham needed to make corresponding moves. Much to the chagrin of Durham fans, outfielder Milt Thompson and shortstop Paul Runge were promoted to Savannah, leaving behind huge holes that no one who followed the team believed could be filled. Pitcher Duane Theiss also went to Savannah after only one week with the Durham club; pitcher Dan Lucia was moved from Savannah to Durham; outfielder Brett Butler was called up from Anderson; and pitcher Russ Kerdolff was released.

Butler got the call he wanted from Atlanta officials the morning of June 23 as he was preparing to play for the South Atlantic League all-star team against the Charlotte O's of the Southern League. A couple of his all-star teammates were Don Mattingly of the host Greensboro Hornets and Andy Van Slyke of the Shelby Pirates.

The Bulls sent Chris Powell, a young member of the front-office staff, to Greensboro and he returned to Durham with Butler after the game. For most of the trip, Powell heard from Butler about how he should have been in Durham from the season's outset, and also that it would not be long before Butler was wearing a big-league uniform. Butler would repeat the refrain to the media once he arrived in Durham.

By the time Powell and Butler got to Durham around midnight, few restaurants were still open so the two dined at a Denny's off Interstate 85 on the north side of town. Powell was not on an expense account, and he got stuck with the twelve-dollar tab, and forever wondered if Butler would reimburse him should he one day make it to the big leagues.

Once in Durham, things did not initially go swimmingly for Butler. Over his first seven games, he collected four hits, carried a .174 batting average and was caught twice in three stolen base attempts. Then he was asked by Pete Bock, the club's general manager, to spend about 30 minutes as a representative of the team in a visit to a children's hospital in Durham. Butler was enthralled by the youngsters and stayed for two hours.

"It just hit me, that it's been all about me," Butler told Bock in the car on the return trip to the ballpark. "I'm not hitting. The world's coming to an end. What I'm doing is just a gift."

A relaxed Butler produced two hits, including a home run, that night against Winston-Salem. That sparked a 15-game hitting streak in which he batted .446 and stole 13 bases. He quickly made Durham fans forget what Thompson had done for the club in the first half of the season.

In the same manner, Zuvella made fans forget about Runge. Like Butler, Zuvella also got off to a rocky start but most of the problems he encountered were off the field. When he signed with Atlanta, Zuvella requested that he first attend graduation ceremonies at Stanford. So he reported later than the other Braves draft picks to Bradenton, where he played in two games as a shortstop, a position he had not played since high school. Then the Braves shipped him to Durham where he was slated to play his new position every day.

When Zuvella arrived at the Raleigh-Durham Airport, no one from the Bulls organization was there to greet him. He picked up a copy of the *Durham Morning Herald* to learn the Bulls were playing that evening in Hampton, Virginia. After a couple of phone calls he also learned that Bulls President Miles Wolff was in Savannah, Georgia, on business, and Bock had taken a few vacation days at the beach. So Zuvella called the Atlanta Braves.

"I had a feeling he was going to quit and come home," said Richard Zuvella, his father from California. "He was really a mixed-up kid."

The Braves arranged for Zuvella to fly to Virginia where a limousine greeted him and ushered him to War Memorial Stadium in Hampton. Zuvella collected three singles, including one that gave Durham the lead in the fifth inning, in his Bulls' debut. More importantly, Zuvella manned shortstop, allowing Jeff Matthews to move to his more natural second base position. It was a much needed move as in one game with Matthews at shortstop, Glen Bockhorn played second base and made four errors.

Zuvella played third base his sophomore year at Stanford, and when future major-leaguer Dave Meier came on board for Zuvella's junior year he was shifted permanently to second base. No one knew what to expect when Zuvella was assigned to Durham as a shortstop.

"When the Braves told me they were sending us somebody who played second base in college ... " said Al Gallagher, completing the sentence by tossing his arms up in disbelief.

Zuvella then went about making a believer of everyone. He collected a hit in 22 of his first 32 games, and made only eight errors during that stretch. At one point, he went 11 games and 47 chances without an error.

"He's been the biggest surprise on this team," Gallagher said.

Zuvella was not your typical minor-league baseball player. For one, he stretched, and stretched, and stretched. Teammates laughed about how the Bulls gained a Yoga instructor when Zuvella jumped on board. Between every pitch, Zuvella was seen leaning to one side or the other in an effort to stretch his arms or his lower legs. Then he worked between pitches to lengthen his back or work a kink out of his neck. Zuvella soon earned the nickname "Gumby."

At Stanford, Zuvella also earned a degree with a double major of communications and economics. The former skills were put to use nightly around the Durham batting cage where Zuvella provided a play-by-play account of the action. The practice struck his teammates as odd, but no more so than seeing Zuvella board a bus for road trips with a couple of books tucked under his arm. Upon his arrival, Zuvella was tackling "*War and Remembrance*," the 1,000-page, Herman Wouk novel. At breakfast with teammates on the road, Zuvella worked crossword puzzles.

Not so well received was Lee, at least by the fans in the third base bleachers at Durham Athletic Park. Lee was sent to Durham under orders from Atlanta to play every day at third base. That was devastating news to a group of students from the Carolina Friends School in Durham who had formed a "Tommy Thompson Fan Club."

Upon Lee's arrival, Gallagher immediately called Thompson into his office.

"I'm going to be honest," Gallagher said. "I've got to play this guy a little more. But I'm going to find a way to get you in the lineup."

Thompson appreciated the honesty from his manager and continued to accumulate at-bats as the team's designated hitter, second baseman, catcher and occasional third baseman. Lee struggled mightily, suffering mostly from having played his entire amateur career with an aluminum bat. Batted balls that landed for extra-base hits at

Florida Southern were often broken wood-bat pop ups in Durham. His teammates privately kept a count of broken bats Lee produced because he rarely hit a ball on the barrel of the bat.

The problem was that Lee was well-liked by his new teammates. They attempted to comfort him, even after it became apparent he probably should have begun his pro career at Anderson, not Durham. But those third base fans did not take kindly to Lee and his .189 batting average. Nor did they approve of his 18 errors in 47 games at third base. Lee also had the great misfortune of playing poorly the same time that a similarly named country singer released a hit song that June called *Looking for Love.* When Lee made an error, fans naturally taunted him by singing their own rendition with the lyrics, "Looking for a glove in all the wrong places."

For the most part, Butler and Zuvella were the only solid reinforcements among position players for the second half of the season. That the Braves would not send more players to Durham became a bone of contention for Gallagher with the front office. The situation came to a head when injuries left Durham without a catcher in July and barely enough infielders in August.

When catchers Blane McDonald and Steve Stieb went down with injuries, Tommy Thompson was called in for emergency duty in late July. Then Thompson went on the shelf with a spider bite, so the Braves sent Brian Snitker from Anderson where he was serving as a coach. At age 24, Snitker had given up his dream of catching in the big leagues and was eyeing a future in the organization as a coach and manager. His playing days were noteworthy only because he blasted the longest home run in Orlando's Tinker Field history. His emergency duty for Durham covered three games and, amazingly enough, included a two-run triple in a 5-4 victory over Salem.

When Zuvella, Rudd and Mike Garcia were injured in August, Gallagher was forced to move Hall from the outfield back to shortstop and play Tommy Thompson at second base. But the shuffling left the manager without a designated hitter. So he activated himself.

Gallagher had not swung a bat since he was the player-manager for Texas City in the Lone Star League three years earlier. Amazingly, over a six-game span at Kinston and Rocky Mount, he batted .304 at age 34. He later played center field in front of the home crowd in the regular-season finale and collected two singles.

No addition to the Durham roster in the second half was celebrated more than that of Kevin Rigby, who three months earlier had earned a degree from Duke University before Atlanta selected him in the 14th round of the draft. Rigby earned a promotion from Anderson by batting .306 there. A crowd of 3,527 — a boost of about 1,000 fans — greeted Rigby as the "hometown hero" for his August 27 debut at Durham Athletic Park. He responded with a two-run double in the fourth inning and a solo home run in the sixth inning. The home run was Rigby's first since April when he blasted one for Duke against North Carolina in the Atlantic Coast Conference Tournament played in Raleigh. The home run also won $320 for Durham resident George Cates in the Bulls "Home Run for the Money" contest. Cates gave $20 of the winnings to Rigby.

Injuries and ineffectiveness also took a toll on the pitching staff in the second half. Yet the Braves seemed more willing to help Gallagher's cause with the arrivals of Jones from the draft as well as Lucia, Jose Alvarez and Joe Cowley from Double-A Savannah. With Behenna, Smith and Rick Coatney handling most of the starting assignments, the new foursome made the starting rotation even stronger in the second half than the first. Combined, Alvarez, Cowley, Jones and Lucia — all right-handers — made 30 starts, while compiling a 17-6 record and 2.67 earned run average.

Jones came to the Braves through an oversight by the New York Mets the previous year. The Mets mistakenly selected Jones in the third round of the 1979 draft, apparently unaware that he was neither 21 years old nor had completed six months of school at the United States Military Academy. Both were requirements at the time to be eligible for the draft. The selection was voided by Major League

Baseball, and a year later the Braves took Jones in the fourth round. Jones proved to be a solid, sometimes spectacular, pitcher for the Bulls. His 6-5 record belied his 2.61 ERA. During one stretch he did not allow an earned run over 21 2/3 innings and he recorded back-to-back games of 11 and 10 strikeouts.

Lucia hardly looked the part of a pitcher. He stood about 5-foot-9 and barely weighed 165 pounds. But he could throw, and he knew how to pitch. Over five starts with the Bulls he was spectacular, winning three games against one loss with a 2.93 ERA. When he developed soreness in his shoulder, the Braves sent him home to California on July 25 for the remainder of the season.

Alvarez was damaged goods when he arrived in Durham in mid-July. After an outstanding season in which he won 11 games with a 3.00 ERA in Savannah the season before, Alvarez tore up his ankle. There was some question about whether he would ever pitch again. By mid-season of 1980, Alvarez was ready for rehabilitation assignments, first in Rookie ball and then in Durham.

Alvarez showed in his first Durham start that Carolina League hitters were overmatched by his stuff. He dominated a good hitting Lynchburg club, allowing two unearned runs before giving up a two-run homer in the ninth inning of a complete-game win.

The following night at Durham Athletic Park, Gallagher was ejected by the home plate umpire following a dispute that led to Lynchburg's first run in the first inning. Gallagher and Bob Veale were Durham's only two coaches, and Veale's responsibilities rested with the pitchers. So Gallagher turned to Alvarez and handed the pitcher the lineup card.

Midway through the game, teammate and roommate Gil Ryan approached Alvarez.

"If you don't get me in this game, you ain't got a place to stay tonight," Ryan said.

Ryan pitched the final three innings to preserve a 5-2 Durham victory, Alvarez completed his managerial career with a perfect record, and he slept comfortably in Ryan's apartment that night.

In his second start, Alvarez again dominated. He allowed Winston-Salem two runs in the bottom of the ninth inning of another complete-game victory.

A couple of days later, Alvarez joined teammates for a round of golf at Hillandale Golf Course in Durham. Afterward, he returned to Ryan's apartment to find a message from Gallagher on their answering machine. Alvarez called his manager.

"Where the heck have you been?" Gallagher asked.

"Just working out," Alvarez said.

"You've been out playing golf, haven't you?"

"The rules are rules, you can't play golf, right?"

"I know what you were doing. Come down to the park immediately. Get your stuff. They need you in Savannah."

Cowley also had spent the previous season pitching for Savannah. He returned there to begin the 1980 season but pitched in only four games when he succumbed to a shoulder injury. Atlanta's front office wanted him to take the remainder of the season off and return to his home in Kentucky. Cowley had other ideas.

"I was determined to get back … damned determined to get back," he said.

So Cowley suggested he pitch the second half of the season in Durham. Cowley was a colorful character, inclined to do or say anything on the slightest whim. He could fill a reporter's notebook with his wisdom. After a complete-game, 2-1 win over Salem on July 27 in which Cowley struggled all game with the command of his pitches, he said: "Some days you've got to sit in the boat, and other days you've got to row like hell. Today, I was really rowing."

Upon arriving in Durham, Cowley immediately threw a bullpen session for Veale.

"Damn, let's get you right," Veale said.

Veale detected that Cowley was throwing with his right arm too close to his body. Also, Cowley was not driving his shoulder toward the catcher after releasing the ball. From the outset Cowley looked like he should have been pitching at a higher level. He started 10 games for the Bulls, won six without a loss, and put up a 2.81 ERA. At one point he went 20 consecutive innings without allowing an earned run.

Cowley also earned the nickname "Crazy Joe" from his teammates. When the team boarded the bus for the final road trip of the season, Cowley somehow smuggled his small dog on board to the disbelief of his teammates.

Perhaps the saddest day of the season's second half came in late July when Gallagher summoned infielder Andres Forbes to his office. Forbes had just returned from a brief stint in Savannah and there was no room for him on the Durham roster.

"I really loved that kid," Gallagher said of Forbes, who at age 23 was not much of a prospect anymore. "I had to release him, which was awful. He was always so polite and always such a hard worker. He was a good kid. A good kid."

Forbes served as Gallagher's conduit to Spanish-speaking players, both the season before in low Class A Greenwood and in Durham. He was fluent in English and Spanish and taught the newcomers to this country how to order food from a menu, how to speak the basics of a new language and how to adapt to the customs of a foreign land.

"He was the adult for all those kids," Gallagher said.

Aside from Forbes' release, the second half was one of mostly highlights, on and off the field. John R. Corne of Raleigh was Durham's 100,000th fan on July 3, marking the first time a Carolina League franchise had topped that mark in attendance since the Peninsula Grays in 1965. The Bulls also drew a Merchants' Night announced crowd of 6,101 on July 14, just short of the Durham Athletic Park record 6,237 for a game in 1946. On Aug. 18, a crowd of 1,802 pushed the Bulls' season attendance to 152,667, breaking the previous Durham record of 152,095 set in 1947.

On the field, every Durham player represented in the Carolina

League All-Star Game in Kinston on July 16 contributed to the North Carolina Division's 3-2, 10-inning victory over the Virginia Division. Gallagher managed the team. Behenna, who had not won a game for the Bulls since May 26, picked up the win with two innings of no-hit relief. Hall and Bockhorn contributed singles. Thompson doubled. Stieb threw out two potential base stealers. Rudd walked and scored a run, and Pettaway pitched one scoreless inning.

North Carolina won when Rocky Mount's Jim Gabella led off the bottom of the 10th inning with a home run. Gabella, who entered the game without a home run in 250 at-bats and with a .209 batting average, was named the game's MVP and with it earned a fifty-dollar bill.

"I'll probably use it to buy some food," he told reporters afterward. "I'm glad I did something good for Rocky Mount."

Gabella's All-Star Game home run proved to be the high point of a dreadful Rocky Mount season. The Bulls won 18 of 20 games against the Pines, but administered only part of the punishment inflicted on the team by the rest of the league as it finished the season with a mere 24 wins in 138 games.

The Pines' won-loss record was only part of the dismal story. By early July, word was spreading through the Carolina League that the financially troubled team might not finish the season. That would have meant 12 open dates for the Bulls, including six lost gates at Durham Athletic Park. None of the other Carolina League teams could afford for Rocky Mount to fold, either.

The Pines were formed as a stop-gap measure by the Carolina League, which needed an eighth club to facilitate Durham joining the league. Lou Haneles, the team's owner, was a 62-year-old former minor-league player who had success the previous season in owning the Newark Co-Pilots of the short-season Class A New York-Penn League.

Haneles was among the few owners who believed a profit could be made without an affiliation with a major-league team. His thinking was that there were an endless stream of players who wanted to live or re-live the dream of playing professional baseball and would play for little pay. He conducted a camp in Ocala, Florida, that spring that served as a tryout for Rocky Mount players. Players paid $220 to attend the camp with the hope of signing on with Haneles' team, which would be managed by Mal Fichman who managed the Newark club the previous season and also ran Haneles' camp.

The Pines' Opening-Day roster was composed of eight players from the camp, five more from Newark the season before and another cast of rejects from major-league organizations. The city of Rocky Mount was less than welcoming to a team that would post double-digit losing streaks on four occasions during the 1980 season, including one stretch in which the Pines went 18 games without winning. Fewer than 400 fans on average attended Rocky Mount games, which were played both in that city and nearby Wilson.

By the end of June, the club was in dire straits as it listed debts of approximately $17,000. The payroll, which consisted of 19 players and a trainer who were paid $325 apiece per month, was in serious danger of not being met for the final two months of the season.

On June 26, a day prior to a scheduled three-game road trip to Alexandria, Virginia, the players almost staged a mutiny after they met and said they wanted to be paid in cash before they departed. "One of the stipulations was that I take a pay cut," said Fichman, whose salary for the season had dipped to $7,200. The Pines secretary, Liz Howell, who also toiled as a waitress at a Rocky Mount restaurant, saw her paycheck slashed to fifty-five dollars a week. "One thing (Haneles) wanted us to do was discontinue washing uniforms every day. He didn't want us to polish our cleats daily because it cost too much," Fichman said. Haneles also named Fichman the team's athletic trainer and bus driver for the remainder of the season as a way of trimming additional expenses.

The league's board of directors met in an emergency session and agreed to allocate $5,000 from the league's treasury to Rocky Mount to keep the club afloat until July 15. Wolff and a second owner, Ervin Oakley of Winston-Salem, threw in another $1,000 apiece to help the cause, and both agreed to pay all of Rocky Mount's travel expenses for remaining games in their cities. The Boston Red Sox and Pittsburgh Pirates also helped the cause by sending Rocky Mount five players who were not getting playing time in their organizations.

In August, Rocky Mount was the subject of a *Sports Illustrated* story entitled "It's been some rocky year." The magazine did not paint a pretty picture.

It got even rockier for the Pines on Aug. 29 at Durham Athletic Park. The Bulls had trailed Winston-Salem by three games in the standings nine days earlier, but an eight-game winning streak put them in position to capture the second half crown during a season-ending three-game series at home against lowly Rocky Mount.

The opener was one to remember for Durham and its fans. Hall walked on four pitches to lead off the bottom of the first inning and promptly stole second base. It was his 100th steal of the season, making him the ninth minor-leaguer to reach that milestone. After doubling and scoring in the fifth inning, Gerald Perry reached on a fielder's choice an inning later and eventually scored his 100th run of the season on a Stieb single.

Durham's eight runs were enough to win the game and clinch a tie for the North Carolina Division's second-half championship, but Behenna provided the candles for the ceremonial cake by throwing a no-hitter. He walked three and struck out seven in the first nine-inning no-hitter by a Durham pitcher since Bruce Von Hoff beat Rocky Mount in August 1966. Afterward, Durham players hoisted both Hall and Behenna to their shoulders and carried them off the field. Hall then returned and slid into second base to the cheering throng of 3,075.

The next night, Durham got a game-winning single from Butler in the 13th inning to defeat Rocky Mount and secure the second-half title. Afterward, Pettaway broke his season-long silence with the media, granting one interview.

"I don't have no hard feelings," Pettaway said. "I'm friendly to all reporters. I just think a lot of them want to print only the bad about people. Because of that, I just figure, hey, I don't talk to reporters. But we don't have to go back and worry about that. Let's forget that."

The regular-season finale was played before a Fan Appreciation Night crowd of 4,811. Although the game was meaningless insofar as the standings as Durham began to prepare for its playoff meeting with Peninsula, the Virginia Division champion, it served as a final celebration of a summer of stunning accomplishments.

Pettaway was named the club's top pitcher on the basis of an 11-4 record, 2.16 ERA and a franchise-record 20 saves in 50 appearances. Hall was recognized as the team's top position player and was the Bulls' lone representative on the All-Carolina League team. With Hall's 100 stolen bases, as well as 38 apiece from Milt Thompson and Perry, 37 from Butler, and 32 from Rudd, the Bulls swiped a Carolina League-record 296 bases, or four short of Gallagher's preseason goal.

By averaging 2,588 fans per home game while attracting a season total of 175,693, the Bulls more than doubled their preseason goal. It was the second-highest attendance figure in Carolina League history, falling well short of the 223,507 who attended Winston-Salem Cardinals games in 1947 at the height of post-war interest in minor-league baseball.

To draw the kinds of crowds they did required a well-conceived plan, but it also took a certain amount of good fortune. The Bulls could not afford a tarp to cover the field that season, yet lost only an April 29 game against Kinston and a May 14 date with Winston-Salem to rainouts.

If nothing else, the success the Bulls enjoyed, both on and off the field, during the 1980 regular season proved Durham was ripe for the return of professional baseball to the city.

The playoffs proved to be anti-climactic. The Bulls won 42 games in each half, and their season-long .600 winning percentage was among the best in all of minor-league baseball. But the team was no match for the 100 wins accumulated by the Peninsula Pilots, a farm club of the Philadelphia Phillies, the 1980 World Series champion. Not since the 1960 Toronto Maple Leafs, who had the advantage of playing a 154-game International League schedule, had a minor-league team hit triple figures in wins.

The biggest difference between the Bulls and Pilots was roster stability. While Peninsula largely kept its roster intact from start to finish, Durham shuffled players throughout the season's second half. Of the 23 players on Durham's Opening-Day roster, only 13 remained against Peninsula in the playoffs.

As talented as Durham proved to be, Peninsula was stocked with even more talent. Shortstop Julio Franco, who batted .321 and led the league with 99 runs batted in, earned Carolina League MVP honors. Outfielder Wil Culmer led the league with a .369 batting average and slugged 18 home runs. With a 17-6 record and 2.60 ERA, LeRoy Smith was the league's Pitcher of the Year. In addition to Smith, the pitching staff featured Wally Goff (14-4), Don Carman (14-5) and Jim Wright (13-1, 1.85 ERA).

So, it was no surprise when Peninsula swept the Bulls in the best-of-five league championship series, winning the finale in Hampton, Virginia. The Pilots put the Bulls in a checkmate position by winning the first two games of the series in Durham. The Pilots led 9-3 heading to the bottom of the ninth inning in the final game played at Durham Athletic Park in 1980.

When Durham came to bat for the final time in the second game, it marked the last chance for Bulls fans to extend a warm thank you to the Bulls. The cheering began in the left-field bleachers as Gallagher departed the first-base dugout, circled behind home plate and headed for the third-base coaching box.

By the time he got there, the remainder of the crowd was standing and applauding. As Perry stepped to home plate to begin the last half-inning, he sensed what was going on and stepped out of the batter's box. The applause turned into boisterous cheering. Peninsula players in the dugout stepped out to see what was going on. Durham players all moved to the top step of their dugout, a few tipping their hats to the crowd.

The serenade of cheers, for a team that was in the process of losing, was like nothing the players and coaches on both teams had ever before seen. Bulls' fans were essentially saluting themselves. They had come together as one in support of a team that was unique to Durham, a club that represented something strong and bold in a community that had lacked a rallying point for years, perhaps decades. A summer of fun and excitement had united a city behind a cause.

The Bulls were Durham's team, not Raleigh's nor Chapel Hill's. Now, when friends from neighboring communities puffed out their chests in civic pride, Durham residents could retort, "Yes, but we have the Bulls."

Gallagher took note of the celebration going on around him as he bowed and doffed his cap to the crowd.

"That was a great tribute to the fans of Durham and the ballplayers," Gallagher said afterward. "The fans of Durham have proven to me tonight that they have a lot of class. Durham showed me a lot of class.

"When I watched the last inning, I realized it didn't matter whether or not we win the championship. We've already won it as far as Durham is concerned… . I can be pretty hard-nosed sometimes, but that brought tears to my eyes.

"In my 16 years of baseball, I've never seen anything like that. I will never forget that moment as long as I live."

Pine For A Day

The following column appeared in the *Durham Morning Herald* on Sept. 7 under the heading: "Pro Baseball Debut Is One For The Books."

My baseball career ended some nine years ago in Pony League, done in by a throwing arm to match Cheryl Ladd's and a batting average slightly less than Mark Belanger's.

My love for the game never wavered. In my heart baseball ranks right up there with family, religion and Twinkies. So I didn't stop to stutter when Mal Fichman, manager of the Rocky Mount Pines, approached me last Saturday with an idea.

"Would you like to play?" he asked. He probably had been turned down by the bat boy.

By Sunday — the final day of the regular season — when the Pines arrived at Durham Athletic Park, I had pen in hand, prepared to sign a pro contract. There were no squabbles. No long-term agreements. No incentive bonuses. It was probably the easiest negotiation of a player contract since the infamous midget Eddie Gaedel hooked on with Bill Veeck and the Chicago White Sox in 1951.

Unfortunately for Fichman, I would not produce for the Pines what Gaedel did for the White Sox. Gaedel walked in his only plate appearance in the major leagues. In my lone at-bat, I struck out on a three-ball, two-strike pitch from Durham pitcher Dom Chiti in the top of the eighth inning. In the bottom of the eighth, I played right field and made what Durham manager Al Gallagher termed "the weakest throw to the infield in baseball history."

No matter my record, which I shall treasure when it appears in the 1981 *"Official Baseball Guide,"* I can now say I walked a mile in the shoes of a Rocky Mount Pine.

From the time I tied the shoelaces and tugged at my sagging socks until I returned to the dugout drenched in sweat after the eighth inning, I gained some valuable insight to professional baseball. Even more precious was the perception gained from playing with the Pines.

Yes, they may have been, as *Sports Illustrated* termed the Pines, "possibly the worst team in professional baseball history." And, yes, they lost 114 games in a 138-game season. Still, each and every one of the Pines acted in a professional manner right to the bitter end of a 13-1 loss last Sunday.

It was once hard to understand why Mike Brown, the Pines' rubber-armed relief pitcher who appeared in 77 games, would play an entire season for $350 a month on a team that had losing streaks of 18, 14, 13 (twice) and 11 games.

Now, after sitting in the dugout and in the bullpen with this collection of rejects from other organizations, I can better understand.

Baseball is in their blood.

Brown and relief pitcher Dave Thomas both agree that there is no greater thrill than signing an autograph. It's an ego trip, sure, but it's an honor just the same. The feeling of a fan asking you to pose for a picture can quickly erase the memory of a 17-0 loss.

Standing before 4,811 fans, while a frightening experience for me, is a symbol of esteem to a player. "Playing before these people makes it all worthwhile," said Thomas, who pitched in a game in Rocky Mount this year before a "crowd" of 44.

If the fans, the autographs and the attention keep the ego going, the balls and strikes and wins and losses count, too.

Pitcher Scott Gibson, who finished the season without a win in 12 decisions, says he is embarrassed to return to his Florida home. "I hate to tell my friends I was oh-for-Rocky Mount," he says.

Tim Bardin, a late-season signee with the Pines out of Atlantic Christian College, may have analyzed the situation best after a pregame Bible lecture centered on living on fact, not feelings.

"We play on fact and feelings," he said of the Pines. "The fact we always lose is not a good feeling."

PART II:
Aftermath

Lights, Camera, Action!

When the Major League Baseball Players Association went on strike prior to the 1972 season, the result was the cancellation of spring training. The strike extended 13 days into the regular season, costing the major leagues 86 games.

The strike also cost at least one minor-league player his dream of one day playing for the Baltimore Orioles. Ron Shelton was a mid-level prospect in the Baltimore organization, having advanced to Triple-A Rochester for the 1971 season. He batted a respectable .260 that season as a dependable backup to regular second baseman Donato Fazio.

Shelton was realistic about his standing with the Orioles. Davey Johnson was cemented at second base with the big club. Bobby Grich was a budding star in the system, and Bob Bailor was on the way. So when spring training was cancelled in '72, Shelton evaluated his future in the game and determined it was time to go back to school.

If nothing else during his five seasons of professional baseball, Shelton took away a new-found affection for motion pictures. When you are stationed in such minor-league outposts as Bluefield, West Virginia, and Stockton, California, there often is no better way to wile away time than by attending matinee shows at the local theater.

"I could go to a movie every day and get out of the lousy motel or hotel, and often it was the only air-conditioned place in town," Shelton said. "I sort of started going to movies indiscriminately and I fell in love with movies."

Shelton also began to romanticize about writing his own movie manuscript, one with minor-league baseball as the backdrop to a story about life in the game. He certainly was not the first to recognize that nearly every sports-themed movie to that point carried a similar story line and rarely, if ever, strayed from the field of play. Essentially, there were no sports movies about the lives surrounding the games, and all seemed to focus on the cheerful endings of a game-winning home run in the bottom of the ninth inning, clinching touchdown in the final seconds or come-from-behind victory in basketball.

Shelton had other ideas because he believed there was more to sports than what was being portrayed in motion pictures. He could write about a world in sports that he knew better than anyone else in the movie business because he had experienced it.

But breaking into the film-writing business proved to be more challenging to Shelton than climbing minor-league baseball's ladder to the major leagues. Shelton was selected in the 39th round of the 1966 Major League Baseball Draft by the Orioles out of Westmont (California) College. A year later, he returned to school to earn a Bachelor of Arts degree in English literature.

Then, upon leaving pro baseball, Shelton returned to graduate school at the University of Arizona where he earned a master's of fine arts degree in visual arts. Afterward, he moved back to Southern California where he pursued a career as a painter/sculptor and worked a variety of jobs — house painter, carpenter, handyman, landscape flunky — for nearly a decade. He dabbled in screenwriting in his off hours.

By the mid-1980s, Shelton had the shell of a manuscript titled *"The Player To Be Named Later"* and was ready to present it to a film studio — namely to Thom Mount, then the young director of Universal Studies. Over the years, Shelton had developed a friendship with Mount, and Shelton was aware of Mount's interest in baseball through minority ownership in several minor-league teams.

Shelton's pitch to Mount was simple: The movie was *Lysistrata* in the minor leagues. *Lysistrata* was an ancient Greek play in which the title character convinces the women of her country to withhold sexual favors to their husbands until they negotiate peace to end the Peloponnesian War. Shelton said his story would be told by a woman who is wooed by both the pitcher and catcher on the team. It had to be the team's battery because they are the only players on a baseball team who actually talk to each other.

Mount liked the premise, and told Shelton to develop the story further.

"It wasn't very good, but it spoke to me," Mount said of the original script and how it made him recall his days attending minor-league games while growing up in Durham. "Watching those guys, with the young guys on the way up and the old guys trying to stay in the game on the way down. You see that as a kid and it's very affecting, or it was for me anyway, very affecting. I thought there was an emotional center in this. It would have resonance to people."

Mount was born to Lillard and Bonnie Mount while his father was attending law school at Duke University. His father later became a successful and prominent attorney in Durham with an unabashed love of minor-league baseball, more specifically the Durham Bulls. Heaven on earth for the young Mount was sipping a Coca-Cola and eating a hot dog at Durham Athletic Park with his father and his father's friends. Not only did Mount have fond memories of running free in the old ballpark, but also watching the likes of budding stars such as Dick McAuliffe in 1959, and Gates Brown in 1961, when the Bulls were a Detroit Tigers affiliate, and Rusty Staub in 1962 when Durham was a farm club of the Houston Colt .45s.

Mount left Durham at age 16, months before his scheduled graduation from Durham High School. He earned an undergraduate degree from Bard College in upstate New York, then accepted a painting scholarship to attend graduate school at California Institute of the Arts in Los Angeles during its first year of operation in 1970.

While in graduate school, Mount began working in the movie business under the legendary Roger Corman, who was known as the Pope of Pop Cinema because of his work on independent films. Like anyone attempting to break into Hollywood, Mount had his turn at reading scripts, including some for actress Jane Fonda. In early 1973, he was a reader at Universal Studios and an assistant to one of its mid-range vice presidents, who turned many projects over to Mount. He also had support from the highly respected Lew Wasserman, chairman of MCA/Universal.

Wasserman saw Mount as a future executive and put the aspiring star in charge of studio relationships with such luminaries as Edith Head, Alfred Hitchcock and Paul Newman. Along the way, Mount worked on such films as *"The Bingo Long Traveling All-Stars & Motor Kings"* and *"Car Wash."* The former movie told the story of a Negro League barnstorming team, and the latter proved to be a box office hit about the day in the life of minority employees at a car wash.

Mount became known early on as a white man producing black movies. More importantly, he was on the cutting edge of infusing black talent into every aspect—from screen writing to acting to producing—of what previously was a nearly lily-white motion picture business. That the movies were making money as well made Mount somewhat of a young sensation.

"Hollywood respects nothing so much as cash coming in over the transom," Mount said. "If that happens, they think they know what you're doing."

Mount knew enough of what he was doing to be named director of Universal Studios in 1974 at the tender age of 26, earning the tag "baby mogul" by *Time* magazine.

A couple of years later, Mount fielded a telephone call from an old friend and baseball fanatic, Van Schley.

"Listen, I think we should buy a baseball team," Schley told Mount.

"Like what?" Mount, a bit perplexed, responded.

"Well, there is a C League team in Texas called the Texas City Stars," Schley said. "They need $10,000 in cash and we need to take on $10,000 to $12,000 in debt."

Each of five investors, including Mount, put up $5,000. Texas City competed in the Class A Lone Star League, which was composed of six teams independent of major-league affiliations. The 1977 season proved to be Schley's foray into independently operated baseball leagues and teams, and he later became the pioneer of teams operating outside the boundaries of organized professional baseball.

The Texas City Stars were not exactly a smashing success in their only year of operation. Al Gallagher, 31 years old and just four years removed from his final days in the major leagues, both played and managed the club to a 35-41 record and last-place finish in the three-team North Division. Fewer than 350 fans on average attended the home games.

At the time, Mount had Willie Nelson under contract to develop movies based on his albums and coerced the great country singer and songwriter to sing the national anthem at one of Texas City's home games. Even that did not help the gate and the Stars' final season attendance figure reached a meager 12,305.

In the end, the entire league folded when the Corpus Christi Seagulls refused to compete in the playoffs for financial reasons. That inauspicious debut into baseball ownership did not deter Mount from future investments in the game with Schley, who later on also roped movie star Bill Murray into part ownership of several teams from Utica, New York, to Amarillo, Texas, to Anderson, South Carolina, to Bellingham, Washington.

In 1979, Mount received another phone call from Schley about investment in a minor-league club. Schley explained that an aspiring writer from North Carolina had recently left the Atlanta Braves and needed investors in the rejuvenation of the Durham Bulls. Schley and Mount each agreed to be minority stock holders in Miles Wolff's club by again contributing $5,000 each.

Mount could not possibly turn down an opportunity to obtain part-ownership of his hometown club. As a youngster hanging out at Durham Athletic Park, Mount learned an appreciation for the struggles of minor-leaguers attempting to realize their dream of one day playing in the big leagues. His father also taught him the nuances of the game, from situations and strategies to the drama that often builds from the first inning to the last.

So, anytime over the years that Shelton or Schley or Wolff pitched the game of baseball to Mount, it was sweet, sweet music to the movie director's ears.

"The thing about baseball that struck Ron and me and Van and Miles is that it's not a sport, and it's not a game, it is in fact a kind of crucible, an X-ray for the totality of the human experience," Mount said during a 2015 interview in what amounted to an unrehearsed soliloquy on the game. "It speaks to all of the decisions we all have to make, everywhere in our lives, over and over again, even inside every game, and it's filled with ethics and quandaries and opportunities and failures.

"All of that weaves together an educational wheel, which is the genius of baseball. It has none of the cut-and-dried brutality of football. It has none of the testosterone nonsense of ice hockey. It has very little of the complex strategy of tennis, for instance. But, somebody used to say to me when I'd say I work in Hollywood, and these people who are disparaging of Hollywood—and there are many of those—well, 'It's not brain surgery.'

"I would say, 'Yes, you're right, it's not brain surgery. It's heart surgery.' It's much more fundamental to the human condition than brain surgery. That's the way I feel about baseball. Of all the sports, I think baseball is heart surgery. I think it touches the heart. It eliminates the dark for us and gives us something we can hold onto that's memorable over multiple generations."

All of that allure of baseball began to shine through with each of the re-writings of Shelton's original screenplay that he presented to Mount earlier. Sometime in late 1985 or early 1986, Shelton telephoned Mount, who was in France working on Roman Polanski's film *"Frantic."*

"I got it figured out," Shelton told Mount.

"What does that mean?" Mount responded.

"Well, here's the thing, it's not just young guys on the way up and old guys on the way down. It's a girl in the middle who is sleeping with both of our guys and trying to make up her mind.

"OK, great. Deal. Done. Now you're talking."

Mount knew the movie project was a huge gamble in Hollywood. First, it was about baseball, which nobody in the motion picture business at the time believed was worth producing. It also was about minor-league baseball, which had even less appeal to Hollywood producers. Finally, Shelton's script was counter to the traditional sports story line where everyone lived happily ever after.

"He jumped off the cliff," Shelton said of Mount's belief in the script, "and we jumped off it together."

Mount first needed a director for the still unnamed movie. Then came selection of actors and a site to begin filming. Shelton had done second-unit directing on occasion, but had never been in charge of a film. No matter, Mount determined that no one could interpolate the script better than the man who wrote it.

Shelton would be the director, and Mount sent him on a scouting mission of minor-league cities in the Class A Carolina League and South Atlantic League. Shelton flew to Raleigh-Durham, rented a car and roamed around North and South Carolina with stops in Anderson, Asheville, Charleston, Columbia, Durham, Kinston, Greensboro and Winston-Salem.

"My big concern was had the minor leagues changed since I had played in them because the major leagues had changed dramatically," Shelton said. "The major leagues had become big money. Guys had become very distant, had agents and publicists. Major league baseball players used to be regular guys, and suddenly they had become celebrities and had become off-putting in many cases.

"I discovered, immediately, the minor leagues hadn't change a bit. They made no money. It was unglamorous. You could still talk to the girls you were trying to get a date with in the stands. You could send notes. Everybody was real close. You knew people in the town. All of that stuff hadn't changed. The stork kind of hung over everybody, so you could get released at any second. Everybody was a dreamer and most of the dreams didn't come true."

Mount swore to himself not to unduly influence Shelton in his decision about where the movie would be filmed. Shelton needed no input. He found everything he wanted in Durham. He liked the idea that Durham was rundown with vacated tobacco warehouses and boarded up downtown storefronts. He found a down-and-out, minor-league town that represented his story well.

Shelton also liked that fans could still walk to games from nearby neighborhoods. Vacant warehouses could be converted to studios, thus eliminating the cost of transporting sets around the city during filming. Durham Athletic Park was perfect, a cozy ballpark with surrounding buildings tight to the outfield fences. It personified a small-town atmosphere.

Mount could then work on a name for the movie. He liked an indirect link from the movie to its title. So, he would not name a movie about a meteor crashing to earth, "Meteor." He had just named a soon-to-be-released movie about the drug-dealing community, "Tequila Sunrise." He wanted a title name that suggested a context that was more memorable than obvious.

"Bull Durham" it would be.

"What I liked about *Bull Durham* is they are the Durham Bulls," Mount said. "Bull Durham chewing tobacco — for those who remember — conjures up another era, another time, and Bull Durham is the city, and it's as much about the city as it is about the ballgame."

Mount and Shelton wanted a young, up-and-comer as the lead character, and Kevin Costner was on their A list. Hollywood already had recognized Costner as a rising star, even though he had been cut out of the film *"The Big Chill."* Costner's credits included *"Silverado,"* but not in a lead role. He had two movies in the can: *"No Way Out,"* and *"The Untouchables."*

Shelton knew Costner's agent, J.J. Harris, and presented her with the script. Harris loved it and turned it over to Costner. When Costner read it, he wanted to show off his athletic skills to Shelton and the two met at a batting cage. Costner wanted the role of "Crash Davis," the aging career minor-leaguer who was on his last legs as a pro baseball player, and Shelton was impressed by how Costner could hit a baseball.

Despite stories over the years that several other big-name actors, such as Kurt Russell and Harrison Ford, were approached about the lead role, Shelton said Costner was the only actor who was ever considered.

In need of financial backing, Mount and Shelton pitched the movie to Fox, Paramount, Warner Brothers, Universal, Tri-Star and Disney. Every studio turned down the movie. One studio director said he might accept the movie if Mount dumped Costner and put someone else in the lead role. Fox's director said the proposed budget needed to be slashed in half, because "no one would ever see this movie," according to Mount. Generally, Mount was told the movie lacked commercial appeal, and it could not attract a foreign audience, which was a prerequisite at the time.

Finally, Mount took the script to Orion, which had taken a liking to Costner, and three years earlier had produced *"Under Fire,"* which was co-written by Shelton and Clayton Frohman. Orion allocated a rather paltry $9 million for producing the movie, and allowed only an eight-week shooting schedule. The studio did grant Shelton much creative freedom in producing the movie.

The movie now had a start date and enough financing to begin making offers and start auditioning. The story of how Shelton landed Susan Sarandon as "Annie Savoy," the beautiful girl who was wooing both the player on his way up and the player on his way down, has taken on a life of its own over the years. It has been reported numerous times that several actresses, including Kay Lenz, Ellen Barkin and Kim Bassinger, turned down offers for the lead role.

Several actresses did audition, and Shelton was impressed by their performances. But the studio kept changing the list of "acceptable actresses for lead role," and Shelton believed he was dealing with a moving goalpost. The final casting decision was made by committee, and Sarandon was not on the original list.

Finally, the studio added Sarandon, and she agreed to fly from Italy to California with her young daughter to audition. She won over the audience and, according to Shelton, was the only actress offered the lead role.

Next, the movie needed an actor to play the role of a young, budding star on his way to the big leagues. This proved to be a most difficult task because not just any young actor would do. Shelton wanted someone very different from Costner in every way. His reasoning was that if the script had two players going after the same girl, he did not want them to be carbon copies of each other. They had to be different physically as well as in style and tone.

Tim Robbins fit the bill as "Nuke LaLoosh." He stood 6-foot-5. Costner was 6-foot-1. Robbins was much more out-going than the reserved Costner. Robbins, at least in the movie, comes across as knee-jerk in his reactions on and off the field. Costner, in his role, is the wiser, more cautious decision-maker.

Costner's character was named after Lawrence Columbus "Crash" Davis who played 148 games as a utility infielder for the Philadelphia Athletics over three seasons from 1940 to 1942. He was drafted into the Navy during World War II. Upon being discharged from the Navy in 1946, Davis returned to graduate school at Duke, his alma mater. Over the next seven seasons, Davis played 636 minor-league games in a failed attempt to get back to the big leagues. Shelton met Davis when the director was scouting for cities to locate the film, and liked the name. The two later became friends.

Annie Savoy was named in deference to women who hang around ballparks and are called "Baseball Annies" by the players. One day while Shelton was writing at his desk, he picked up a matchbook from "Savoy Bar," which could have come from a famous hotel bar in London or perhaps a bar and restaurant in Albuquerque, New Mexico. Either way, it stuck as Annie's last name.

For Nuke LaLoosh's name, Shelton had to travel to Columbia, South Carolina, where he was preparing one evening to dine at the Radisson Hotel. As he sat down for a cocktail, the waiter greeted him.

"Hello, sir, my name is Ebby Calvin LaRouche, and I'll be your server tonight," the waiter said, "but you can just call me 'Nuke.' "

Shelton jotted the name down on a napkin, wondering whether "Nuke" was spelled like a nuclear meltdown or like the nickname "Newk," as in the former Brooklyn Dodgers pitcher Don Newcombe. He went with the former, then altered the last name because he did not want it associated with the radical leftwing LaRouche Movement authored in the 1970s and 1980s by Lyndon LaRouche.

Shelton worried ever after that the waiter would one day demand royalty fees from the movie for using his name as Robbins' character. He never got the call.

Wolff was one of the few who got a sneak preview of the script, and he was intrigued. Like most who were curious about the filming of a movie at Durham Athletic Park, Wolff believed the interest would pass. He never believed the film would have any impact on his franchise, one way or the other.

"Once they started filming, I was less than enthused," Wolff said. "Shoots kept being changed and in my minor-league heart, I felt they were spending stupid money."

When he purchased the Bulls franchise from the Carolina League prior to the 1980 season, Wolff immediately changed the Durham Athletic Park color scheme, painting over the traditional staid green that characterized most minor-league parks since forever. By painting the park a shiny blue, Wolff had essentially spruced up the park. Movie producers wanted the old color, so before shooting began, the entire stadium and surrounding buildings were painted green. When filming was completed, the production company returned the stadium and all buildings back to Wolff's blue color scheme.

Because filming was conducted in the dead of winter, the park's Bermuda-grass playing surface had deteriorated from green to brown and was painted green. The frosty breath of several of the actors could be seen against the cold air in several scenes as temperatures occasionally dropped to the freezing mark. Extras acting as fans occasionally had to remove their winter jackets to make scenes look like summer nights.

To ensure the grandstands were filled for one scene, producers passed out pamphlets at a Pink Floyd concert in nearby Chapel Hill asking patrons to be part of a movie by coming to Durham Athletic Park afterward. In one movie scene, several fans are noticeable wearing Pink Floyd T-shirts.

Producers wanted a big crowd, in particular, for an afternoon scene and went to Wolff for help. He agreed to send a letter to all season-ticket holders, essentially advertising the film, but also offering a free hot dog to all those in attendance. Once the crowd of maybe 2,000 fans was in the park and ready to go, producers had a change of heart and decided it might be better if the filming was done at night. Wolff was told not to give away the hot dogs until that night, so the crowd might stay. He refused.

In one scene, Annie Savoy gives pitching instructions to Nuke LaLoosh. Originally, the scene was to be shot at the ballpark, but then Shelton decided it was best to shoot it at Savoy's home, so in quick order, Bulls groundskeeper Bill Miller had a truck of dirt shipped to the nearby house and he constructed a pitching mound in the backyard.

Most of the Bulls involvement in the movie's filming centered on Pete Bock, who had left the club as its general manager five seasons earlier to serve as the GM of the Hawaii Islanders in the Pacific Coast League. He returned to the Durham area to form, along with Wolff, a baseball management company that consulted with minor-league operators on how to successfully run their clubs.

Mount knew of Bock through Wolff. So, the movie's producer hired the former minor-league umpire and general manager as a baseball consultant. Bock's charge was to make certain actors and ballplayers looked the part, that baseball scenes looked as realistic as possible, and that there would be no left-handed catchers or shortstops. If a scene called for a baserunner to be thrown out at third base, Bock would make sure he had the proper players in position to make the play occur, and appear realistic.

Prior to filming, Bock set up what essentially was a spring training complex for tryouts. Most of the 84 "actors" he hired were professional baseball players who had time on their hands during the offseason, when the movie was filmed. He needed that many players because some scenes were filmed in other North Carolina locales such as Asheville, Greensboro and Rocky Mount. Essentially, he needed about four teams of players, including those who were the "extras" among the Durham Bulls.

One such player hired was Paul Devlin, whose eligibility as a player at the University of North Carolina had expired. He was set to debut the following spring for the New York Mets Class A affiliate in the Carolina League. In one of the movie's classic scenes, Devlin was tipped off by the catcher — Crash Davis — that the next pitch from Nuke LaLoosh would be a fastball. After Devlin crushed that pitch for a home run, Davis visited his pitcher on the mound and told him that any pitch hit that far should have "a stewardess on it."

One night — actually, it was around 2 in the morning — during filming, Shelton was looking for an actor he had hired to be the preacher for a wedding scene at home plate between a Durham Bulls player and an avid fan. Nowhere to be found, Shelton turned to Bock and said, "You can do it."

Bock was wearing gloves and a couple of sweat suits to help him deal with the cold of the late night. He went to a trailer to try on a suit for the scene, but the suit was a size 38, several notches below what Bock wore at the time.

"Well, that rules me out," Bock said.

"No, no, no," an assistant in the trailer replied. "We'll take care of it."

Bock arrived for the scene in the suit, which had the back of the jacket and pants ripped out so it would fit. The adjustments could not be detected with straight-on shots of Bock from the film crew. Thus, Bock played the role of the preacher.

Back in California, during the cutting and re-editing of the film, Mount and Shelton were battling over compromises in changes to the film, not all of which met Shelton's approval.

At about the same time, Mount was in conversations with Charles Glenn, then the executive vice president of advertising for Orion, about ways to promote the movie. Among other things, Glenn decided to produce a poster depicting a sultry Annie Savoy with her arm draped around Crash Davis as they sat atop the hood of a car outside a baseball stadium.

"It really made the movie," Mount said. "The idea was that it was both about baseball and sex, which we couldn't talk about very openly in newspapers at that time, but it really worked."

The picture was taken at a ballpark in California at sunset. The movie is pitched on the poster as "Bull Durham: A Major League Love Story in a Minor League Town," with the additional subtext: "Romance is a lot like baseball. It's not whether you win or lose. It's how you play the game."

The movie's premiere was held in June of 1988 at the Carolina Theater in downtown Durham, a few blocks from Durham Athletic Park. Shelton and Mount were there to introduce the movie to city dignitaries, Bulls employees, friends and family. Before the showing, Mount took the stage with his mother, Bonnie, sitting in the front row.

"I want you to know," Mount told the audience, "if there are any cuss words in here, my mother made me put them in." The crowd howled. Bonnie Mount never forgave her son for the comments.

Unlike today, movies then did not have to open in massive numbers of theaters or produce outrageous earnings on the first weekend of showings. To be successful then, a movie could open modestly and hold for several months.

That is what happened with *"Bull Durham."* It did about $5 million in ticket sales the first weekend in 1,238 theaters, and continued to produce a similar dollar figure every week through the entire summer of 1988. It represented how successful movies worked in those days, mostly by word of mouth, and eventually grossed $50 million.

Interestingly enough, the *Durham Morning Herald* panned the movie after the premier showing. The local newspaper was virtually alone in its criticism. Nationally, the movie picked up steam as review after review was glowing in its praise. Perhaps the best representative of the national reviews was written by David Ansen for Newsweek magazine. Ansen wrote that *"Bull Durham"* "works equally as a love story, a baseball fable and a comedy, while ignoring the clichés of each genre."

As much steam as the movie gained throughout theater showings in the summer of 1988, it really was only the beginning of a lasting impact on baseball. No other baseball movie, before or since, has resonated so powerfully with fans and players quite like "*Bull Durham*." Some would argue otherwise, but most agree that the movie remains the greatest ever produced about baseball, and among the best sports films of all-time.

The movie landed in Durham because of Mount's association with the Bulls, and because Shelton believed the city and Durham Athletic Park best represented what minor-league baseball was all about at the time.

In the years following the movie, attendance spiked at the old ball park as fans from all over the country wanted to get a glimpse of the park and somehow again connect with what they saw in the movie. Even today, nearly three decades after the movie was released and after the Durham Bulls long since moved into a new stadium, baseball fans still park their cars and walk around the exterior of Durham Athletic Park. Or, they just park their car down the third-base line and reminisce about what minor-league baseball must have been like in the 1980s.

Dream Fulfilled

Little did I know at the time that Allan Simpson, who was born and raised in Kelowna, British Columbia, shared the same obsession with baseball that I had from my days growing up in Wyoming, and had the same sense of appreciation for the vital role statistics played in the game.

Like almost all Canadian kids, Simpson obsessed over ice hockey growing up, and learned to skate and play the game at a young age. He was a huge fan of the six-team National Hockey League, in particular the Detroit Red Wings, and a die-hard follower of the old Okanagan Senior Hockey League, and vividly remembered, as a 6-year-old, when the OSHL's Penticton Vees, representing Canada, defeated Russia 5-0, to win the 1955 World Hockey Championship. He also listened intently three years later when his own Kelowna Packers lost the 1958 Allan Cup, symbolic of senior hockey supremacy in Canada, in seven games to Ontario's Belleville McFarlands.

Unlike American kids, Simpson had limited exposure to baseball — particularly after he began attending boarding school as a 9-year-old 30 miles north of his Kelowna home. The school followed a distinct English curriculum, and he learned to play cricket, and not baseball, as a youngster. But he got his big break when he made a trip with his family to California over the Easter break in 1960, and not only was he exposed to the sweet, infectious sounds of Vin Scully calling Dodgers pre-season games on the radio while in Los Angeles, but saw his first televised baseball game on the same trip and even coerced his parents into taking him to his first game, on Easter Sunday — April 17, 1960, to be exact — at San Francisco's sparkling new Candlestick Park.

From that point, he was hooked and soon began to devour all the baseball news he could get his hands on, especially as it pertained to his beloved Cincinnati Reds, and his favorite player, center fielder Vada Pinson.

The only trouble was, the nearest major-league baseball team from where he lived was more than 1,000 miles away, in San Francisco. Furthermore, his access to games on TV was limited to maybe one game a week. Though he could pick up an occasional Giants game via radio, it generally was only when the team played at home on a Tuesday or Friday, when it was dark and he could pick up a radio signal. It also wasn't uncommon for him to get into a car and drive into the mountains above Kelowna in search of a stronger radio signal to tune in a game, if one was available. Neither his local paper, nor the two dailies in Vancouver, some 300 miles away, published box scores of major-league games or had any sense of meaningful major-league coverage.

While Simpson developed an insatiable appetite for baseball as a young teenager, his limited access to the game from his remote location in Canada left him thoroughly unfulfilled. That's when he began turning his attention to the next best thing, the minor leagues, and he became an avid follower of Pacific Coast League teams in Vancouver, Seattle and Spokane, Washington — and even Portland, Oregon — though none was closer than a five-hour car ride away. At least he could tune in most of their games on radio, and did on almost a nightly basis. He even talked his father into taking him to PCL games once or twice a summer, especially when the San Diego Padres (which included future members of the Cincinnati Reds) were in the area.

At the time, Simpson's real lifeblood to the game became *The Sporting News*. He patiently awaited its arrival in the mail every Wednesday, and immediately began devouring every story, every box score, every statistic that appeared in the weekly publication. It didn't matter that the average big-league box score might be 10 days or even two weeks old.

One season, Simpson used the comprehensive baseball coverage *The Sporting News* provided each week to tally box scores from all Pacific Coast League games, enabling him to compile his own set of statistics. He was forever a fan of fellow Canadian and future Hall of Famer Ferguson Jenkins after compiling his game-by-game statistics, and those of all the Arkansas Travelers that 1964 season, in the basement of his family's home.

The more time and energy Simpson invested in baseball, the more he wanted to make it a career, with his ultimate goal of someday working for a major-league team — even though, as a Canadian, he knew his employment opportunities might be limited because of immigration issues. Another trip to California in 1971, this one in search of available opportunities in the game, led Simpson to Ted Bowsfield, a Penticton native and rare Canadian with a big-league pedigree. Bowsfield was working for the California Angels at the time. He directed Simpson to Tom Sommers, the Angels farm director who a few years earlier, while attending the University of Southern California, had played for a summer college team in Fairbanks, Alaska. Sommers suggested he contact that club, the Alaska

Goldpanners, which Simpson did and he was hired to be the team's assistant general manager the following summer.

Not only that, he would serve the dual role of temporary sports editor of the local daily paper, the *Fairbanks Daily News-Miner*, as Don Dennis, the general manager of the Goldpanners, also happened to be the executive editor of the newspaper. The Goldpanners were obviously treated favorably by the local paper.

As a condition of Simpson's employment by the paper, Dennis needed to secure a temporary work visa, which he successfully did. But less than a month into his tenure as sports editor, Simpson's visa was revoked once it was determined that he was filling a position that could have been occupied by an American. Rather than return home, he simply bided his time for another three or four weeks until his summer tenure with the paper was scheduled to end anyway.

Meanwhile, his real reason for being in Fairbanks was to gain valuable experience working for a baseball team, and this was no ordinary baseball team. The Goldpanners won the National Baseball Congress World Series all three years Simpson was in Fairbanks, and over the years sent more than 200 players to the major leagues. While in college at the time, first at Everett (Washington) Community College and then at San Diego State, Simpson managed to return to Fairbanks two more summers, to both work for the newspaper and the baseball team — even as his working visa had been revoked. He simply had to tell a few "fishing stories" to immigration authorities at various border crossings between Canada and the United States in order to seamlessly pass undetected. Simpson kept a low profile while continuing to work at the *Daily News-Miner* for fear that his status as an illegal immigrant would be exposed. It was not.

His memorable experience in Fairbanks only fueled Simpson's fire to get into the game full-time despite the many hoops he knew he would have to jump through when it came to obtaining a work visa. Married in 1974 following the baseball season, Simpson and his wife, Jill, also a Canadian, decided that border-hopping was no way to make a living.

But while he was on his honeymoon, Simpson got word that the Montreal Expos, Canada's lone major-league team at the time, would be locating a farm team in Lethbridge, Alberta, in 1975, as a member of the Rookie-level Pioneer League. Simpson happened to be back east at the time and dropped by the Expos offices in Montreal to inquire about the general manager's position in Lethbridge. Jim Fanning, then Montreal's general manager, liked what he heard from Simpson and recommended to the local Lethbridge organization that they hire him.

Watching baseball up close fulfilled Simpson's dream of being part of the game, but the reality of earning $700 a month over the course of the summer, while working for the only professional baseball team in western Canada, quickly dashed that dream. Simpson came to the reality that he needed to get on with his life without baseball. He knew he had reached a dead end.

Over the next five years, Simpson returned to school, earned a degree in accounting from Western Washington University in Bellingham, Washington, and worked as a public accountant in Vernon, British Columbia, just north of his hometown of Kelowna. Simpson's intent was to become a chartered accountant — the Canadian equivalent of a CPA — though it would take at least three more years to complete the necessary articling and course requirements. By 1980, he no longer had the stomach for being an accountant even though it nicely supported his wife and two young children.

One day in May 1980, while baseball was coincidentally in the early stages of making a stirring comeback in Durham, North Carolina, half a continent away and a country removed, Simpson was mowing his lawn in Vernon. He was deep in thought about how to resurrect a career in baseball. An idea was hatched. Simpson promptly turned off the lawnmower, marched into his house and declared to his wife that he was going to launch a baseball newspaper.

"Well," Jill responded without hesitation, "let's do it."

Within eight months, the first issue of All-America Baseball News rolled off the press. Despite having no publishing experience, a limited journalism background and a badly undercapitalized bank account, Simpson made the calculated gamble to publish a niche newspaper as a one-man operation out of the garage of his newly located home in White Rock, British Columbia.

Despite the words of advice from his parents throughout Simpson's childhood — "If you want to do something badly enough, then go ahead and do it," and, "If you're going to do something, then do it the right way, do it to the best of your ability" — they believed their son had lost his mind.

Simpson's parents wondered if their son's obsession with baseball had clouded his judgment — as did everyone else he sought out for advice. Yet his wife was in favor of the move, as risky and impractical as it was, and Simpson was convinced in his own mind that the timing was never better for a new baseball publication, especially with his growing dissatisfaction with the direction *The Sporting News* had taken.

Simpson faced a number of major hurdles with the new publication, not the least of which were his Canadian address and citizenship. He knew he faced uncertain odds of ever obtaining a working visa, either temporary or permanent, that would enable him to move freely to the United States, although his contact with a Seattle law firm that specialized in immigration matters outlined a few scenarios where it might be possible. He also knew the chances of a publication about baseball succeeding in the United States were slim if it was based in another country.

Undaunted, Simpson and his wife packed up their young family and moved some 300 miles to White Rock, located 25 miles south of Vancouver, late in 1980. That community was strategically chosen as a home base because of its close proximity to the U.S. border. That would enable Simpson to cross into the state of Washington on a daily basis to conduct as much business as the immigration authorities he encountered every day would allow. He was forbidden from establishing an office in the United States.

He contracted with the *Bellingham Herald*, home of the local daily newspaper in Bellingham, some 30 miles south of the border, to have the paper printed. He established a mailing house in Seattle, some 100 miles down Interstate 5, to handle everything related to mailing the product. Most importantly, he established post office boxes in both Bellingham and just across the border in Blaine, Washington — anything to give the impression to potential subscribers that the soon-to-be-launched publication was located in the state of Washington and was an American product, and not the work of some crazy Canadian north of the border who probably knew more about hockey than he probably could ever hope to know about baseball.

But Simpson was hardly a Canadian who was naïve about baseball, or lacked passion for the game. While most of us remember precisely where we were upon learning of President John F. Kennedy's assassination in 1963 or man's first landing on the moon in 1969, Simpson could tell you where he was on June 8, 1965 when Rick Monday became the first player selected in the inaugural Major League Baseball draft.

While others might closely follow the drafts of more mainstream sports like football or basketball — or even the hockey draft, for those in Canada — Simpson developed a fascination from the start with baseball's annual dispersal of amateur players. In so doing, Simpson often asked himself a question: Why is it that baseball can be so popular and compelling at the major-league level in the mainstream media, and yet such an afterthought in some of the more subtle areas of the game at the grassroots level, like the draft, or the minor leagues, or college baseball, or even summer baseball from his days with the Goldpanners, so as to receive little or no national exposure?

Simpson met with Randy Adamack, public relations director for the Seattle Mariners, to get some direction on various areas of the game he needed to consider, while also gaining insight on some of the pitfalls he might want to avoid.

He attended baseball's Winter Meetings in Dallas in 1980 and hooked up with, among others, Tracy Ringolsby, who was covering the Mariners at the time for the *Seattle Post-Intelligencer.* Among other things, the two established a network of correspondents who would provide some token major-league coverage for the publication, but Ringolsby, a future Hall of Fame baseball writer, understood the focus from the start was on player development and proved an invaluable consultant as he also had a passion for some of the more subtle areas like the coverage of prospects and the draft, and was well connected at the grassroots level with scouts, as well as minor-league coaches and instructors.

On the same trip to Dallas, Simpson also made a side stop to Chicago and contracted with D. William Berry & Associates, predominantly a marketing and fulfillment company, to perform such duties as sell advertising for the publication on a commission basis, while establishing a marketing campaign.

Mainly through a direct-mail campaign and advertising the publication in *The Sporting News,* of all places, Simpson had 1,500 subscribers before printing the first issue. He carried that first batch of charter subscribers to Seattle in a baby-food box where the names and addresses were key-punched into a computer, and mailing labels were processed. One-year subscriptions for the scheduled 22 issues of *All-America Baseball News* — bi-weekly February through November, monthly in December and January — went for $16.50, or half the cover cost of $1.50 per issue. Half-year subscriptions were offered for $8.25.

Meanwhile, Simpson began working on the charter edition in his impromptu office: an unheated two-car garage in White Rock where empty beer bottles, winter snow tires and golf clubs were every bit as much a part of the decor as a primitive typesetting machine and homemade layout table. The typesetter, purchased for $4,000, had almost no memory, and Simpson could see only one line of copy on his screen at a time. If the processor ate the copy, as it was inclined to do, it was lost forever.

Getting the first issue into print was an adventure. Simpson wrote much of the content himself, while various outside contributors used the mail, or a telecopier to provide copy. Simpson quickly abandoned the idea of typesetting all the copy himself and recruited a friend, an airline ticket agent who could type at twice the speed he could, to come to his aid. The night before the much-anticipated inaugural issue was scheduled to go to publication, Simpson still had galleys of copy hanging from the girders in his garage with several of the 24 pages still blank. Headlines, as well as captions for photos, needed to be written, and corrections were made on the fly. Any notion of proofreading would have to wait for another issue.

Simpson greeted readers on page two of the premier February 28, 1981 issue with a letter from the editor that read, in part:

"*All-America Baseball News* will make a determined effort to bridge the gaps, to make information more accessible to religious followers of the game who cannot begin to follow baseball at all levels, in all regions of the country, through the regular channels.

"It's not a publication designed for the casual baseball observer. That we make clear at the outset. Only if you want in-depth coverage of the minor leagues and college baseball, an inside look at the major leagues, and a myriad of statistics and data-related material directed your way, will *AABN* be likely to prove satisfying to you."

That first issue was jammed with information, including an extensive recap of the 1980 draft. Various columns covered the major leagues and an extensive minor-league notebook was tucked back in the issue.

The bulk of that inaugural issue concentrated on college baseball, and Simpson showed right away that he knew what he was writing about by selecting Arizona State as the publication's pre-season No. 1-ranked team. The Sun Devils eventually won the College World Series that year, and five of Simpson's top 20 teams in the preseason played in Omaha in the CWS. His pre-season All-America team also bore a striking resemblance to the first round of that year's draft.

The lone ad in the inaugural issue was Merle Harmon's FAN FAIR and ran over two-thirds of a page. While the ad might have sold a few $11.95 waste baskets with major-league team logos for Merle Harmon, it did not go a long way in balancing the budget for Simpson's Pacific Northwest Sports Publications, Inc., the corporate name for Simpson's fledgling company. While various other advertisers came aboard, it was not until the fourth issue that Simpson landed his first full-page ad, that one for "Pennant Drive," a baseball board game.

Without much advertising and a subscription base that was not growing significantly, Simpson faced serious financial problems after the first few issues were published. The $20,000 in capital that Simpson used for start-up costs was long gone.

Then there was the toll each publication was taking on what essentially was a one-man operation.

After the first issue went to bed in February of 1981, Simpson was so exhausted from the better part of two nights without sleep that he could not complete even the 30-mile drive from Bellingham, where the paper was printed, to his home in White Rock. He had to pull his car into a rest area on Interstate 5 that became a familiar pit stop in the coming months, and slept for a half hour before completing the journey. The following day he returned to Bellingham to pick up the 4,000 printed copies — the extras were for promotional purposes — and trucked them to Seattle for mailing. In those days, the newspaper was delivered in bulk mail. Some issues reached subscribers, some did not. Because postal officials insisted that the publication needed an office in the United States, which could be inspected to verify the paper's authenticity, it was not until the fifth issue that Simpson somehow convinced the right person in the U.S. Postal Service of the viability of his product and gained second-class postage privileges.

But it was not much longer before Simpson was not only out of money, his bills were accumulating. It was apparent that the publication was at a crossroads. Along with his father, he met with Bill Berry of Chicago-based D. William Berry & Associates in Seattle, and the decision was made to cease publishing. Berry agreed to work out an agreement with *Baseball Bulletin*, a rival periodical with a limited readership, to assume his subscriber list.

For three days, Simpson lived with the reality that his dream of publishing a baseball newspaper was dead. But he was unable to walk away from his decision with a clear conscience — that he had given it his best shot and it just did not work out. It particularly nagged at him that his deal with *Baseball Bulletin* required him to pay that publication $5,000 for the rights to his subscriber names, and was not the other way around as was customary in the industry.

With that at his driving motivation, Simpson changed his mind, and his first order of business was to immediately back out of the agreement with *Baseball Bulletin*. To keep the publication going, he then borrowed $22,000 from his father to satisfy various cost overruns and general publication costs.

Simpson might have been alone, but he believed in his product. He had developed a loyal following of readers, and the baseball industry was quickly gaining respect for Simpson and rallying to his cause because of the quality content that was appearing in the paper, much of it gathered through excellent reporting and thorough source development. He was determined to keep the publication afloat while actively pursuing a buyer to move it to its rightful home in the United States — hopefully in a deal that would enable Simpson to move with it, pending the resolution of his unresolved immigration issues.

His pre-draft issue shed light and valuable insight on the normally anonymous baseball draft like never before, especially after it correctly touted Oral Roberts University right-hander Mike Moore and Wichita State University outfielder Joe Carter as the first two selections in the 1981 draft by the Seattle Mariners and Chicago Cubs, respectively. He also accurately forecast eight of the top 10 selections, and his draft projections overall were amazingly on target, especially considering no one had ever previously mined scouting offices in any detail for inside information on top prospects.

It also did not hurt Simpson's cause that college baseball unofficially and unexpectedly came of age in 1981, both with the emergence of the College World Series as a viable TV product on a fledgling network devoted exclusively to sports, known as the Entertainment and Sports Programing Network, or ESPN, and a dramatic swing in the number of more-recognizable college players that were selected in the first two rounds of the draft than ever before. Players were now being drafted that the average fan could see on TV and even relate to.

Then Simpson got the first big break he needed to keep the publication afloat in the form of Major League Baseball's 54-day strike in the summer of 1981. Without major-league baseball to quench their thirst for the game, fans quickly turned to the next best alternative, the minor-league game, and that played perfectly into the hands of *All-America Baseball News*, which by then already was providing significant coverage of the minor leagues.

With each passing day of the strike, media outlets like ESPN and the new national daily newspaper, *USA Today*, were desperate for summer content and turned their attention to the minor leagues, providing publicity that the minors had never known. The more exposure the minors received, the more a growing legion of fans began looking for additional news on this previously untapped area of the game, and new readers were drawn to *All-America Baseball News*. Soon it — and no longer just *The Sporting News* — had become a definitive source for information on the minors.

Soon thereafter, *All-America Baseball News* began breaking out rankings on the top prospects in each minor league, as well as in each organization. Such coverage became a staple of the paper's coverage through the years.

Slowly but surely, *All-America Baseball News* began to grow, and some of the pressing financial issues that almost sunk the publication began to dissipate, especially when the first wave of subscribers began renewing at rates considered superior to industry average, and more and more advertisers came on board.

One person who witnessed first-hand all the attention that was showered on minor-league baseball during the summer of 1981 was Miles Wolff, whose Durham Bulls benefited from fans wanting to watch any kind of baseball in person that summer.

Wolff also had recognized during the 1980 and 1981 seasons the need for a publication that covered baseball exclusively, and his father's background in the newspaper business sparked interest in what Simpson was doing with *All-America Baseball News*.

Wolff became one of the publication's charter subscribers, and it was not long before the inevitable paths of Simpson and Wolff crossed.

During his brief time as general manager of the Lethbridge Expos in 1975, Simpson had come into contact with Bob Freitas, a long-time, highly respected baseball executive and ambassador for the game, and then a field representative for the National Association of Professional Baseball Leagues, or simply the minor leagues. It was Freitas' duty to travel from city to city in the minor leagues, mostly in a trouble-shooting role, and he met Simpson shortly after Simpson took over as general manager of the Lethbridge club.

Simpson quickly developed a friendship with Freitas that lasted long after he decided to throw in the towel in Lethbridge after one year and return to school in order to seek a job in the business world. Meanwhile, Wolff had also struck up a special friendship with Freitas through the years as a result of his various front-office endeavors in the game.

Freitas was keenly aware of Simpson's financial troubles and the immigration hurdles he was encountering. Like Simpson, he believed the publication needed to move to the United States to have a real chance to succeed, and he began actively seeking a buyer on Simpson's behalf. Naturally, Wolff was one of the people Freitas contacted.

In mid-May of 1982, Simpson made the cross-country trek to Durham to meet with Wolff, and before he left two days later the two had struck a deal for Wolff to buy *All-America Baseball News,* effective July 1. Though Wolff bought the publication in its entirety, in part to remove any doubt in the minds of probing immigration officials on the ownership structure while it was in transition, the deal included options for Simpson to eventually buy back up to 45 percent of the stock of the new company, at cost, over for a period of 10 years, and in time he exercised all his options.

As a condition of the deal, Simpson would move to Durham to continue in his role as the publication's editor. Wolff would effectively become the publisher. But the sale was only conditional, and it all hinged on one very important detail: Wolff's availability to secure a visa for Simpson that would allow him and his family to legally come to the United States.

After consulting with various legal officials locally, Wolff was given the impression that obtaining a temporary visa would be a much more difficult task than securing a long-term visa. When he trekked to Charlotte, some two hours from Durham, in late July with the purpose of talking to the Department of Naturalization and Immigration Service about the protocol for obtaining a visa, Wolff expected a long and drawn-out process. He was taken aback when immigration authorities sent him on his way home to Durham after little more than a half hour . . . with a visa in hand. Much to his surprise, Simpson's visa was processed expeditiously with a minimum of paperwork and almost no questions asked.

Effectively, the visa had a five-year life and Simpson, for immigration purposes, was classified as an inter-company transfer, at liberty to move from the new company's branch in Canada to its home base in Durham.

With that hurdle cleared, Wolff and Simpson finalized their deal to move *All-America Baseball News* to its adopted home in North

Carolina. While the deal was effective as of July 1, it was agreed that Simpson would continue to publish the product out of his garage in Canada, with all business-side activities moving to Durham immediately. In time, Simpson would move with his family, though most likely not before the first of the year.

The move had far-reaching implications for Simpson as it meant uprooting his family from their Canadian home, and relocating them some 2,500 miles. Simpson was not sure how his wife Jill might react to moving to North Carolina, and he was not about to break the news to her, not on Aug. 2, 1982, the day that Wolff let Simpson know that he obtained the visa. Jill was in hospital, in labor, in the process of delivering the couple's third child. The announcement of a pending move to the United States south would have to wait for another day.

Over the next six weeks, Wolff and Simpson began plotting a course of action for *All-America Baseball News* and it led them to Boston, where they attempted to strike a long-term business relationship with Howe News Bureau, the long-time baseball statistics service that was also under new ownership and in the process of making some of the same inroads on the game at the minor-league level that *All-America Baseball News* was making.

In Boston, or more specifically at the Wareham, Massachusetts, home of new Howe owner John Wylde, a historic development happened in the evolution of *All-America Baseball News* as the name of the publication was officially changed to *Baseball America.* Simpson, Wolff and Wylde were all in agreement that the original name was a little long and unwieldy, and possibly even reflected too much of a college-oriented theme. They tossed around various potential titles, and *Baseball America* quickly became the popular choice.

When Simpson relocated to Durham in January 1983, *Baseball America's* base had ramped up to about 6,000 subscribers, though it continued to be a struggle financially, even under new ownership. Wolff routinely had to tap into the coffers of the highly successful

Bulls, then about to begin their fourth year of operation, to make ends meet.

It was not long before *Baseball America,* now located across the street from Durham Athletic Park in a converted old restaurant that was also used as the Bulls souvenir store, gained more credibility in the industry and soon became its most-influential voice in the minor leagues. The more *Baseball America* grew, the more inroads it continued to make on its chief competition, *The Sporting News,* which continued to diversify into an all-sports product but was also becoming increasingly wary of the challenge being posed to its core product, baseball, by this young, ambitious upstart.

In its haste to counter the growing challenge posed by *Baseball America, The Sporting News* enacted various measures that ranged from threatening to fire correspondents if they also wrote for *Baseball America,* to rejecting ads and the purchasing of mailing lists aimed at building *Baseball America's* circulation. *The Sporting News* made various subtle attempts to inflict their considerable will on *Baseball America* with the intent of eliminating it as a competitor—to a point of even trying to acquire *Baseball America.*

As *Baseball America* grew by leaps and bounds, the more the staff grew, and soon the publication moved from its primitive location at Ballpark Corner, on Morris Street opposite Durham Athletic Park, to a new location in 1985 on Duke Street. While it initially occupied only the bottom floor of a two-story structure, it soon took over both floors as *Baseball America's* subscription base grew exponentially to a point that it had upwards of 75,000 subscribers in the early-1990s, and a readership of more than 250,000.

Simpson continued to serve the paper in his role as editor, though the long-term future of his position came into question in 1987 when the temporary visa that enabled him to move to North Carolina in 1982 to oversee the continued growth of *Baseball America* was about to expire. Finally, with his options almost exhausted, and his case in the hands of a New York immigration firm, Simpson's application for permanent residency was approved in early 1990, and within months he had the green card in hand that would enable him and his family to live lawfully in the U.S. and continue in his role of editor of *Baseball America.*

■

Wolff, meanwhile, became less involved with the day-to-day affairs of *Baseball America* through the years, and turned most of the publishing functions over to Dave Chase, his right-hand man. Once Wolff sold the Bulls in 1990 to Raleigh businessman Jim Goodmon for $4 million, he subsequently focused much of his attention on the Raleigh IceCaps, his new East Coast Hockey League team that would be the forerunner to a full-blown National Hockey League team arriving in the Triangle in the form of the transplanted Hartford Whalers, and to his blossoming role as the godfather of independent baseball in the form of the revamped Northern League.

Believing he had taken *Baseball America* as far as he was capable of taking it, especially with on-line publishing becoming critical to the future of the newspaper industry, Wolff sold the publication in 2000 to an Atlanta-based internet financial-services company. The sales price: $2.1 million. Simpson also agreed to cash out his remaining interest in the paper, though consented to stay on in his existing role as *Baseball America's* editor in chief.

Over the next few years, Simpson was increasingly at odds with the paper's new management group and the direction it was taking with a product he created. Believing he, too, had run his course with the publication, he resigned in 2006, six days shy of the 25th anniversary of the first issue, and immediately went to work for Perfect Game USA, an Iowa-based company he had cultivated a relationship with as a corporate partner of *Baseball America.*

Perfect Game was quickly gaining a foothold in the game as a baseball event company, especially as it pertained to the showcasing and scouting of the nation's top high-school baseball talent. It only continued to thrive over the next decade—much as *Baseball America* did, too, under the direction of Will Lingo and John Manuel, who jointly succeeded Simpson in his role as editor. Lingo eventually became *Baseball America's* publisher.

This Is Durham!

Miles Wolff, Allan Simpson and I met for lunch in the winter of 2013 at the Tobacco Road Sports Café, which sits high above the left field wall at Durham Bulls Athletic Park, just across the railroad tracks from downtown Durham. From our perch, we peered out to see renovations being undertaken at one of the finest Triple-A minor-league ballparks in the country. The porch of the restaurant provided a spectacular view of a gorgeous stadium.

Mostly what the three of us could see that day was just how far the Durham Bulls, minor-league baseball and the City of Durham had progressed during our adult lives.

Thirty years earlier, Wolff, Simpson and I held a similar meeting, about a mile away, across West Corporation Street from the old Durham Athletic Park in a cramped one-room building that had served as a souvenir shop for the Durham Bulls and soon would be the national headquarters of a fledgling baseball publication just renamed *Baseball America*. The view that day was of a hastily hung curtain, drawn to separate the publication's offices from the souvenir shop. The curtain might as well have been a set of blindfolds because none of the three of us could possibly foresee what was to come.

At the time, Wolff was the principal owner and president of the four-year-old Bulls, as well as principal owner and publisher of *Baseball America*. Simpson, who founded *Baseball America*, had just recently moved to Durham to serve as the publication's editor after selling a majority interest in *Baseball America* to Wolff several months earlier. I was there, both in my role as the baseball beat writer for the Durham Morning Herald and as a contributing editor for *Baseball America*.

All three of us knew about Durham, a city few would argue was — at the time — considered the armpit of the Research Triangle. There was little pride in the city of Durham. The tobacco industry was dying a slow death. Jobs were difficult to find. Crime had skyrocketed. The local public schools had fallen behind those of their neighbors in Raleigh and Chapel Hill. Raleigh had the state capitol and North Carolina State University. Chapel Hill had the ambience of Franklin Street and the University of North Carolina. The Research Triangle Park, an ecosystem for high-tech innovation and technology located between the three communities, was just emerging on the national scene, but the majority of its employees were establishing roots either in Raleigh and its suburbs or in Chapel Hill.

Durham had Duke University, but the relationship between the two was icy at best. The prestigious university operated on a virtual island within the city limits. Any interaction between the two was strictly because geography dictated it. Duke certainly did not boast publicly about being located within a city considered downtrodden in comparison to its neighbors.

Then the Durham Bulls came to town. Suddenly, Durham had something it could embrace. Even better, Raleigh did not have professional baseball. Nor did Chapel Hill.

"Durham was still kind of the weaker link in the Research Triangle, you might say," said Jim Wise, a reporter for 34 years at the *Durham Herald-Sun* and later the *News and Observer* of Raleigh, and a Durham historian. "That's an image that a lot of people in Durham had. There were various attempts at building up a better image, and making Durham feel better about itself and conveying a more positive image, but it wasn't particularly effective.

"When the Bulls returned, I think it served as a real sort of unifying element in the city. The response, as I recall, was this real burst of enthusiasm that Durham had something to rally around and get interested in. It got people out at a time when going out in the evening in Durham just wasn't done. So, it was sort of a meeting point and a rallying point.

"It gave the city a sudden shot of adrenaline and a shot of pride."

Right out of the gate in 1980, the Bulls established themselves as one of the top franchises in minor-league baseball. That proved to be true over the next seven seasons when annual attendance at Durham Athletic Park ranged from 142,370 in 1983 to 217,012 in 1987.

Then came the movie *"Bull Durham,"* and that changed the dynamics of the franchise forever. No longer was the old ballpark quaint and cute. It was undersized and bursting at the seams. While it once was nice to walk a few blocks to the ballpark, now fans were being asked to park their cars a half-mile or farther away. Squeezing 12 fans into a bleacher bench suited for 10 was no one's idea of an enjoyable night at the ballpark.

"There are so many times this stadium isn't able to serve the fans," Wolff said late in the 1988 season. "When you can't find a seat, the idea of a new stadium sounds pretty good."

Home attendance that season — the same summer as the release of the movie — soared to a Class A-record 271,650, an average of 4,116 fans in the 5,000-seat park. The following season attendance was 272,202, then an unthinkable 300,499 in 1990.

Adhering to the belief that the old ballpark was part of the appeal for fans flocking to see the Bulls, Wolff first conducted a feasibility study with the idea of expanding Durham Athletic Park. At the same time, Durham began to consider other downtown sites — University Ford and Briggs Avenue — for possible construction of a new stadium.

Renovation of Durham Athletic Park fell to the bottom of any list of proposals because of poor access, failing infrastructure, subpar roadway systems, outdated utilities, parking concerns and visibility in a neighborhood setting. As much as everyone loved the old ballpark, there was no feasible way for it to meet the demands of its growing fan base.

Plus, remaining at Durham Athletic Park sealed Durham's fate as forever being a Class A or Double-A franchise. Wolff had bigger ideas.

"With the right stadium and parking, I think we could draw half a million in this market," Wolff said. "If Triple-A ever does come to the market, it'd be a dynamite franchise."

Pushing the issue of a new stadium for Durham was the approval by Raleigh voters in 1988 of a $3.5 million bond issue for a new stadium on North Carolina State University land near its football stadium. Recognizing that many Bulls fans made the 20-mile drive from Raleigh to Durham, Wolff obviously did not want the competition of another team.

Under National Association of Professional Baseball League rules, Wolff held territorial rights to any franchise located within 10 miles of Durham. The outer city limits of Raleigh and Durham were 9.5 miles apart at the time. An initial proposal was made to build the stadium at the state fairgrounds adjacent to N.C. State's Carter-Finley football stadium, land that was not within any incorporated city and, thus, not covered by the territorial rights rules.

Wolff went to work at the 1988 Baseball Winter Meetings and got approval from NAPBL leaders to amend and extend the territorial limits restriction to 35 miles from home plate to home plate.

Steve Bryant, an advertising executive, had purchased the Columbus (Georgia) Astros franchise in the Double-A Southern League during the 1989 season with a design on moving it to Raleigh. When the plan to build a stadium next to Carter-Finley Stadium was spurned by Wolff's territorial rights, Bryant instead built a stadium 12 miles east of Raleigh — and 36 miles away from Durham Athletic Park's home plate — outside the tiny town of Zebulon and re-located the Columbus franchise there for the 1991 season as the Carolina Mudcats.

Durham city officials, meanwhile, had begun to recognize the value of the Bulls franchise to the city. But financing for a public-private venture was an iffy proposition for a cash-strapped city like Durham.

"The city of Durham is not as wealthy as some of our neighboring municipalities," said Durham Mayor Wib Gulley. "We've got to plan a little harder and be a little more financially conscientious than others might have to be."

The city decided to put a vote to the public about building a new ballpark on the University Ford site in the form of an $11.3 million Durham County bond referendum. It was a low-turnout election in March of 1991, and most voters were from outside the Durham city limits. The referendum had no chance to pass. It failed not because of a lack of interest in the Bulls, but rather because Durham's citizens saw such an entertainment investment as frivolous at a time when the more pressing issues were education and public transportation.

"The sucking sound out of downtown was accelerated," said Bill Kalkhof, then the president of Downtown Durham Inc.

Frustrated that the Durham public could not see the economic value of such an investment, Wolff threw up his hands in defeat. One week after the referendum failed, Wolff sold the team to Jim Goodmon, the owner of Raleigh-based Capitol Broadcasting Company.

Goodmon's initial plan was to move the team to the Research Triangle Park, to a location equal distance from Durham, Raleigh and Chapel Hill, and get several municipalities there to build a stadium that could serve Raleigh as well as Durham.

Sensing that Durham could lose the Bulls, a group of business and political leaders formed Downtown Durham Inc., to begin figuring out a way to revitalize and develop the city's central core.

Kalkhof was hired to direct the group.

"The ballpark was one of the first projects I delved into," Kalkhof said. "For me, it was never about just the ballpark. We were envisioning Camden Yards."

Kalkhof began lobbying then-mayor Harry Rodenhizer and city council member Chuck Grubb to help keep the most prominent aspect of Durham's city pride: the Bulls. Goodmon was on board, if the city would build a new stadium.

City leaders visited Baltimore to see what Camden Yards, the home of the Orioles, had done for that city's downtown revitalization. They liked what they saw, but still ran into public opposition to funding for a stadium in Durham.

Downtown Durham Inc. then came up with a plan to use certificates of participation as a means to fund the new stadium. Certificates of participation allow a city to borrow money and pay it back through taxes. While they are more costly than bonds, it was a more attractive option than going back to the voters to approve bonds for a stadium.

"There was an uproar in the community about it, obviously," Kalkhof said. "What the hell are you doing? Guys like me were out on the stump saying it's not just about the ballpark, it's about keeping the Bulls. It's going to be a cornerstone or an anchor for downtown revitalization.

"Of course, 90 percent of the community thought we were nuts. Our selling point was that it was never just about the ballpark. It's what that public investment would be as a catalyst going forward. I can't say we overly convinced a lot of the public at the time, but we convinced people who needed to be convinced."

That was, in particular, the 13 members of city council who took a huge political risk and approved $16 million in May of 1992 to fund construction of a new baseball stadium. The cost eventually climbed to $18.5 million and was designed by Populous (formerly HOK), which also designed Camden Yards and carried the same "old-style" ballpark to Durham.

The 7,000-seat Durham Bulls Athletic Park opened for the 1995 season and immediately became the showcase of minor-league ballparks with a brick façade, 32-foot high green monster wall in left field, plush clubhouses, wide seats and fan amenities that matched any major-league ballpark.

Attendance jumped from 254,266 the previous season at Durham Athletic Park to 390,486 in 1995 at the new ballpark. Two years later, it was apparent that the Bulls had outgrown the Class A Carolina League, which came in perfect sync with major-league expansion. When Tampa Bay joined the American League as an expansion club for the 1998 season, it hooked up with Durham as its Triple-A International League affiliate.

That effectively ended an 18-year affiliation the Bulls had with the Atlanta Braves, their parent club throughout the duration of their time in both Durham and the Carolina League. While Goodmon continued to own and operate the old Bulls franchise, it initially relocated to Danville, Virginia, before moving to Myrtle Beach, South Carolina.

To meet Triple-A standards, Durham Bulls Athletic Park was expanded to 10,000 seats. The larger stadium and the jump in level of play also meant another leap in attendance for the Bulls, who drew 381,589 fans the previous season in the Carolina League and 477,709 in their first season in the International League. Every season since, the Bulls have averaged more than 500,000 fans including a franchise-record 547,156 in 2016.

"The Durham Bulls today are clearly one of our flagship franchises," said Pat O'Conner, president of Minor League Baseball, in early 2016. "If you're talking about game production, yes, they are on a short list. If you're talking about game operation, yes, they're on a short list. Physical plant? Yes. Ownership? Yes. Management? Yes.

"The embodiment of what minor-league baseball should be as far as engrained and immersed and meshed into the city? Yes. On any metric, the Durham Bulls are on a short list, absolutely."

The Bulls essentially led minor-league baseball's resurgence into again being part of the fabric of American society. "*The Encyclopedia of Minor League Baseball*" termed 1946-51 as "The Golden Age" of the minors and 1992 to today as "The Boom Years." As they did during that first period, baseball fans began to recognize minor-league baseball as being family affordable entertainment.

In 1991, minimum standards for minor-league ballparks were established and that touched off the biggest building boom in history. Cities across the country began constructing new stadiums to house their minor-league clubs. From 2000 to 2015, minor-league baseball clubs opened 61 new ballparks.

As a result, attendance soared. A record 42,812,812 fans attended minor-league games during the 2007 season. A year later, that record reached 43,263,740, and has remained at the same level with 41,377,202 attending games in 2016, marking the 11th consecutive season of surpassing 41 million fans.

By 2016, there were 176 teams in 15 leagues, and eight of those teams set single-season franchise attendance records.

Along the way, Durham clearly has been the leader in minor-league baseball's resurgence.

"What was accomplished in Durham with the Bulls in the old ballpark, through the movie, and then into the transition to the new ballpark and elevated status in the game as far as classification, it's clearly one of the better stories that we are able to tell," O'Conner said. "We can tell a lot of stories (in the minor leagues), but it is one of the better success stories from the standpoint of letting creativity come to the fore."

With that creativity working at the ballpark from the beginning in 1995, Durham city officials next began to explore developing the area surrounding Durham Bulls Athletic Park and in downtown Durham. The American Tobacco campus, across Blackwell Street from the ballpark, was the next order of business. Nearly all the buildings were vacant and in severe disrepair. A few developers, when shown the property, were not the least bit interested. One developer looked around, noticed that the calendars on the walls were still turned to August of 1987, and sneered. The primary use of the property was for SWAT training by the Durham police department.

Goodmon again stepped in.

"As a company and a family we have a fundamental belief that our company cannot be successful unless the community around us is successful," said Michael Goodmon, Jim Goodmon's son and the vice-president of Capitol Broadcasting.

In addition to being on the hook for the $3 million to expand the stadium in 1998, the elder Goodmon and his company first built in 2001 the Diamond View office building beyond the right field wall at the ballpark. To secure financing for the building, Capitol Broadcasting worked a handshake deal with Duke University, Compuware and GlaxoSmithKline, a pharmaceutical company, to lease 300,000 square feet of space. While not necessarily a sound financial move, all parties agreed it was in everyone's best interest for downtown Durham's revitalization. Today, several office buildings rim the outfield walls at Durham Bulls Athletic Park.

In 2004, Capitol Broadcasting purchased the American Tobacco warehouses. Soon, restaurants began to move in as tenants. Mostly, though, the buildings became office rental property.

Recognizing that a half-million baseball fans were coming to the ballpark every spring and summer, companies took to the idea of locating their offices nearby. The McKinney+Silver advertising agency and the investment firm InterSouth, among others, rented space.

The architectural details of the 19th century industrial complex includes such landmarks as a water tower, a smokestack and overhead conveyors and walkways retained from the American Tobacco plant. An amphitheater and river were added to the courtyard area, a YMCA fitness center soon landed in the complex as well as biking and jogging trails.

"It made Durham go from the lowest rents and the highest vacancy in the Triangle, to the submarket with the highest rents and lowest vacancy in the Triangle in the span of less than 10 years," said Scott Selig, Duke University's associate vice-president for capital assets and real estate.

Duke went from renting 70,000 square feet of office space in downtown Durham in 2004 to renting one million square feet by 2016. The university employed 150 people downtown in 2004 and 2,600 11 years later. Duke did it because it was important to the university to be a vital cog of a vibrant community.

"It's absolutely critical," Selig said. "We are competing with Palo Alto (California) and Boston (Massachusetts) and cities like those for the best faculty, staff and students in the world. It doesn't matter that we can give them similar facilities on campus. It matters what they can do afterwards and on weekends.

"If they can have a higher quality of life and yet have the same educational facilities, we tend to now win the competition for the best and brightest faculty, staff and students. Plus, we live here. We want that interesting thing going on, on more than just the campus."

A turning point for Duke University's melding more into the fabric of the Durham community occurred in 1995 when Tallman Trask was hired as the school's executive president, a position he previously held at the University of Washington. At Washington, Trask cut his teeth on revitalization projects with satellite campuses in historic districts in both Seattle and Tacoma.

"When he came here, it didn't take him more than 20 seconds to figure out the power Duke had to not only build new buildings but to move their human resources around," said Reyn Bowman, past president of the Durham Convention and Visitors Bureau, of Trask. "It's his genius."

Trask said he had watched other universities which ended up living in intolerable urban places, and it proved to be of little benefit to those schools. He also recognized that, unlike cities such as Baltimore and Chicago, Durham's size made such revitalization and integration of Duke much more manageable.

"Duke didn't want to sit next to an abandoned downtown," Trask said. "What we finally decided was we are going to need to build some office space," Trask said. "It just seemed to me that going downtown served multiple purposes where building another office building at Duke didn't help anybody. So we took the money we would have spent building office buildings on campus and basically invested in for-profit real estate deals in downtown Durham."

Duke University played another role in moving Durham away from its long-held image of being a "tobacco town" to one that now boasts of being the "City of Medicine." The first season (1980) of pro baseball's return to Durham also marked the opening of a $94.5 million, 616-bed Duke Hospital north of the school's original hospital, bringing the number of patient beds to 1,000. Fourteen years later, the Duke University Medical Center embarked on the busiest period of new construction in decades, resulting in the Levine Science Research Center, Medical Sciences Research Building, a renovation of the Duke Clinic, additions to the Morris Building for cancer care and research, a new Children's Health Center, a new ambulatory care building and new parking garages.

By the turn of the century, Duke was gaining recognition as one of the top medical centers in the country. In turn, a greater light was shone on the city in which it resides.

Duke also brought greater recognition to Durham with the enormous success of its men's basketball program. The unknown coach, Mike Krzyzewski, who was hired a few months before the Bulls opened play in 1980, became the winningest college basketball coach in history while leading Duke to national championships in 1991, 1992, 2001, 2010 and 2015.

Over the years, Krzyzewski helped enhance Durham's profile nationally by boasting that he and his family loved calling the city home.

And why not? Durham now has as much or more to offer than its neighboring cities in the Research Triangle. The Durham Performing Arts Center opened in 2008 near Durham Bulls Athletic Park as the largest such facility in either North Carolina or South Carolina at a cost of $48 million. The center hosts more than 200 performances a year, and is one of the largest grossing venues on the Broadway theatre circuit.

While the American Tobacco campus and ballpark sparked a rebirth of downtown Durham, it soon became just one of seven districts in the central part of the city. Nearly 50 shopping locations, more than 40 restaurants and multiple entertainment venues give Durham residents and visitors a wide variety of daily options.

"The downtown stadium has kicked off so much for downtown Durham to where we now have national magazines writing about our entrepreneurial culture, our start-up culture, the 'foodiest' town in the southeast, the most tolerant community," Michael Goodmon said. "That started with the ballpark."

It used to be to reach Durham Athletic Park when arriving in town from the south side of downtown, a visitor would travel along Duke Street, essentially bypassing the central part of the city. Today, it is worth leaving the Durham Freeway and driving along Blackwell Street past Durham Bulls Athletic Park, the American Tobacco complex and the Durham Performing Arts Center, over the railroad tracks and into the City Center district downtown.

Within the City Center a visitor can pass by the old CCB Building, which once housed mostly empty office space atop a bank and now is home to the five-star 21C Museum Hotel, complete with an art gallery. Where once there were an inordinate number of wig shops, there now are numerous fine-dining choices. A glimpse inside the newly renovated Carolina Theatre, where the premiere of "Bull Durham" was staged, is worthwhile, and you can't help but notice the Duke Clinical Research Institute tower that hovers over downtown.

Then it is on to the Central Park District, which surrounds three sides of Durham Athletic Park and includes a farmer's market, YMCA and skate park. The area was featured in a 2014 article in the *New York Times*, which described it as a previously neglected part of town. "Now there's live music, top-notch barbecue, fair trade coffee, and even valet parking on a block that five years ago was deserted after dark," the newspaper wrote.

Trask is more succinct in his assessment of Durham's downtown revitalization.

"Twenty years ago, you go downtown and you might see 10 people, and they were asking you for money," Trask said. "Today, you go downtown and you can't find a place to park."

Meanwhile, the Research Triangle Area has become a mecca of baseball. Between the Triple-A International League Bulls in Durham, the Carolina Mudcats in the Class A Carolina League in Zebulon and the Rookie Appalachian League Royals in Burlington, nearly every level of the minor leagues is represented in the area. Also, USA Baseball, the national governing body of the sport, is headquartered at Durham Bulls Athletic Park. Its National Training Complex is located in nearby Cary.

Collegiate baseball also has grown in the area. The North Carolina Tar Heels reached in the College World Series six times from 2006 to 2013, the North Carolina State Wolfpack appeared in the 2013 College World Series, and Duke produced a first-round draft pick — right-handed pitcher Marcus Stroman by the Toronto Blue Jays — in 2012, and reached the NCAA tournament in 2016 for the first time in 55 years.

Also, North Carolina Central, a historically black college in Durham, has played NCAA Division I baseball since 2007. The Eagles now play their home games at Durham Athletic Park, which has become a reclamation project since the Bulls moved to Durham Bulls Athletic Park for the 1995 season.

The old ballpark was initially used by the Durham Dragons of the now-defunct Women's Professional Softball League and, for a time, the Durham collegiate summer club in the Coastal Plain League. It also hosted the annual Bull Durham Blues Festival.

In 2008, the City of Durham allocated $4 million — the figure eventually increased by another million — for the ballpark's renovation. The ballpark reopened in August of 2009 with a new playing surface and spanking new clubhouses. The renovations kept some of the original flavor of the park with the main grandstands intact and the iconic turret ticket tower outside the park. In many ways, the park is in much greater condition than in any time the Bulls played games there.

The Bulls played single regular-season games at Durham Athletic Park in May of 2010 and 2011.

The ballpark still stands as a monument to one glorious season of Carolina League baseball in 1980, and as a testament to just how far professional baseball and the city of Durham have advanced ever since.

Stuart Coman was born and raised in Durham. As a teenager he and his buddies headed every summer to Myrtle Beach, South Carolina, for fun and frolicking, and to chase girls. Coman remembers well that, when asked by a girl, he and his friends would either lie and say their hometown was "Raleigh" or mumble "Durham" under their breath.

In May of 2015 I had a chance to catch up again with Coman during the Atlantic Coast Conference baseball tournament that was held at Durham Bulls Athletic Park, which had undergone another $9 million in renovations the previous year.

The offices of Coman Publishing are now located across from the ballpark in the American Tobacco complex. Coman gave me a tour of the complex one afternoon during a rain delay at the tournament. At each stop, Coman paused, looked around and marveled at what he saw.

"Can you believe this?" he repeated several times. "This is Durham!"

Where Have You Gone Joe Cowley?

The greatest joy derived in writing about the 1980 Durham Bulls came in my attempts to contact every player and coach associated with the team. Because my son, Luke, is much more adept at using the Internet to locate people, he played a huge role in tracking down as many players as possible.

In the end, there were only a few I could not find. They included Juan Alduey, Joe Cowley, Andres Forbes, Craig Jones, Johnny Lee, Mark Lucas, Alvin Moore, Al Pratt and Miguel Sosa.

Rick Behenna is the only player who is deceased.

Of those I contacted and interviewed, nearly every one went through a withdrawal period from baseball. For some, the transition into life without the game they all loved was more difficult than for others. Pitcher Lance Gore probably summed it up best when I spoke to him by phone one afternoon in late 2015.

"It's tough," Gore began. "You've got to remember, every one of us grew up thinking we were going to be a big-league ballplayer. That was our dream. It's a tough deal to the point where you have reality staring you in the face. I remember, I was kind of upset about it. It makes it hard for people to be that competitive, and have that dream and then not realize it. It's tough. I understand it.

"It was a great time of our lives, not only ours but our families and our friends who were behind us. When your dream doesn't come true, it's tough. It's tough. You have to find another dream, and a lot of people just can't let go, I don't think. It's really difficult, but you just have to be thankful for your life and the blessings you're given and keep plugging away."

JUAN ALDUEY: Throughout his half-season stay in Durham, Alduey spoke little English. Potential interviews with the tall, slender right-hander were off limits and he was not interested in talking through the club's unofficial interpreter, second baseman Andres Forbes.

Alduey had a live arm and began the season with much promise. He had outstanding control, but his fastball had little life and Class A hitters finally began to catch up with it. By mid-July he was caught in a numbers crunch and was released by the Atlanta Braves organization. In 14 games with the Bulls, he went 4-5 with a 5.05 earned-run average.

After Alduey got the news of his release from manager Al Gallagher, he walked behind the grandstand toward the front entrance where groundskeeper Bill Miller was waiting to transport him by car to the airport and ultimately to his homeland in the Dominican Republic.

I happened to cross Alduey on his way out of the park. He stopped, paused, and in near-perfect English cursed me down.

During a phone conversation with Ike Pettaway late in 2015, he swore that Alduey was living nearby in West Palm Beach, Florida, but I could not confirm that.

JOSE ALVAREZ: By the end of the 1980 season Alvarez had proven that, when healthy, he possessed a major-league arm. The right-hander's stay in Durham was brief—two complete-game starts in mid-July—and he concluded the season in Savannah of the Double-A Southern League. He began the 1981 season in Richmond, the Braves Triple-A affiliate, and made his major-league debut as a late-season call up, throwing two perfect innings of relief on Oct. 1.

Alvarez appeared in seven games for the Braves in 1982, then bounced around the minor leagues for the next six seasons. He pitched in the Houston, Montreal and Kansas City organizations. In 1985, Alvarez was pitching for Memphis in the Royals' organization, when his wife, Michelle, sang the national anthem before a July 4 game. Immediately after the game, the Royals released Alvarez.

The following season Alvarez got another chance with the Braves and finally landed a full-time gig in Atlanta's bullpen for the 1988 and 1989 seasons. When he was called to the big leagues in '88, he checked in with an old friend from the minor-leagues, Brett Butler, who by then was playing for the San Francisco Giants. Butler's home was in Atlanta, and he allowed Alvarez and his wife to live in the house over two summers.

Alvarez has three children and lives in Greenville, South Carolina, where he serves as a chaplain—through the Fellowship of Christian

Athletes—to the players, wives and caddies on the PGA's Web.com Tour.

RICK BEHENNA: Maturity, or lack thereof, was an issue for Behenna as a pitcher in Durham during the 1980 season, when he went 8-13 with a 4.15 ERA. So, he returned to the Bulls for the 1981 season and grew up. He won 13 games and was on his way to establishing himself as a starting pitcher for the Braves. He made the big club out of spring training in 1983 and debuted on April 12 by pitching five shutout innings to gain the win against the Cincinnati Reds.

That Behenna reached the major leagues was no surprise to his former Durham teammates. They were, however, stunned that Behenna singled in his first two plate appearances against Reds pitcher Mario Soto. At every step of the way in the Braves' minor-league system, Behenna was generally considered the worst hitting pitcher on the staff.

Behenna appeared in 14 games for Atlanta during the 1983 season, then on Aug. 23 was part of what is roundly considered the worst trade in the history of the franchise. The Braves sent Behenna, along with Butler and infielder Brook Jacoby to the Cleveland Indians for veteran pitcher Len Barker. Behenna pitched parts of three seasons in Cleveland, while Butler and Jacoby became outstanding players. Barker went 9-17 over the next two seasons for the Braves.

Behenna's career ended following the 1985 season and, after first returning to Durham to raise a family, later settled outside Atlanta where he served as the pitching coach at East Coweta High School. He also owned the Newnan Braves collegiate summer team in the Great South Baseball League, but discontinued its operation when he began to battle Stage Four colon cancer in 2010.

Behenna died of cancer on Jan. 31, 2012. He was 51.

PETE BOCK: Bock was the original general manager of the Bulls and remained in the position for the 1981 season, then served in the same capacity for the Hawaii franchise in the Triple-A Pacific Coast League for the next five seasons. He returned to Durham to partner with Bulls owner Miles Wolff in a consulting business that catered to minor-league franchises, then was GM of the Raleigh IceCaps East Coast Hockey League hockey team from 1991 to 1996. The success of the team was instrumental in the Research Triangle area landing a National Hockey League franchise, the Carolina Hurricanes, two years later.

When the IceCaps were sold, Bock was a driving force in founding the Coastal Plain League, a summer collegiate wood-bat league with teams in North Carolina, South Carolina and Virginia. He served as the league's president until 2015 when he left to own and operate the expansion Holly Springs franchise, located just outside of Raleigh.

On Feb. 15, 2015, just before the franchise's inaugural season, Bock slipped on a patch of ice outside of his home and broke both his neck and back. He suffered paralysis from the waist down, although a year later he had movement in his left leg and toes on both feet. His wife, Cindy, broke her hip slipping on the same patch of ice.

Bock, who uses a wheelchair, continues to work several days a week with the Holly Springs franchise.

GLEN BOCKHORN: Bockhorn's baseball career was the classic case of a player who had batting skills that could have taken him to the big leagues, but the Braves could never find a position for him. Unfortu-

nately, baseball organizations do not generally develop designated hitters.

During the 1980 season for the Bulls, Bockhorn got tryouts at first base, second base, third base and the outfield while hitting 15 home runs, which tied him for the club lead. He even caught one game, and that experiment extended to the 1982 and 1983 seasons in Durham and Savannah. He looked as if he might make his way through the system and reach Atlanta when he batted .287 in 1983 with 20 home runs and 80 runs batted in for Savannah. But not having a defined position eventually led to the end of his career following the 1986 season with Buffalo, a Triple-A affiliate of the Chicago White Sox where he was again a teammate of ex-Bull Tommy Thompson.

Bockhorn returned to his hometown of Round Rock, Texas, where he embarked on a career in sales for Veritiv Corporation, a leading North American business-to-business distributor of print, publishing, packaging, facility and logistics solutions. He and his wife were married in 1981 and have two children.

Bockhorn continued to correspond periodically over the years with Frankie Parrott, the blind longtime Bulls fan who died at age 65 in May of 2014.

BRETT BUTLER: Of all the players on the Bulls roster in 1980, Butler, far and away, had the most outstanding major-league career, one that included playing for five teams over 17 seasons. After hitting .366 and stealing 36 bases in 66 games for the Bulls, he played for the

Braves from 1981-83. His best season was 1991 when he was an all-star with the Los Angeles Dodgers. He batted .296 that season with 38 stolen bases and led the National League in games played (161), runs scored (112) and walks (108). He finished seventh in voting for the National League Most Valuable Player award. He retired following the 1997 season with a .290 career batting average and 2,375 hits over 2,213 games.

Butler was diagnosed in May of 1996 with throat cancer. Despite being told by most people he came in contact with that he would never play baseball again, he returned to the Dodgers' lineup in September. Butler began chewing tobacco and dipping while playing in the minor leagues.

"I actually quit because I didn't want to get throat cancer," Butler said. "Fifteen years later, I got throat cancer. Could it have been a contributing factor? Maybe. When I go to share my story about that, I say, 'Yes, it could have, or it wouldn't have happened.' "

After retiring, Butler remained in the game as a coach and manager, mostly in the minor leagues with the Arizona Diamondbacks organization. In 2014 and 2015, he was a coach for the Miami Marlins.

Throughout his playing and coaching career, he retained a friendship with retired Durham police officer Ray Evans. One night prior to a Bulls game during the 1980 season, Evans tossed Butler a pack of Levi Garrett chewing tobacco. Butler took his bubblegum, wrapped it in chewing tobacco, stuck it back in his mouth, and produced a couple of hits that night. A ritual was established with Evans tossing Butler another pack of chewing tobacco before every home game.

"It's a wonderful memory of a relationship between a player and a fan that could last our lifetimes," Butler said.

ARCILIO CASTAIGNE: There was much suspicion during the three weeks that Castaigne, better known as R.C., wore a Bulls uniform during the 1980 season that he was considerably older than the 23 years of age listed by the Braves. Fudging on ages was commonplace in professional baseball then, particularly among players who were born outside the United States.

Turns out, the suspicions about Castaigne were warranted. He actually was born in 1955 — not 1957 — in Holguin, Cuba, making him 25 when he pitched for the Bulls.

"My response always was, 'Hey, I don't get people out with my birth certificate,' " said Castaigne, who was reared in Dallas, Texas. Castaigne said he still is not certain how his age got changed, but it apparently happened shortly after he attended Texas Wesleyan, his fourth Texas college in four years, and before he was drafted in the 30th round by the Braves in 1979.

Castaigne picked up two saves in three games for the Bulls before being demoted to Anderson of the Class A South Atlantic League for the remainder of the 1980 season. He then pitched for three seasons in the Dominican Republic before retiring from the game. For the last 32 years, he has worked for the City of Dallas and kept his hand in baseball by coaching at Lakehill Prep School in Dallas. He has two sons.

DOM CHITI: The left-handed throwing Chiti, a second-round pick of the Braves in 1976, never was healthy during his 1980 season in Durham and went 1-1 with a 2.90 ERA in 25 appearances. In his previous four seasons in the Braves system, Chiti was a starting pitcher with much promise. But an arm injury curtailed his career and he was finished playing following the 1981 season.

Chiti, the son of former major league manager Harry Chiti, subsequently became a baseball lifer. He spent nine seasons, beginning in 1982, in the Baltimore Orioles organization primarily as a coach, then another 12 seasons with the Indians organization as a roving instructor, advance scout and as the major-league club's bullpen coach. In five seasons with the Texas Rangers, Chiti was the director of player personnel and later big-league bullpen coach. Five more seasons with the Braves saw Chiti serve as a scout and special assistant to the general manager.

Chiti returned to the Orioles in 2014 where he served as their bullpen coach through the 2016 season. He returned to the Braves for the 2017 season as the team's director of pitching. He and his wife have two children and three step-children.

RICK COATNEY: Coatney compiled a 9-2 record with a 4.60 ERA for the 1980 Bulls, and although he would pitch another five seasons in the minor leagues, that season would be the apex of his career. He pitched for the Bulls again in 1981 and 1982, and reached Savannah in the Braves organization. He also pitched at the Double-A level in the Rangers organization, but a series of injuries chased him from the game following the 1985 season.

Coatney admittedly struggled with life after baseball. He was married all three seasons in Durham, and later divorced. He settled back in his home state of Arkansas and married his current wife, Arline, in 1994. Between the two marriages, Coatney has four children.

He finally found a substitute for baseball in golf and has won numerous amateur tournaments over the years. He has failed in attempts to qualify for the U.S. Open and the U.S. Senior Open, but continues to play golf often. For the past 12 years he has worked for WeatherBarr Windows and Doors in Fort Smith, Arkansas.

JOE COWLEY: Even while rehabbing an arm injury, Cowley was far too advanced for the Class A Carolina League during his 10 games for the 1980 Bulls. He posted a 6-0 record with a 2.81 ERA to prove his point. By the 1982 season, Cowley was pitching for the Braves in the start of a five-year major-league career with the Braves, New York Yankees, White Sox and Philadelphia Phillies.

Over 95 big-league games, Cowley registered a 33-25 record with a 4.20 ERA. During the 1984 and 1985 seasons as a starting pitcher for the Yankees, Cowley compiled a sterling 21-8 record with a 3.81 ERA.

On Sept. 19, 1986, Cowley threw a no-hitter for the White Sox against the California Angels. He walked seven and struck out eight in the 7-1 victory. The Angels scored their run in the sixth inning when Cowley issued walks to the first three batters and allowed a sacrifice fly. Cowley remains the only pitcher in major-league history to never win another game after throwing a no-hitter.

Cowley is believed to be living in Lexington, Kentucky, but repeated attempts to reach him were unsuccessful.

LARRY EDWARDS: Edwards pitched for three seasons in the Milwaukee Brewers organization, before joining the Bulls in 1980. In 15 games, he went 5-2 with a 4.15 ERA. Following the 1980 season, Edwards was traded to the White Sox for catcher Jeff Vuksan, who would play 37 games for the '81 Bulls as a reserve catcher. Edwards eventually reached Triple-A in the White Sox organization in his last year of professional baseball, 1982.

He injured his arm playing winter ball and moved to Iowa with his wife. When they divorced, Edwards returned to his hometown of

Cumberland, Md., where he has worked the past 21 years as an assistant manager for Frito-Lay.

During a phone conversation in October of 2015, Edwards revealed that he was getting married the next day to his longtime friend, Joanie.

ANDRES FORBES: The 1980 season was the end of the line for Forbes in professional baseball, his .243 batting average with one home run for the Bulls not enough to keep him in the game.

Gallagher always had heard that Forbes landed a job with the United Nations, perhaps because he was so skilled at speaking both English and Spanish. In all likelihood, though, Forbes returned to his native Dominican Republic where he is certain to be just as nice a guy today as he was with the Bulls.

AL GALLAGHER: Gallagher took many phone calls from me throughout 2015 and 2016 from his home in Fresno, California. He turned 70 years old in October of 2015 and suffered through a mild stroke. Yet he carried an enthusiasm for the subject matter through each conversation that told me the 1980 Durham Bulls

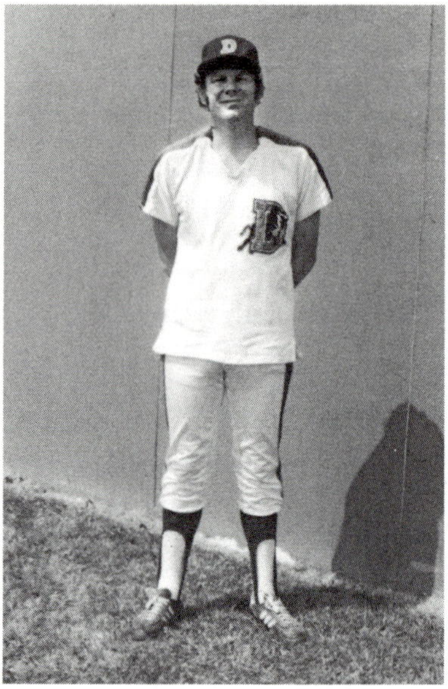

still carried a special place in his heart.

"I've got memories of a fantastic team," Gallagher told me one evening. "I never had, nor will I ever have, a bunch of kids that I liked more than that team. I had so many guys that played the game the way I liked to play it: balls out, let's go get 'em."

Then, in a conversation at a later date, he added: "I have fond memories of my boys. That was my favorite team, by far, because we had characters. I love characters because I'm a character."

Dirty Al was that, and his propensity to sometimes make the game more about him than his players probably cost him a shot at his dream job of managing in the major leagues. Gallagher returned to Durham in 1981 and he continued to tussle with Braves management and with players through a mediocre 70-68 season. After he was not re-hired by the Braves beyond the 1981 season, he landed in the Cleveland organization at Double-A Chattanooga in 1982 and Triple-A Buffalo in 1983.

Then Gallagher essentially was black-balled by Organized Baseball. His managerial style of making winning paramount, even in the minor leagues, never meshed with the mission of the Atlanta and Cleveland organizations.

Thus began an on-again, off-again, 30-year odyssey for Gallagher as a manager in independent baseball. At some point, Gallagher managed an independent team in the Class A California League, as well as in the Western League, Northern League, American Association, United League Baseball and North American League. Wolff, forever indebted to Gallagher for his contributions to the early success of the Bulls franchise, occasionally landed Gallagher managerial jobs in the independent leagues where Wolff served as commissioner. Gallagher's last managerial stint was in McAllen, Texas, of the since-disbanded North American League.

In 1988, when no longer active in the game, Gallagher underwent alcohol rehabilitation, and has not had a drink since. During treatment he met his current wife, Nancy. On their 25th anniversary, they renewed their wedding vows at home plate in the ballpark in Harlingen, Texas. "It meant a lot to me when I got out there," Gallagher says. "Baseball is so much a part of me. I don't realize that."

Gallagher was married to his first wife Terry while he was in Durham and their marriage lasted 24 years. The two had three children together and remain close friends with both living in Fresno. Gallagher also inherited three children from Nancy's first marriage. Together, the couple has seven grandchildren and four great-grandchildren.

Gallagher still follows the San Francisco Giants religiously on television. He cannot stand it when they lose.

MIKE GARCIA: More than three decades after playing parts of the 1980, 1981 and 1982 seasons with the Bulls, Garcia still shakes his head at his good fortune.

"I was so blessed," Garcia says. "Look at me. I caught the last out in the College World Series to be a national champion the year before. Then the next summer, I find myself in that 1980 Durham Bulls uniform. I don't know how you get, at that age, two better experiences in baseball. It was absolutely priceless."

Garcia caught the final out at second base to secure Cal State Fullerton's championship victory over Arkansas in the 1979 College World Series. A year later, he played 29 games for the Bulls, batting .280. By the conclusion of the 1982 season, Garcia was out of baseball after a couple of brief stops in Double-A Savannah.

Upon being told of his release in spring training of 1983, Braves farm director Hank Aaron offered Garcia a job as a roving infield instructor in the organization's minor-league system. But Garcia was also offered the head coaching job at California's Canada (pronounced Can-yah-duh) College, where he played before transferring to Cal State Fullerton. He often served as a volunteer assistant coach at Canada College while playing in the Braves system prior to accepting the role as the team's head coach.

Garcia was Canada's head coach from 1984 through 2002 and has served as its athletics director ever since. Garcia's teams were 451-220, won six conference championships and made 14 consecutive appearances in the California junior college state tournament. Five of Garcia's players eventually reached the major leagues. Garcia was inducted into the California Community College Baseball Hall of Fame, the San Mateo County Sports Hall of Fame and the Canada College Athletics Hall of Fame.

In 2001, Garcia was driving the bus with his Canada team on board to the state Final Four tournament in Fresno. In an effort to steer the bus away from a stalled 18-wheeler, Garcia took the brunt of the force from the driver's seat, broke his jaw, six ribs and his right foot. One of his assistants suffered a broken back, but the remaining coaches and all the players were unscathed.

Garcia, who ran the Garcia Baseball Academy for youth kids for two decades, has a daughter and son and lives in San Carlos, Calif.

LANCE GORE: Gore made quite an impression on the Braves' brass during his first full season of pro ball at low Class A Greenwood in 1979 and made an extraordinary jump to Double-A Savannah to begin the 1980 season.

His Greenwood statistics were stunning: In 45 games, all but two in relief, Gore won 13 games, lost 11 and saved seven. He had a 2.52 ERA over 100 innings pitched. But the jump to stiffer competition at Savannah combined with an arm injury proved too much for Gore and he was sent to Durham on July 17.

Gore appeared in 11 games out of the Bulls bullpen, going 1-2 with a 4.80 ERA, and was released following the season.

He returned to Cal State Fullerton, earned a business degree and worked for 20 years for the Nitta Corporation of America, a manufacturer of industrial belting. Since then he has worked for Forbo Movement Systems, which sells industrial conveyor and processing belts.

Gore and his wife, Cindy, have two children and reside in Lake Elsinore, California.

ALBERT HALL: Hall sped to the major leagues as quickly as he did around the bases for the Bulls when he stole 100 bases during the 1980 season while hitting .283. He played the 1981 season in Savannah, then made his big-league debut late in the season with the Braves. He had late-season call-ups again in 1982 and 1983, before settling in as pretty much a regular in the Atlanta outfield from 1984 through 1988.

Hall's most productive season with the Braves was 1987 when he batted .284 and stole 33 bases in 92 games. During that season's final week, in a Sept. 23 game against the Houston Astros, Hall put his name in the Braves record book by hitting for the cycle. He was the first Braves player to do so since Bill Collins in 1910 when the franchise was located in Boston, and remains the only Atlanta player to achieve the feat.

Hall's career with the Braves came to a premature end following the 1988 season at age 30 when he went to the club and admitted to being a drug addict. He was released by the team in spring training the following year, but not before his case went before an arbitrator who ruled in the Braves favor that he was let go because of subpar performance, not for his involvement with drugs. He hooked on with Pittsburgh in 1989 and played 20 games for the Pirates to conclude his professional career.

"I wasn't a liability to me and my family," Hall said about his drug addiction over a meal in Birmingham, Alabama, in July of 2014. "But there was no way I could blame anybody for that than me."

Even 25 years later, Hall looked as if he could still steal bases in a major-league game, and carried the same toothy smile as during his days in Durham. He was fit and proud to say he had been alcohol and drug free since leaving baseball. He has worked for 24 years for a tubing products company in Birmingham, where he lives with his wife of 34 years.

CRAIG JONES: Jones came out of the U.S. Military Academy in 1980 and took the Bulls by storm. He was a hard-throwing right-hander who went 6-5 with a 2.83 ERA. He eventually reached Richmond in the Braves system and pitched for that club during the 1982, 1983 and 1984 seasons.

Jones fell just short of the major leagues. He is believed to be in the real estate business in New York.

RUSS KERDOLFF: The minor-league baseball numbers game and Kerdolff's status as a late-round draft pick by the Braves caught up to him with Durham in 1980.

The 6-foot-5, 195-pound right-hander posted outstanding numbers in stops in 1979 with the Braves Rookie League club and with Greenwood. Combined, Kerdolff was 6-1 with a 1.72 ERA.

He did not pitch poorly in 17 relief appearances for Durham (0-3, 4.28 ERA), but when it came time to trim the roster, the Braves saw Kerdolff as a 38th-round pick, in whom they had little investment. He was released.

Kerdolff was inducted into the Northern Kentucky University Athletics Hall of Fame in 1999. He was 28-5 with a 2.28 ERA in four seasons at Northern Kentucky, earning All-America honors in 1979. He also was a two-time Academic All-American.

Kerdolff returned to Northern Kentucky after his playing days, and today is the school's comptroller.

GENE LANE: One of Lane's biggest challenges as athletic trainer for the 1980 Bulls was getting the players to eat healthy. Players were allotted $6.50 daily for meals on road trips only. Many players wanted to pocket the money and eat cheaply at fast-food restaurants. On trips to Kinston, Lane arranged for the team to eat after games at a local steak house, which cut a deal with the club so the cost of the meal would not exceed the amount each player received from the club.

Lane says that Durham became a prime stop for athletic trainers in the Braves minor-league system.

"I've told people that in my entire life, in the major leagues as well, I had more fun in Durham than anyplace else," he said.

Lane eventually reached the big leagues with Atlanta, then served as an athletic trainer on the PGA and Senior PGA Tours. He spent almost two decades in various parts of the Saint Thomas Health Services network and currently is the vice-president of client services for Applied Health Analytics in Nashville, Tennessee. He is married and has three children.

JOHNNY LEE: Lee never could hit professional pitching. After batting .189 in 47 games for the 1980 Bulls, he managed a .231 average for Anderson the following season. Lee had a tremendous arm across the diamond from third base, though, and the Braves converted him to pitching late in the 1981 season.

Despite a 10-9 record and a 4.81 ERA for Anderson in 1982, Lee was released following the season.

MARK LUCAS: Lucas got caught in a numbers squeeze when he started the 1980 season with the Bulls after finishing the previous season in Savannah. Gallagher simply could not find playing time for Lucas and he was released after playing only three games.

DAN LUCIA: Just when it looked as if Lucia was set to overcome his lack of size (5-foot-10, 168 pounds) when he pitched for the Bulls, the right-hander was beset with back and shoulder injuries. In five games, he went 3-1 with a 2.90 ERA. He returned to the Bulls for the 1981 season, but his career was done.

Lucia returned to his native California where he worked for Coca-Cola for 12 years, then the past 22 years with Boggeri Sales and Marketing. He has coached the San Marin High School girls basketball team for the past 10 years.

JEFF MATTHEWS: Matthews proved to be the typical Class A-level ballplayer during his Durham days, which stretched over 87 games in 1980. He was a solid player, yet not considered a prospect. He

was called up to Savannah and played 12 games that season for the Braves Double-A club, but that was mainly to fill in for injured players.

Matthews, who hit .295 with one homer and 32 RBIs for the Bulls, was never going to play in the big leagues. Yet his value to the team was immeasurable. He could play every infield position, played all-out every game, and proved to be a leader-by-example to teammates both on and off the field. In return, Matthews experienced the time of his life in professional baseball with the Bulls.

"It was a pretty big deal for somebody like me to have experienced that," Matthews said. "Nine of (my teammates) got to the show, but that, I guess, was my show, which ain't all bad.

"A lot of people that's all you've got to say is, 'I played for the Bulls,' and everybody knows who the Durham Bulls are."

Matthews returned to his native Minnesota after being released by the Braves following the 1980 season. He played town ball for about a decade in the Minneapolis area and later coached for 10 years at Holy Angels High School in nearby Richfield. He now works for ExpressPoint Technology Services, helping with the organization of repair operations in the United States and Mexico.

Matthews was one of the few married players while in Durham. He remains married to Deb, and they have three children.

BLANE MCDONALD: Even today, McDonald admits that Durham was not a great experience for him. He was unhappy with the Atlanta

organization and feuded with Gallagher. In 81 games during the 1980 season, he hit .260 with five homers and 33 RBIs. When he showed up for spring training the following year with an injured shoulder, his professional career was finished.

"The truth of the matter is, I probably wasn't mentally tough enough at the time," McDonald says. "I was still a little full of everything in the world being fair. There were a couple of unfortunate incidents that happened that were complete misunderstandings, but the personalities involved had different agendas.

"The bottom line was, the experience in Durham, I enjoyed the fans, I enjoyed the notoriety of the uniforms being different, we had a lot of fun, I enjoyed playing. I just didn't enjoy the organization at that particular time. It was not my favorite year in professional baseball, let's put it that way."

After baseball, McDonald first worked in Florida, then in Texas for 15 years. For the past five years he has worked for Capital One Auto Finance in Atlanta where he resides with his wife of 22 years. The couple has two children and three grandchildren.

BILL MILLER: Miller became the groundskeeper for the Bulls in 1980 despite not having a day of experience in the field. By the time he left the Bulls during the 1995 season he was regarded throughout the minor leagues as one of the best in the business.

Miller later served as general manager of the Durham Dragons of the Women's Pro Softball League, then spent a few years tending athletic fields for Durham area recreation departments. He now works in commercial landscape maintenance and resides in Durham.

ALVIN MOORE: Outfielder Alvin "Zeke" Moore of the Bulls was not to be confused with outfielder Alvin "Junior" Moore, who played for the Braves in 1976 and 1977. While in Durham, Moore served a valuable role for Gallagher's club as a fourth outfielder during the 1980 and 1981 seasons, batting .242 the first season and .282 the next.

There are some simply inexplicable happenings at every level of baseball. What Moore did for the Bulls from May 24 to June 9 of the 1981 season falls into that category. Completely out of the blue, Moore scorched the baseball like perhaps no one in the history of the franchise. He remarked during a 17-game hitting streak that the baseball appeared to be the size of a beach ball as it approached home plate.

During the streak, Moore batted .492, scored 16 runs, drove in 24, belted eight doubles and seven home runs. Teammate Brad Komminsk was the Carolina League player of the year that season and he never had a string of hitting prowess to come even close to Moore's.

Before and after that streak, Moore batted .209. He was released by the Braves at the end of the season, but anyone who was there to witness Moore's three-week assault on Carolina League pitching that season has not since forgotten it.

GERALD PERRY: No one doubted that Perry would play in the big leagues. The man could hit, and led the Bulls in run scored (102), homers (15), RBIs (92) and walks (94). He also worked tirelessly at his craft, including making himself into a decent fielding first baseman over a 13-year career with the Braves, Kansas City Royals and St. Louis Cardinals.

He batted .265 with 59 home runs for his career. His best season was 1988 with St. Louis when Perry was an all-star, and finished fifth

in the National League in hitting with a .300 average. Late in his career, Perry became a pinch-hitting specialist. He set the St. Louis record for pinch-hits in a season with 24 in 1993 and in 1995 became the Cardinals' all-time leader in pinch-hits with 70.

That was his final season in the big leagues, and he later served as hitting coach for the Seattle Mariners, Pirates, Oakland Athletics and Chicago Cubs. He has since taken his coaching to the minor leagues.

IKE PETTAWAY: Unfortunately for Pettaway, he found his game was best suited to be a relief pitcher too late in his professional career. He was 25 by the time he became a dominant closer for the Bulls in 1980, going 11-4 with a 2.08 ERA and 30 saves. He was back in Durham in 1983, then pitched in Double-A that season in the Yankees system. He gave it one last try with the Marlins' Class A club in the Florida State league at age 30 in 1985, but his career was finished.

Pettaway was forever grateful to Gallagher and pitching coach Bob Veale for believing in him as a pitcher who could get outs in the eighth and ninth inning of games for the Bulls. The 1980 season proved to be the highlight of Pettaway's minor-league career.

Today, Pettaway says he still has one regret about that season. His policy of not talking to the media might have labeled him as a bit of a malcontent, at least in the eyes of Braves management.

"I didn't talk to anybody," Pettaway said in 2015 from his home in West Palm Beach, Florida. "That was my biggest mistake. That was the biggest mistake I could have made. I was a great guy. I just didn't talk to the media. I don't have any idea why."

Pettaway is married and has two children. He drives a Vac-Con truck for the City of West Palm Beach. He says he talks to everybody, and was more than happy to talk to me after all these years.

AL PRATT: About seven years after Pratt's one season in Durham in which he went 8-4 with a 5.22 ERA, he was spotted by his former Bulls teammate Tommy Thompson. The two happened upon each other at a tryout in Sarasota, Florida, at the White Sox spring training complex. Thompson was in his final season of professional baseball. Pratt was 30 years old, trying out under an alias.

"I looked at him," Thompson said. "I knew him. I knew him. Then it came to me and he said, 'Shhh, shhh, I'm going by a different name.' "

Different name. Different age. It did not work. The real Al Pratt's final season in professional baseball was 1985 when he pitched three games for the independent Miami Marlins in the Class A Florida State League.

GARY REITER: Midway through the 1982 season with the Bulls, Reiter remarked to a reporter that he had been in Durham so long he should consider purchasing a house. Three years later, when his professional career concluded at Triple-A Richmond, Reiter returned to Durham and bought that house.

Reiter, who hailed from Ohio and attended Bowling Green State, remains the only member of the '80 Bulls to still make Durham his home. Reiter met and married Donna Underwood of Raleigh and never left. The couple has two children. Reiter works for North Carolina Siding and Windows in Raleigh, and occasionally lands jobs as a technician for televised sporting events throughout the southeast.

Over the 1980, 1981 and 1982 seasons, Reiter pitched in 124 games covering 247 innings for the Bulls. He compiled a 17-17 record with 19 saves and a 3.79 ERA. He once held the Durham record by appearing in 61 games for the '82 Bulls. For the 1980 team, he went 3-4 with a 4.72 ERA.

KEVIN RIGBY: After a late-season call up from Anderson to Durham in 1980, Rigby reversed the order the following summer in his final year of professional baseball. By the end of that '81 season, Rigby realized it was time to put his economics degree from Duke to better use. He played in just five games for the 1980 Bulls.

So Rigby entered the banking world in New York, first working 11 years for Goldman Sachs, then 16 years for Deutsche Bank, and most recently for Wells Fargo in corporate finance.

Rigby and his wife, Jane, of 26 years have two sons and reside in Greenwich, Conn.

RONNIE RUDD: Rudd produced a very respectable season for the Bulls in 1980, batting .276 with 56 RBIs and 33 stolen bases in 99 games. His path up in the Braves organization was blocked by a plethora of outfielders including Butler, Hall and Milt Thompson.

Rudd returned to Durham in 1981 in what proved to be a bizarre season for him. Early in the season, he was traded to the Orioles organization and sent to Hagerstown of the Carolina League. He played in four games for Hagerstown in Durham. Shortly thereafter, Rudd was returned to the Braves and finished his final season of pro baseball in Durham.

Rudd has owned and operated Rudd Appliance in Richmond, Virginia, since 1982.

PAUL RUNGE: Runge rocketed to the major leagues from Durham. After hitting .261 with eight homers and 37 RBIs in 74 games, he spent the second half of the 1980 season playing for Savannah, then played most of the following season with Richmond.

He was called up to Atlanta late in the 1981 season and played parts of eight seasons with the Braves. His career .232 batting average never did lend itself to a full-time job in the big leagues and he retired from playing the game following the 1990 season with Syracuse, the Triple-A affiliate of the Toronto Blue Jays.

Runge immediately went into coaching and managing. He managed 15 seasons in the Atlanta farm system, including 1997 in Durham when the Bulls went 63-76 under his guidance. For the past six years, Runge served as minor-league field coordinator for the Astros. Then he was hired for the 2017 season by the Braves to manage their new Class A team in the Florida State League.

He and his wife, Rae, have two children and reside in Jupiter, Florida.

GIL RYAN: Back and elbow injuries cost Ryan much of his career in professional baseball. The 1980 season with Durham was his finale. He went 5-6 with a 3.67 ERA. Had he come along today he likely would have undergone Tommy John surgery and prolonged his career. Back then, you simply retired.

Ryan was a Texas native and returned to San Antonio following his baseball career. He moved to Memphis, Tennessee, in 1989 where he worked for a real-estate development company for 15 years. He established Ryan Commercial Properties in 2004 and has been a retail shopping center developer ever since.

Ryan is married to Jerri and has two children. They reside outside Memphis.

MIKE SMITH: No one had more fun playing professional baseball than Mike Smith. Even 35 years after his two seasons of pitching for the Bulls, Smith still tells stories in his thick Boston accent. Like when two or three players would head out for lunch at the local mall on road trips. The players would stand perfectly motionless, and the first one to crack had to pay for everyone's meals. Or, when he and his teammates played baseball with a Nerf ball in their hotel rooms on the road.

Smith was the best storyteller, and perhaps the funniest guy on that 1980 team. At 6-foot-5 and 215 pounds, he could be intimidating to some, but he was good-natured and fun-loving at heart.

Smith was a mainstay in the Durham rotation in 1980 and 1981, then reached Savannah in 1982 and Richmond in 1983 before injuries curtailed his quest to pitch in the major leagues.

He returned to Massachusetts following his playing days, coached Pop Warner football for 20 years and high school baseball for 17 years, including his last stint as the head coach at Littleton High in Lowell, Massachusetts.

He now works for Ace Hardware in his hometown of Newton, and has two sons.

BRIAN SNITKER: Late in the 1980 season, the Bulls suffered a spate of injuries to catchers. Both McDonald and Steve Stieb were sidelined, so the Braves temporarily promoted Snitker from Anderson to Durham. Snitker had been serving as a coach in Anderson.

When Tommy Thompson was felled by an injury, Snitker stepped in and caught three games. Later he filled in for ailing catchers at Savannah, and that was the end of his playing career.

But Snitker remained in the Braves organization, mostly as a manager over the next three decades. His managerial stops included the 1983, 1984 and 1987 seasons in Durham, where he never had a winning season and was not well-received by fans because of that. Snitker was considered an excellent teacher and developer of talent.

Snitker was Atlanta's bullpen coach in 1985 and 1988-90, then was the Braves' third base coach from 2006-2013. He was the manager for Gwinnett, the Braves' Triple-A affiliate in the International

League, until May 17, 2016, when Atlanta fired manager Fredi Gonzalez and Snitker was named interim manager. Following the 2016 season, Snitker was named Atlanta's manager for the 2017 season.

Snitker and his wife, Ronnie, reside in Lilburn, Georgia. They have two children.

MIGUEL SOSA: Sosa arrived in Durham late in the 1980 season and played in five games. Then he spent the next two seasons as the Bulls everyday shortstop, which was both a good and a bad thing. It meant the Braves thought enough of his play to give him an everyday job, but two full seasons at the Class A level can only stagnate a player's professional career.

Time finally ran out on Sosa and he was released by the Braves following the 1985 season. He attempted to hook on with the Detroit Tigers and Yankees organizations the following season, but his pro career was done. It is believed that Sosa returned to his native Dominican Republic.

STEVE STIEB: Stieb was considered an excellent defensive catcher in both the 1980 and 1981 seasons for the Bulls. But he never could hit, and his three-year foray in the Braves organization concluded with a .217 career batting average in 194 games.

Perhaps figuring that what worked for his younger brother Dave, who pitched for 15 seasons in the big leagues, the Bulls tried Steve's arm out on the pitching mound twice during the 1980 season and five more times in 1981.

That did not pan out for Stieb, either, and he was out of baseball following that '81 season.

PETE TEIXEIRA: The long home run Teixeira surrendered to lose the 1980 season-opening game at Winston-Salem signaled the pending end to his professional baseball career. He pitched three more times unsuccessfully out of the Durham bullpen and soon was released.

Teixeira returned to his home in Miami, Florida, and worked the remainder of that summer loading trucks for a trucking company. He then went back to his alma mater and earned a graduate degree in counseling from the University of Florida.

Teixeira worked for several years in the University of Florida athletics department, then for Xerox Corporation in Jacksonville, Florida. For nearly 30 years he has worked for Epicon Products, a Johnson and Johnson Company that sells medical instruments.

Teixeira and his wife, Tacey, have three children and reside in Oviedo, Florida.

For the longest time, Teixeira could not follow the game he once loved, finally returning to enjoy it when his nephew, Mark Teixeira, reached the major leagues and enjoyed a productive 14-year career.

DUANE THEISS: Theiss spent only one week in Durham. He arrived from Anderson on June 16 and departed for Savannah on June 23. In between, he pitched three innings of shutout relief over two games.

Theiss was a 12th-round selection by the Braves in 1975 out of Marietta College in Ohio. Two seasons later, he pitched 17 games for Atlanta. He appeared in two more games late in the 1978 season for Atlanta, but an injury sidelined him during the 1979 season with Richmond.

His attempts to come back from the injury ended during his three-team swing through the Braves system in 1980.

Theiss later was a pitching coach at Marietta College and at Ohio State University. He was inducted into the Marietta Athletics Hall of Fame in 1988. He lives in Westerville, Ohio.

MILT THOMPSON: When it comes to evaluating talent, scouts generally look for five tools—hitting ability, power, speed, fielding ability and arm strength. Thompson lacked a power swing, yet displayed the other four tools in abundance during his half-season with the Bulls, hitting .290 with two homers, 36 RBIs and 38 stolen bases. Four seasons later, Thompson began to show off those skills at the highest level in a big-league career that covered 13 seasons with the Braves, Phillies, Cardinals, Astros, Dodgers and Colorado Rockies.

Thompson batted .274 for his career, including .302 for the Phillies in 1987 and .307 for the Cardinals in 1991. He also stole 46 bases in 1987. Thompson batted .294 for the Phillies in the 1993 World Series loss to the Blue Jays.

Following his playing career, Thompson immediately went into coaching and served in that capacity over the years with the Tampa Bay Rays, Phillies, Astros and Royals. He was the hitting coach for the 2008 World Series champion Phillies and a year later on their pennant-winning team. Thompson, Larry Bowa and John Vukovich are the only Phillies to both play and coach in a World Series.

Thompson lives in the off-seasons in Washington Township, New Jersey. He has four daughters.

TOMMY THOMPSON: There is no more compelling story among the 1980 Bulls than that of Thompson. He will coach a seventh consecutive season in the White Sox minor-league system in 2017, sans drugs or alcohol. Thompson, who admits to an addiction to drugs during his playing and coaching careers, is a recovering alcoholic.

As a player, Thompson hit .241 with nine homers and 56 RBIs for the 1980 Bulls, and returned to Durham in 1981 and '82. Left-handed hitting catchers who can also play the corner infield posi-

tions are difficult to find in the minor leagues. He was never considered a major-league prospect, but nonetheless was a valuable commodity both in the Braves and later the White Sox systems because of his versatility.

Thompson reached Triple-A in 1985 with the Braves, then played at that level with the White Sox in 1986, 1987 and 1988. He never got the call to the big leagues.

Thompson was the perfect candidate to coach, and the White Sox recognized that. He bounced around the White Sox and Braves organizations as well as in independent league baseball as a coach and manager, then was a roving catching instructor for the White Sox from 1997 through 2005.

In 2006, Thompson checked himself into a drug rehabilitation clinic in New York.

"I never drank a lot. They used to call me 'two-beer Tom,' " Thompson said. "I was screwed up. Got into cocaine. Got into crack. Crack, I thought was a little better high. The weed got me high, but when I got to crack, I just kept wanting more."

Thompson believes he first turned to alcohol and drugs as a way of dealing with his father's death at age 54. Thompson was a student at the University of Oklahoma at the time. Then, in 2003, he sunk further into the alcohol and drug abyss following the imprisonment of his son, Michael, the divorce from his first wife, Mary Jo, and the death of his mother.

He returned to manage Frederick, Baltimore's Class A affiliate in the Carolina League for the 2007 season. But 49 games into the 2008 season, he had returned to drug and alcohol abuse and volunteered to leave the club.

"I just told them I'm not finished, but I need to go take care of myself," Thompson said. "Maybe I was sick of me. I was sick of being sick. I knew if I didn't go take care of myself, I thought I had a chance to die."

Through the winter of 2008, Thompson lived in his car in Upstate New York, homeless.

"That's when I had to look deep down and say, 'What's going on?' " Thompson said. "I hit a down of all downs. I laugh at it now. When I go speak, I tell them this story. All I wanted was a hit of coke. I wanted a hit. I was living in my car, and I thought I was living large in the winter in New York, freezing my butt off. That's how sick I was."

He returned to baseball and managed in 2009 at Windy City, an Independent club in Crestwood, Illinois, of the Frontier League, where Thompson proved he could make it through a season without the aid of alcohol and drugs. The White Sox kept tabs on Thompson that season, and asked him to speak the following spring training to their minor-league players and coaches about the ills of alcohol and drug abuse.

"When I was talking, I was balling and they were balling," Thompson said. "It was unbelievable. They didn't have to hire me back, but they had given me another opportunity."

The only condition upon the White Sox hiring Thompson was that there would be no more chances. Thompson had to remain clean, and he has since managed clubs in Kannapolis and Winston-Salem, North Carolina.

"I still have thoughts," Thompson said of his past addictions. "We play a game and it's hot. I know if I drink a beer, that beer might lead me to wanting a hit of crack. You know what I'm saying? When I talk to my sponsor in the (rehabilitation) program, I see that God is challenging me every day."

Thompson and his son have reconciled their differences and now have a healthy relationship. Thompson married Leeanne Vinson in April of 2013, and they reside in Pine Mountain, Georgia.

BOB VEALE: Veale stood 6-foot-6 and weighed around 225 pounds when he served as pitching coach for the Bulls. He was still an intimidating force on the pitching mound despite being six years removed from a 13-year major league career at age 45. If he thought a Bulls player was getting too comfortable in the box during batting practice, Veale would heat up his fastball and mix in a few nasty curveballs.

Off the field, "gentle giant" was always the most apt description of the man. He proved to be a father figure to many of the pitchers he coached, not only on how to bend a breaking ball but also how to conduct themselves professionally off the field.

During a visit with Veale in 2014 at his home in Graysville, Alabama, he admitted that his two years in Durham were tainted by an inability to get along with Hank Aaron, Atlanta's farm director at the time. Veale eventually landed a job as a pitching coach in 1983 for the Utica (New York) Blue Sox, an independent team in the Class A New York-Penn League. During the season, the club celebrated "Bob Veale Day."

Among those who helped salute Veale was former Pirates teammate Willie Stargell, who said "there are givers and there are takers in the world. Bob Veale is a giver," according to Joseph Gerard in a 2014 article for the Society for American Baseball Research.

Upon leaving baseball, Veale returned to his native Alabama, where he resides today.

"At the age of 58, Veale stayed connected to his baseball roots by working as a groundskeeper at Rickwood Field (in Birmingham) two days a week," Gerard wrote. "He played an important role in preserving the storied old ballpark he played in as a child."

Veale was inducted into the Alabama Sports Hall of Fame in 2006.

MILES WOLFF: Wolff sold his interest in the Bulls in 1990, the ECHL's Raleigh IceCaps hockey team in 1997 and *Baseball America* magazine in 2000.

He was not done with his interest in baseball, however, and pioneered the growth and development of independent professional baseball with the creation of the Northern League in 1992. The league, with Wolff as its initial commissioner, fielded teams in the upper Midwest — most notably St. Paul, Minnesota — and was an overnight hit.

With traditional minor-league baseball going through a wave of popularity at the time not seen since the heyday of the minor leagues in the late 1940s, independent baseball jumped on the bandwagon, and soon other independent leagues sprung up around the country. Teams landed in communities in the United States and Canada starved for some form — any form — of professional baseball, but otherwise shut out of the limited spots available in the traditional affiliated leagues in the minors.

Beginning in 1989, Wolff owned and operated a team in Quebec City, Quebec, as a member franchise in the far-flung Northern League. He soon spent several months of the year north of the border running the Quebec Capitales, and oversaw its growth into one of the premier franchises in independent baseball, even as it transitioned from the Northern League to the short-lived North East League in 2003, and to the fledgling Can-Am League in 2005. He later took an active role with the Ottawa Champions of the same league.

Forever in search of the next Durham Bulls franchise, Wolff also has owned the Burlington, North Carolina, franchise in the Rookie Appalachian League since 1997, and the Elmira, New York, franchise in the independent New York State League since 2009. Previously, he owned teams in Asheville, North Carolina; Butte, Montana; Pulaski, Virginia; and Utica, New York.

Wolff served as commissioner of the North East League from 2003-04 and of the Central Baseball League from 2002-05. He currently serves as commissioner of the Can-Am League, the successor to the North East League, and the American Association, both independent leagues.

Wolff was selected as the 79th most important person in baseball history by John Thorn and Alan Schwarz in the eighth edition of *Total Baseball: The Ultimate Baseball Encyclopedia.*

During off-seasons, Wolff resides in Durham with his wife, Michelle. They have two children.

PAUL ZUVELLA: Durham was a mere pit stop on Zuvella's run through the Braves farm system. He managed late-season call-ups to Atlanta in 1982, 1983 and 1984, before finally sticking with the big club beginning in 1985.

In parts of nine big-league seasons with the Braves, Yankees, Indians and Royals, Zuvella batted .222. He left his major-league career with a couple of claims to fame. His name is fourth from the end alphabetically in the *Baseball Encyclopedia*, just ahead of George Zuverink, Dutch Zwilling and Tony Zych.

Zuvella also made a brief appearance in the 1986 movie Ferris Bueller's Day Off. "Mr. Rooney," a character in the movie, is watching a June 5, 1985 game between the Braves and Cubs on a television in a Chicago bar. Zuvella is seen as the runner at first base when Claudell Washington hits a foul ball that is caught by the film's title character, who was supposedly sick at home from school. Zuvella recalls signing a waiver during the filming of the movie, excluding him from any possible royalties.

Following his playing career, Zuvella was a coach and manager in the Rockies organization from 1992-98. He was named the Rockies player development "Man of the Year" in 1993 and one of *Baseball America's* top managerial prospects in 1997.

After leaving baseball, Zuvella returned to his home state of California and was inducted into the Samuel Ayer High School Hall of Fame in 2007 in Milpitas where he was valedictorian of his senior class. Zuvella continues to sell real estate in Danville. He and his wife, Laurie, have two children and reside in San Ramon.

PART III:
Appendix

1980 Durham Bulls Game-by-Game Results

FIRST HALF

NO.	DATE	OPPONENT	W/L	SCORE	RECORD	ATTENDANCE
1	April 11	@ Winston-Salem	L	3-2	0-1	
	April 12	@ Winston-Salem, ppd.				
	April 13	@ Winston-Salem, pdd.				
2	April 14	@ Winston-Salem	L	3-0	0-2	
3	April 14	@ Winston-Salem	W	4-3 (10)	1-2	
4	April 15	Salem	W	12-8	2-2	4,418
5	April 16	Salem	W	4-1	3-2	642
6	April 17	Salem	W	6-5 (12)	4-2	884
7	April 18	Alexandria	W	11-4	5-2	2,316
8	April 19	Alexandria	W	5-4	6-2	5,791
9	April 20	Alexandria	W	7-4	7-2	2,722
10	April 21	@ Salem	W	6-5	8-2	
11	April 22	@ Salem	W	8-7	9-2	
12	April 23	@ Salem	W	12-9	10-2	
13	April 24	@ Salem	W	4-0	11-2	
14	April 25	@ Alexandria	W	12-2	12-2	
	April 26	@ Alexandria, ppd.				
	April 27	@ Alexandria, ppd.				
15	April 28	Kinston	L	5-9	12-3	2,121
	April 29	Kinston, ppd.				
16	April 30	Kinston	W	3-2	13-3	
17	April 30	Kinston	L	1-0	13-4	1,879
18	May 1	Kinston	L	10-2	13-5	1,217
19	May 2	Peninsula	W	7-6	14-5	3,311
20	May 3	Peninsula	L	7-3	14-6	4,591
21	May 4	Peninsula	L	3-0	14-7	1,887
22	May 5	@ Lynchburg	W	4-3	15-7	
23	May 6	@ Lynchburg	W	5-1	16-7	
24	May 7	@ Lynchburg	W	6-4	17-7	
25	May 8	@ Lynchburg	L	5-1 (15)	17-8	
26	May 9	@ Peninsula	L	11-1	17-9	
27	May 10	@ Peninsula	W	9-4	18-9	
28	May 11	@ Peninsula	W	15-3	19-9	
29	May 12	Winston-Salem	W	11-9	20-9	2,586
30	May 13	Winston-Salem	W	6-3	21-9	2,011
	May 14	Winston-Salem, ppd.				
31	May 15	Winston-Salem	W	4-3 (8)	22-9	
32	May 15	Winston-Salem	W	5-4	23-9	2,912
33	May 16	@ Kinston	L	5-4	23-10	
34	May 17	@ Kinston	W	9-8	24-10	
	May 18	@ Kinston, ppd.				
35	May 19	*@ Rocky Mount	W	8-2	25-10	
	May 20	@ Rocky Mount, ppd.				
36	May 21	@ Rocky Mount	L	5-3	25-11	
37	May 22	*@ Rocky Mount	W	6-4	26-11	

NO.	DATE		OPPONENT	W/L	SCORE	RECORD	ATTENDANCE
38	May 22	*@	Rocky Mount	W	4-0	27-11	
39	May 23		Lynchburg	W	2-1	28-11	3,009
40	May 24		Lynchburg	L	5-4	28-12	4,699
41	May 25		Lynchburg	W	13-8	29-12	2,162
42	May 26		Rocky Mount	W	5-4	30-12	2,225
43	May 27		Rocky Mount	W	13-0	31-12	1,890
44	May 28		Rocky Mount	W	12-6	32-12	2,283
45	May 29		Rocky Mount	W	4-3	33-12	1,943
46	May 30	@	Winston-Salem	L	5-3	33-13	
47	May 30	@	Winston-Salem	L	6-2	33-14	
48	May 31	@	Winston-Salem	L	10-7	33-15	
49	June 1	@	Winston-Salem	L	5-4	33-16	
50	June 2		Salem	W	8-4	34-16	1,416
51	June 3		Salem	L	7-3	34-17	2,010
52	June 4		Salem	W	3-1	35-17	2,392
53	June 5		Salem	L	4-3	35-18	1,903
54	June 6		Alexandria	W	5-1	36-18	2,852
55	June		Alexandria	L	6-2	36-19	3,490
56	June 8		Alexandria	W	13-7	37-19	1,489
57	June 9		Alexandria	L	10-4	37-20	1,261
58	June 10	@	Salem	L	3-2	37-21	
59	June 11	@	Salem	W	7-6	38-21	
60	June 12	@	Salem	L	8-3	38-22	
61	June 13	@	Alexandria	L	9-3	38-23	
62	June 13	@	Alexandria	L	5-4 (12)	38-24	
63	June 14	@	Alexandria	L	5-2	38-25	
64	June 14	@	Alexandria	L	5-4	38-26	
65	June 15	@	Alexandria	W	9-1	39-26	
66	June 16	@	Alexandria	L	3-1	39-27	
67	June 17		Kinston	W	11-5	40-27	
68	June 17		Kinston	W	2-1	41-27	3,192
69	June 18		Kinston	W	5-3	42-27	2,063
70	June 19		Kinston	L	4-1	42-28	2,237
Total First-Half Attendance							**81,804**

END OF FIRST HALF

NO BULL

SECOND HALF

NO.	DATE	OPPONENT	W/L	SCORE	RECORD	ATTENDANCE
71	June 20	Peninsula	W	8-2	1-0, 43-28	5,122
72	June 21	Peninsula	W	8-7	2-0, 44-28	2,342
73	June 22	Peninsula	L	8-7	2-1, 44-29	2,851
74	June 23	Peninsula	W	9-1	3-1, 45-29	1,972
	June 24	@ Lynchburg, ppd.				
	June 25	@ Lynchburg, ppd.				
75	June 26	@ Lynchburg	L	4-2	3-2, 45-30	
76	June 26	@ Lynchburg	L	4-0	3-3, 45-31	
77	June 27	@ Peninsula	L	8-6	3-4, 45-32	
78	June 28	@ Peninsula	L	13-4	3-5, 45-33	
79	June 29	@ Peninsula	W	3-1	4-5, 46-33	
80	June 30	@ Peninsula	L	6-5	4-6, 46-34	
81	July 1	Winston-Salem	W	4-3	5-6, 47-34	2,279
82	July 2	Winston-Salem	W	6-2	6-6, 48-34	1,988
83	July 3	Winston-Salem	W	6-3(11)	7-6, 49-34	2,899
84	July 4	@ Kinston	L	5-4	7-7, 49-35	
85	July 5	@ Kinston	W	5-4	8-7, 50-35	
86	July 6	@ Kinston	L	7-2	8-8, 50-36	
87	July 7	@ Kinston	W	6-3	9-8, 51-36	
88	July 9	@ Rocky Mount	W	14-8(10)	10-8, 52-36	
	July 10	@ Rocky Mount, ppd.				
89	July 11	@ Rocky Mount	W	3-1	11-8, 53-36	
90	July 11	@ Rocky Mount	W	4-1	12-8, 54-36	
91	July 12	Lynchburg	L	6-4	12-9, 54-37	3,387
92	July 13	Lynchburg	L	4-2	12-10, 54-38	2,369
93	July 14	Lynchburg	W	6-4	13-10, 55-38	6,101
94	July 15	Lynchburg	W	5-2	14-10, 56-38	1,737
95	July 17	Rocky Mount	W	7-0	15-10, 57-38	1,211
96	July 18	Rocky Mount	L	7-3	15-11, 57-39	3,393
97	July 19	Rocky Mount	W	6-4	16-11, 58-39	2,777
98	July 20	@ Winston-Salem	W	5-2	17-11, 59-39	
99	July 21	@ Winston-Salem	L	11-6	17-12, 59-40	
100	July 22	@ Winston-Salem	W	2-0	18-12, 60-40	
101	July 23	Salem	L	5-3	18-13, 60-41	904
102	July 24	Salem	W	5-4(10)	19-13, 61-41	1,527
103	July 25	Salem	L	10-2	19-14, 61-42	2,544
104	July 26	Alexandria	L	12-3	19-15, 61-43	4,597
105	July 27	Alexandria	W	2-1	20-15, 62-43	1,159
106	July 28	Alexandria	W	9-2	21-15, 63-43	1,572
107	July 29	@ Salem	L	5-2	21-16, 63-44	
108	July 30	@ Salem	L	4-3	21-17, 63-45	
109	July 31	@ Salem	L	8-1	21-18, 63-46	
110	Aug. 1	@ Alexandria	W	7-3	22-18, 64-46	
111	Aug. 2	@ Alexandria	W	5-4	23-18, 65-46	
112	Aug. 3	@ Alexandria	L	6-4	23-19, 65-47	
113	Aug. 5	Kinston	W	2-1	24-19, 66-47	2,252
114	Aug. 6	Kinston	W	4-0	25-19, 67-47	3,088
115	Aug. 7	Kinston	W	6-0	26-19, 68-47	2,296
116	Aug. 8	Peninsula	W	8-2	27-19, 69-47	2,407

NO.	DATE	OPPONENT	W/L	SCORE	RECORD	ATTENDANCE
117	Aug. 9	Peninsula	L	7-6	27-20, 69-48	1,983
118	Aug. 10	Peninsula	L	7-5	27-21, 69-49	2,259
119	Aug. 11	@ Lynchburg	L	4-3	27-22, 69-50	
120	Aug. 11	@ Lynchburg	W	8-5 (8)	28-22, 70-50	
121	Aug. 12	@ Lynchburg	W	2-1 (11)	29-22, 71-50	
122	Aug. 13	@ Lynchburg	L	5-4	29-23, 71-51	
123	Aug. 14	@ Peninsula	L	8-3	29-24, 71-52	
124	Aug. 16	@ Peninsula	L	9-0	29-25, 71-53	
125	Aug. 16	@ Peninsula	W	3-2	30-25, 72-53	
126	Aug. 17	Winston-Salem	W	6-4	31-25, 73-53	2,080
127	Aug. 18	Winston-Salem	L	8-4	31-26, 73-54	1,802
128	Aug. 19	Winston-Salem	L	11-10	31-27, 73-55	2,782
129	Aug. 20	@ Kinston	L	4-0	31-28, 73-56	
130	Aug. 21	@ Kinston	W	10-6	32-28, 74-56	
131	Aug. 22	@ Kinston	W	10-5	33-28, 75-56	
132	Aug. 23	*@ Rocky Mount	W	2-0	34-28, 76-56	
133	Aug. 23	*@ Rocky Mount	W	9-8 (13)	35-28, 77-56	
134	Aug. 24	*@ Rocky Mount	W	11-0	36-28, 78-56	
135	Aug. 26	Lynchburg	W	7-6	37-28, 79-56	2,391
136	Aug. 27	Lynchburg	W	9-8	38-28, 80-56	3,527
137	Aug. 28	Lynchburg	W	10-3	39-28, 81-56	2,790
138	Aug. 29	Rocky Mount	W	8-0	40-28, 82-56	3,075
139	Aug. 30	Rocky Mount	W	5-4(13)	41-28, 83-56	3,885
140	Aug. 31	Rocky Mount	W	13-1	42-28, 84-56	4,811
Total Second-Half Attendance						**94,159**
Total Season Attedance						**175,963**

** Games played at Wilson, N.C.*

END OF REGULAR SEASON

Carolina League Playoffs

(Best of five series)

NO.	DATE	OPPONENT	W/L	SCORE	ATTENDANCE
1	Sept. 1	Peninsula	L	7-2 (10)	2,389
2	Sept. 2	Peninsula	L	9-4	2,412
3	Sept. 3	@ Peninsula	L	8-2	1,281

1980 Durham Bulls Statistics

BATTING	AGE	G	AB	R	H	2B	3B	HR	RBI	SB	CS	BB	SO	AVG	OBP	SLG	OPS
Rick Behenna	20	27	1	0	0	0	0	0	0	0	0	0	1	.000	.000	.000	.000
Glen Bockhorn	23	105	370	61	79	17	2	15	69	2	0	54	95	.214	.316	.392	.708
Brett Butler*	23	66	224	47	82	15	6	2	39	36	15	67	30	.366	.513	.513	1.027
Andres Forbes	23	57	177	32	43	3	2	1	14	4	0	18	15	.243	.318	.299	.618
Al Gallagher	34	7	26	5	9	1	0	0	4	0	0	3	2	.346	.414	.385	.798
Mike Garcia	23	29	82	11	23	1	0	1	5	8	1	24	14	.280	.444	.329	.774
Albert Hall#	22	125	491	95	139	16	7	4	41	100	27	77	52	.283	.389	.369	.757
Johnny Lee	21	47	169	16	32	2	0	0	8	2	1	12	27	.189	.242	.201	.443
Mark Lucas*	24	3	9	0	2	0	0	0	0	0	0	1	2	.222	.300	.222	.522
Jeff Matthews	24	87	285	40	84	8	0	1	32	0	4	46	35	.295	.392	.333	.725
Blane McDonald	23	81	260	34	68	9	0	5	33	1	0	26	36	.262	.334	.354	.688
Alvin Moore	22	106	314	54	76	14	1	8	51	8	5	55	44	.242	.359	.369	.728
Gerald Perry*	19	138	497	102	124	19	5	15	92	37	20	94	77	.249	.372	.398	.770
Ike Pettaway	25	51	0	0	0	0	0	0	0	0	0	1	0	.000	1.000	.000	.000
Kevin Rigby*	22	5	22	5	6	2	0	2	5	1	0	4	1	.273	.385	.636	1.021
Ronnie Rudd*	21	99	373	52	103	9	4	5	56	33	10	31	54	.276	.329	.362	.691
Paul Runge	22	74	245	37	64	8	4	8	37	12	8	53	55	.261	.396	.424	.821
Brian Snitker	24	3	10	0	2	0	1	0	3	0	0	0	0	.200	.273	.400	.673
Miguel Sosa	20	5	23	5	8	3	0	1	5	0	1	1	4	.348	.375	.609	.984
Steve Stieb	24	91	270	32	61	11	1	3	29	7	1	20	64	.226	.289	.307	.596
Milt Thompson*	21	68	255	49	74	12	3	2	36	38	3	42	62	.290	.393	.384	.777
Tommy Thompson*	22	111	361	46	87	16	2	9	56	1	1	51	42	.241	.340	.371	.711
Paul Zuvella	21	48	149	21	47	7	0	2	19	3	4	23	12	.315	.409	.403	.812
TEAM TOTALS	**22**	**140**	**4613**	**744**	**1213**	**173**	**38**	**84**	**634**	**293**	**101**	**703**	**724**	**.263**	**.364**	**.372**	**.735**

PITCHING	AGE	W	L	ERA	G	GS	CG	SHO	SV	IP	H	R	ER	HR	BB	SO
Juan Alduey	23	4	5	5.05	14	13	2	1	0	73	95	50	41	8	15	41
Jose Alvarez	24	2	0	2.00	2	2	2	0	0	18	14	6	4	1	5	12
Rick Behenna	20	8	13	4.15	27	27	6	2	0	180	181	97	83	16	81	107
Arcilio Castaigne	23	0	0	7.20	3	0	0	0	2	5	4	4	4	2	5	2
Dom Chiti*	21	1	1	2.90	25	3	0	0	3	62	56	23	20	4	28	31
Rick Coatney	20	9	2	4.60	26	12	0	0	0	94	95	53	48	6	56	55
Joe Cowley	21	6	0	2.81	10	10	2	0	0	64	57	26	20	6	25	44
Larry Edwards*	21	5	2	4.15	15	0	0	0	1	26	30	18	12	0	10	14
Lance Gore*	22	1	2	4.80	11	0	0	0	1	15	14	8	8	2	5	12
Craig Jones	21	6	5	2.83	13	13	3	2	0	86	69	34	27	3	34	77
Russ Kerdolff	22	0	3	4.28	17	0	0	0	1	40	48	24	19	5	10	22
Dan Lucia	21	3	1	2.90	5	5	0	0	0	31	31	14	10	2	12	14
Ike Pettaway	25	11	4	2.08	51	0	0	0	20	91	65	32	21	2	48	95
Al Pratt	23	8	4	5.22	18	14	2	0	0	88	109	64	51	9	45	64
Gary Reiter*	23	3	4	4.72	22	12	1	0	0	80	91	52	42	7	57	51
Gil Ryan	21	5	6	3.67	29	8	3	0	2	103	91	50	42	3	56	65
Mike Smith	21	11	3	3.73	22	21	5	3	0	140	145	73	58	10	51	77
Steve Stieb	24	0	0	0.00	2	0	0	0	0	4	1	0	0	0	0	3
Pete Teixeira	23	1	1	7.71	4	0	0	0	1	7	8	6	6	2	4	2
Duane Theiss	26	0	0	0.00	2	0	0	0	0	3	2	0	0	0	1	0
Tommy Thompson	22	0	0	9.00	1	0	0	0	0	1	2	1	1	0	1	1
TEAM TOTALS	**21.9**	**84**	**56**	**3.84**	**140**	**140**	**26**	**10**	**31**	**1212**	**1208**	**635**	**517**	**88**	**549**	**789**

•Left-handed. # Switch-hitter.

APPENDIX

Acknowledgements

No one was more important to the undertaking of this project than Allan Simpson, the founder and former editor of *Baseball America*. Allan was more than giving of his time to both edit and make suggested changes to the original manuscript. From the outset he believed in the book and kept pushing me over time to keep after it, all the way to the completion of the finished product. Allan and his wife, Jill, were most generous in housing me on a couple of visits to Durham and allowed me to use their condo in Myrtle Beach, South Carolina, for a week of writing.

My wife, Kim, and son, Luke, told me from the beginning that this book was worth writing. Then Kim lent her valuable edits and Luke turned detective in hunting down many of the players on the 1980 Durham Bulls who had scattered around the country following their pro careers.

My father, Leo, steered me to sports at an early age and I developed the same love for athletics that he did both during his professional softball career and in his sports broadcasting endeavors. My mother, Pat, instilled in each of her eight children a love of the English language, and I was no exception. We cursed her (under our breath) when we were youngsters as she corrected our grammar, but thanked her later in life for her diligence in making certain we both spoke and wrote properly.

When you grow up as one of eight children, you learn to be a team player, and that means lending support throughout your life to your brothers and sisters. A special thank you for their support along the way to Rick and Cindy Morris, Sue and Ray Randolph, Becky Barsell, Judy and Bill Woodward, Ann and Steve Hartman, Molly and Randy Youngberg, and Sarah Moyer and Rick Young.

Barry Jacobs is one of the top sportswriters in the country and a dear friend. He taught me more about journalism and dealing with subject matters during our frequent breakfast conversations than any class I took in college. I am forever grateful.

Special editing kudos to the aforementioned Simpson, along with Mike Chibarro, John Godwin, Bruce Winkworth and Bill Woodward. All took great care in reading through early manuscripts and offered expertise.

Most of the reporting in the book was done through my own notebooks, scorebooks and clippings. The scrapbook kept by the Durham Bulls front office was invaluable, and made available to me by Miles Wolff, who only once asked if I ever planned to return it. I am thankful also to all the Durham area writers who provided reporting during that 1980 season, including Elson Armstrong, Connie Ballard, Bryan Black, Elton Casey, Hal Crowther, Frank Dascenzo, Keith Drum, John Evans, Al Featherston, Gerry Garte, Ron Green Jr., Tom Harris, Barry Jacobs, Carol Jova, Wendy McBane, Phil Pitchford, Charles Rowe, Bob Sherrill, Carol S. Smith, William M. Smith, Ron Swaim, Joe Tiede, Gene Upchurch, and Will Wilson. They recorded the history well.

Of the more than 50 people I interviewed, no two gave me better insight and were more willing to grant me time — even at odd hours of the day or night — than Al Gallagher and Tommy Thompson. Both have amazing recall and are tremendous storytellers. Others who I interviewed included Jose Alvarez, Jean Bradley Anderson, Buddy Bailey, Bill Bell, Pete Bock, Glen Bockhorn, Reyn Bowman, Brett Butler, Arcilio Castaigne, Rick Coatney, Stuart Coman, Larry Edwards, Mike Garcia, Michael Goodmon, Lance Gore, Chuck Grubb, George Habel, Albert Hall, Gene Lane, Bill Kalkhof, Dan Lucia, Rick Marzan, Jeff Matthews, Blane McDonald, Bill Miller, Thom Mount, Pat O'Conner, Ike Pettaway, Chris Powell, Kevin Rigby, Paul Runge, Gil Ryan, Larry Schmittou, Scott Selig, Ron Shelton, Red Shuttleworth, Mike Smith, Allan Simpson, Paul Snyder, Pete Teixeira, Tallman Trask, Bob Veale, Jim Wise, Miles Wolff and Paul Zuvella.

Other friends who have lent their hand in some way include Art Chansky, Mary Gould, Matt Mackelcan, Bill Miller, Nikki Morris, Chris Powell, Len and Georgianne Spungin and Neil White.

The folks at Baseball America, most importantly Will Lingo, John Manual, Ronnie McCabe and Sara Hiatt McDaniel, were fantastic to deal with all along the way. Also, thanks to Lauren Havens, Sonya Hinsdale and Lynn Richardson at the Durham County Public Library; Heather Darnell and Sam Poley at the Durham Convention and Visitors Bureau; Patrick Cullom and Keith Longiotti at the University of North Carolina's Wilson Library; Joe Billetdeaux and Don Hart of the Pittsburgh Pirates; Larry Leathers and his sports information staff at Vanderbilt; Matt Sutor of the Durham Bulls; and Dave Lezotte of the Gwinett Braves.

Sources

For the most part material for this book was gleaned from my notebooks and clippings as a reporter for the *Durham Morning Herald* during the 1980 season. Unless otherwise noted, additional clippings were used from the *Durham Morning Herald*, *Durham Sun*, *The Spectator*, *The Chapel Hill Newspaper*, *Raleigh Times*, *News and Observer* of Raleigh, *The Carolina Times* and *The Anvil*. *Texas Monthly* magazine was used as well as media guides from the Carolina League and the Durham Bulls.

Baseball-reference.com was invaluable in culling statistics from players and teams. Other sites used to gather information included Bob Godfrey's bobspoint.blogspot.com, and Main Street Carolina Timeline at mainstreet.lib.unc.edu.

Most books used were cited throughout, but included:

Anderson, Jean Bradley. *Durham County, A History of Durham County, North Carolina.* Duke University Press, 1990.

Berchelmann, David A. III. *Legendary Locals of El Paso*, Arcadia Publishing, 2015.

Chrisman, David F. *The History of the Piedmont League* (1920-1955). Maverick Publications, 1986.

Holaday, J. Chris. *Professional Baseball in North Carolina.* McFarland & Company, Inc., Publishers, 1998.

Holaday, Chris. *Baseball in the Carolinas.* McFarland & Company, Inc., Publishers, 2002.

Holaday, Chris. *Baseball in North Carolina's Piedmont.* Arcadia Publishing, 2002.

Johnson, Lloyd and Wolff, Miles. *Encyclopedia of Minor League Baseball, third edition.* Baseball America, 2007.

Lamb, David. *Stolen Season, A Journey through America and Baseball's Minor Leagues.* Random House, 1991.

Simpson, Allan. *The Baseball Draft, The First 25 Years 1965-*

1989. Baseball America, 1990.

Sumner, Jim L. *Separating the Men from the Boys, The First-Half Century of the Carolina League*. John F. Blair, Publisher, 1994.

Photo Credits

Pages 9, 10, 27, 44, 55, 73, 86, 117, 158, 174, 177, 178, 227, 263: North Carolina Collection, Durham Herald-Sun Collection, University of North Carolina Library at Chapel Hill, N.C.

Pages 106, 147: National Baseball Hall of Fame and Museum.

Pages 130, 194: Courtesy of Baseball America

Page 212: Ben Casey

Pages 228, 230, 232, 234, 235, 237, 237, 238, 241, 242, 244, 245, 246, 248, 248, 249, 250, 251, 252, 254, 257, 259, 261: Bill Miller personal collection

Page 278: Courtesy of The State newspaper, Columbia, S.C.

Index

F

G

H

I

J

K

L

M

About The Author

Ron Morris began a half-century career in journalism as a young stringer for The Associated Press in Cheyenne, Wyoming. He worked at *The Salisbury Post* in North Carolina during his high school and college days, and graduated from UNC Charlotte in 1977, the year the 49ers reached the Final Four in men's basketball.

Morris has won numerous state and national awards at the *Chapel Hill Herald* and *Durham Herald-Sun* in North Carolina, as well as the *Tallahassee Democrat* in Florida and *The State* newspaper in Columbia, South Carolina. He was a five-time South Carolina sportswriter of the year by the National Sportscasters and Sportswriters Association.

He is author of the 1988 book *"ACC Basketball: An Illustrated History."* He continues to write occasional columns for the *News and Observer* of Raleigh, North Carolina as well as *Basketball Times*, and most recently was a consultant to the City of Columbia, South Carolina.

Morris has hitch-hiked across the country, run a marathon, counted the number of times a basketball bounced in a college game and recently took up baking.

Morris and his wife, Kim, reside in Lexington, South Carolina. They have one son, Luke.

Contact Morris at ronmo@sc.rr.com.